KEYS TO CHINESE LANGUAC
(Book I)

Keys to Chinese Language
(Book I)

漢語入門
(上冊)

By Jing-Heng Sheng Ma

馬盛靜恆 著

The Chinese University Press

Keys to Chinese Language (Book I)
   By Jing-Heng Sheng Ma

ISBN 962–996–210–1

THE CHINESE UNIVERSITY PRESS
The Chinese University of Hong Kong
SHA TIN, N.T., HONG KONG
Fax: +852 2603 6692
      +852 2603 7355
E-mail: cup@cuhk.edu.hk
Web-site: www.chineseupress.com

Printed in Hong Kong

CONTENTS

INTRODUCTION

Keys to Chinese Language is a comprehensive package of course material for elementary learners of Mandarin Chinese. It is a set of two volumes of textbooks, workbooks, and an interactive tutorial software (CD-ROM).

In each lesson of the textbooks, a pinyin text precedes a Chinese character text. All the lessons basically include (1) a short text (most of them are in the form of conversation); (2) an annotated vocabulary list with illustrated sentences; (3) sentence pattern drills; (4) a Sentence Building section; and (5) a Questions and Responses section.

In the pinyin texts of some of the lessons, extra sections — Cultural Notes and Fun Activity — are included. The Cultural Notes section is designed to explain some of the cultural difference between China and the western world. Interesting genres such as songs, word-play, and tongue-twisters are also introduced in the Fun Activity section, to enliven and vary the language experience.

In the Chinese character texts of each lesson, a reading section is included at the end. In this reading section some characters and expressions not covered in class are deliberately introduced, providing learners with an opportunity to take the initiative to learn outside class.

The pinyin text focuses on pronunciation, accuracy of intonation and fluency of speech, while the Chinese character text stresses character recognition and reading comprehension. Therefore, the pinyin text should be used prior to the Chinese character text.

A list of the 18 most frequently-used radicals and a set of flash cards (numbered with proper stroke order) are included for reference.

The workbooks contain different drillings, namely, (1) New Character Practice; (2) New Word and Expression Practice; (3) Grammar Practice; and (4) Reading and Writing Exercises. All of these exercises are designed in such a way that learners can revise what they have learnt efficiently.

An interactive tutorial software (CD-ROM) comes with the text. It is designed to help learners prepare class assignments. Each lesson consists of four sections: (1) Listening Comprehension; (2) Vocabulary (Chinese to English and English to Chinese translations); (3) Illustrative Sentences; and (4) Audio-Only Grammar Exercises (Sentence Patterns, Sentence Building and Questions and Responses.) In the Listening Comprehension section, one is asked to listen to a dialogue and complete a multiple-choice, self-correcting quiz. In the Vocabulary section, one will take part in an interactive flashcard game. The Illustrative Sentences section provides one with listening exercises combined with the Chinese characters for each sentence and images to aid in comprehension. The Audio-Only Grammar Exercise section allows one to listen to native speakers reading exercises while they follow along in their textbook. The tutorials give the language learner a concrete sense of accomplishment for work done on that lesson. What's more, through the online tutorials, one can receive immediate feedback and recognize their progress.

Traditional Chinese characters are used in *Keys to Chinese Language*. According to many experienced educators, it is easier for learners to begin with learning traditional Chinese characters, before switching to simplified Chinese characters. The phonetic transcription used in the book is the pinyin system adopted by the People's Republic of China after 1949.

There are ten lessons in *Keys to Chinese Language (Book I)*. Although only ten new characters are introduced in each lesson, one will actually be learning 20 to 30 compound words, idioms and / or expressions. One will have learned a total of 225 characters, 347 compound words/expressions, and 117 basic sentence patterns from *Keys to Chinese Language (Book I)*. When finishing the materials of this package, one should also be able to use familiar everyday expressions (e.g., greetings, self-introduction, requests, and preferences) and some basic phrases for making conversations, telephone conversations, letter and e-mail writing.

Keys to Chinese Language (Book II) consists of 12 lessons. A total of 120 new characters, 361 compound words/expressions, and 89 sentence patterns are introduced. With the successful completion of this set of materials, one will be able to report on events in the past, discuss plans for the future, make comparisons, express cause, effect and purpose, talk about holidays and birthday parties, ask permission, express emotion, give advice and make suggestions.

Keys to Chinese Language is based upon and constitutes a logical continuation of the introductory course materials *Keys to Chinese Character Writing*, in which a systematic instruction in the writing of Chinese characters is introduced. It is strongly recommended to use both of the texts together for more effective learning.

ACKNOWLEDGEMENTS

Many people have helped shape this project. This project would not have succeeded without institutional support, especially the technology resources from Wellesley College and many of my colleagues and students at Wellesley. My thanks go to my colleagues, Dai Chen and Weina Zhao, for their hard work on the reading section and grammar section of the workbook, respectively. My thanks also go to my colleagues, Dai Chen, Ann Huss, Haoming Liu, and my husband Wei-Yi Ma, for recording the texts. I would also like to express my gratitude to Li Yu and Minji Yao for the many hours they spent on typing the texts. Special thanks go to my student, Ee Cheng Ong — she has helped throughout the preparation of this project. My thanks also go to Stephani Cho for her wonderful illustrations and book cover designs.

Many people have helped develop the online tutorial program accompanying the texts. I am grateful to Kenneth B. Freundlich, Director, Instructional Technology, and Andrew W. Waldron, Director, Knapp Media & Media Technology Center; for their excellent technical support and advice. Special thanks must go out to Heather Elizabeth E. Woods, Project Leader, for her inspiration during the development of this project, her excellent technical advice and software design throughout the project. If not for the incredible effort Heather put into it — discussing the project with me for the past ten months, designing the Flash template, and organizing the students, the project would never have been achieved. Special thanks to Wellesley Knapp Instructional Technology Summer 2003 Interns, Jiayang Chien and Gowun Kim — lead designers for the project, Daphne Francois, Joyce Hsu, Tara McGovern, and Kate Tetreault. Chinese Department Interns Julia Zhang, Joyce Lo, Wen-chi Alice Tiao, and Minji Yao for the hundred of hours they devoted to the project; I am in awe of their technological skills! My deepest thanks and love go to my husband, Wei-yi Ma for his endless support.

I am indebted to the work of a number of linguists who have contributed to the study of the Chinese language, especially John DeFrancis, Charles N. Li, Sandra A. Thompson, Chao Yuen-ren and Wang Hai.

I am special grateful to my editor, Helene Schulman, for helping me shape the book and for her patience, support, and her detailed commentary. She has been invaluable to this project. My deepest gratitude go to the editors of The Chinese

University Press. They offered generous advice, assistance, and excellent editorial suggestions in the course of preparation of *Keys to Chinese Language*. Any remaining errors and infelicities are of course my own responsibility.

This project was generously funded by special gift contributions from Mrs. Elizabeth Tu Hoffman, her husband, Mr. Rowe Hoffman, and Mrs. Ann Munro. Their support was extremely valuable and no words can express my appreciation for their support and encouragement.

Jing-Heng Sheng Ma
Wellesley, Massachusetts
June 2006

ABBREVIATIONS OF PARTS OF SPEECH

Adj	Adjective	xíngróngcí	形容詞
Adv	Adverb	fùcí	副詞
As	Aspect Marker	tǐmào cíwěi	體貌詞尾
AV	Auxiliary Verb	zhùdòngcí	助動詞
Conj	Conjunction	liáncí	連詞
CV	Coverb	fǔdòngcí (jiècí)	輔動詞(介詞)
Det	Determinative	zhǐshìcí	指示詞
DO	Direct Object	zhíjiē bīnyǔ	直接賓語
EV	Equative Verb	duìděng dòngcí	對等動詞
IE	Idiomatic Expression	xíguàn yòngyǔ	習慣用語
IO	Indirect Object	jiànjiē bīnyǔ	間接賓語
IV	Intransitive Verb	bújíwù dòngcí	不及物動詞
MA	Movable Adverb	kěyí fùcí	可移副詞
MW	Measure Word	liàngcí	量詞
N	Noun	míngcí	名詞
Neg	Negative	fǒudìngcí	否定詞
Nu	Number	shùcí	數詞
O	Object	bīnyǔ	賓語
Pron	Pronoun	dàimíngcí	代名詞
PW	Place Word	dìfāngcí	地方詞
QP	Question Particle	yíwènyǔ zhùcí	疑問語助詞
QW	Question Word	yíwèncí	疑問詞
S	Subject	zhǔyǔ	主語
SV	Stative Verb	jìngtài dòngcí	靜態動詞
TW	Time Word	shíjiāncí	時間詞
V	Verb	dòngcí	動詞
VO	Verb-Object	dòngbīn fùhécí	動賓複合詞

CAST OF CHARACTERS

Mǎ Sīwén
馬思文

Mǎ Àiwén
馬愛文

Mǎ xiānsheng
馬先生

Mǎ tàitai
馬太太

Xǔ Xiǎoměi
許小美

Lín Hǎiyīng
林海英

Mǎ Hóng
馬紅

Jīn Jiàn
金建

Wáng lǎoshī
王老師

18 MOST FREQUENTLY-USED RADICALS

Radical (部首)	Chinese Character (漢字)				
人/亻	來	大	今	們	他
口	呢	和	哥	問	喝
土	報	在	坐	地	土
女	姓	好	妹	姐	媽
彳	從	待	得	後	很
心/忄	愛	怕	快	慢	想
手/扌	才	拿	找	指	手
日	是	早	晚	明	日
木	樂	本	林	樹	木
水/氵	酒	湯	海	汽	水
火/灬	熱	燙	災	煩	火
竹/⺮	笨	等	第	筆	竹
糸/糹	給	緊	累	紅	紙
艹	花	菜	葉	茶	草
言	請	話	說	誰	許
足/𧾷	跟	路	跳	跑	足
辵/辶	進	過	送	遠	近
金/釒	鉛	錶	銀	錢	金

第一課　你姓甚麼？
Lesson 1　What is your family name?

Lesson 1
Pinyin Text

• •

CONTENTS

chinese pal...n
pronaunttation tool.

✵ Text

Nǐ xìng shénme?

What is your family name?

Lǎoshī	:	Tóngxué zǎo! Wǒ xìng Wáng. Wǒ shì nǐmen lǎoshī. Nǐ xìng shénme?	Good morning, students! My family name is Wang. I am your teacher. What is your family name?
Xuésheng 1:		Wǒ xìng Xǔ.	My family name is Xu.
Lǎoshī	:	Nǐ xìng shénme?	What is your family name?
Xuésheng 2:		Wǒ xìng Mǎ.	My family name is Ma.
Lǎoshī	:	Nǐ ne?	And you?
Xuésheng 3:		Wǒ yě xìng Mǎ.	My family name is also Ma.
Lǎoshī	:	Nǐ shì tā jiějie ma?	Are you his elder sister?
Xuésheng 3:		Bú shì. Wǒ shì tā mèimei.	No. I am his younger sister.
Lǎoshī	:	Nǐ xìng shénme?	What is your family name?
Xuésheng 4:		Wǒ xìng Linden.	My family name is Linden.
Lǎoshī	:	Nǐ xìng Lín, hǎo ma?	Your family name is Lin, okay?
Xuésheng 4:		Hǎo.	Okay.

X → english 'sh' with tongue behind lower front teeth

✿ Vocabulary and Illustrative Sentences

1. tóng   **same, similar, be the same** (SV)

☞ **tóngxué**   be in the same school, fellow student, schoolmate; a form of address used in speaking to a student (N)

(1) Tā hé wǒ shì tóngxué.	He and I are classmates.
(2) A: Tóngxuémen, nǐmen hǎo ma?	Students, how are you?
B: Wǒmen hǎo, laǒshī.	We are fine, teacher.

2. xué   **study, learn; imitate, mimic; knowledge, subject of study** (V)

(1) Nǐ yào xué shénme?	What do you want to study?
(2) Tā xué wǒ shuōhuà.	He imitates the way I speak.

☞ **xuéwèn**   learning, knowledge, scholarship (N)

(1) Tā hěn yǒu xuéwèn.	He is very knowledgeable.
(2) Yàoshi nǐ xiǎng yǒu xuéwèn, nǐ děi "xué" yě děi "wèn."	If you want to have knowledge, you have to "study" and "inquire."

3. shēng   **give birth to; unfamiliar, unacquainted** (V)

☞ **shēngrì**   birthday (N)

A: Míngtiān shì nǐ shēngrì ma?	Is tomorrow your birthday?
B: Shì. Míngtiān shì wǒ shēngrì.	Yes, tomorrow is my birthday.

☞ **xuésheng**   student, pupil, disciple, follower (N)

(1) Tā shì hǎo xuésheng.	He is a good student.
(2) Jīntiān lǎoshī gěi xuésheng zhǐ hé bǐ.	Today the teacher gave the students pens and paper.

4. shì   **be, am, is, are; correct, right, yes** (EV)

(1) A: Tā shì Wáng lǎoshī ma?	Is he Professor Wang?
B: Shì.	Yes.

(2) A: Mǎ lǎoshī shì Rìběnrén   Is Professor Ma Japanese?
ma?

B: Tā yěxǔ shì Rìběnrén.   He may be Japanese.

5. **lǎo**   **old, aged** (SV); **always (doing something)** (AV)

(1) Tā shì wǒ lǎo tóngxué.   He is my old schoolmate.

(2) Wǒ xiǎo mèimei lǎo ài hē   My little sister always loves to
qìshuǐ.   have soft drinks.

☞ lǎorén   old people (N)

Lǎorén dōu hěn ài shuōhuà ma?   Do all old people like to talk?

6. **shī**   **teacher, master** (N)

☞ lǎoshī   teacher (N)

(1) A: Nǐ de lǎoshī xìng shénme?   What is your teacher's family
name?

B: Tā xìng Jīn.   Her family name is Jin.

(2) Wǒmen lǎoshī hěn ài wǒmen.   Our teacher loves us very much.

7. **shén**   **very, extremely, more than** (AV)

8. **me**   (suffix for shénme, zhème, nàme, zěnme and duóme)

☞ shénme   what (thing) ? (QW)

(1) A: Zhè shì shénme?   What is this?

B: Zhè shì qián.   This is money.

(2) A: Nà shì shénme?   What is that?

B: Nà shì qiānbǐ.   That is a pencil.

(3) A: Nǐ shuō shénme?   What did you say?

B: Wǒ shuō wǒ yào hē qìshuǐ.   I said I want to have soft drinks.

☞ zhème   so, such, this way, like this (Adv)

(1) Māma jīntiān zhème kuàilè.   Mother is so happy today.

(2) Nǐmen jīntiān dōu zhème máng ma? | Are you all so busy today?

☞ nàme　like that, in that way; then, in that case (Adv)

A: Nǐ nàme ài nǐ jiějie ma? | You love your elder sister that much?

B: Shì. Wǒ hěn ài wǒ jiějie. Tā yě hěn ài wǒ. | Yes. I love my elder sister very much. She also loves me very much.

9. bù/bú　**no, not** (Neg/Adv)

(1) Wǒ bú ài hē jiǔ. | I don't like to drink wine.

(2) Wǒ bù xiǎng qù Rìběn. | I don't want to go to Japan.

(3) A: Nǐ jīntiān lái-bu-lái wǒ jiā? | Are you coming to my house today?

B: Wǒ jíntiān bú qù, míngtiān qù. | I am not going today, but I will go tomorrow.

☞ bú dà　not very, not too (AV)

(1) Wǒ jiějie zuìjìn bú dà kuàilè. | My elder sister has not been very happy lately.

(2) Tā gēge bú dà ài shuōhuà. | His elder brother does not like to talk much.

☞ búguò　but, however (Conj)

A: Tā ài nǐ ma? | Does he love you?

B: Tā ài wǒ, búguò wǒ bú ài tā. | He loves me, but I don't love him.

10. mǎ　**a surname; horse** (N)

Wǒ māma xìng Mǎ. Tā yě yǒu mǎ. | My mother's family name is Ma. She also has a horse.

🐾 Pattern Drills

1.1 THE EQUATIVE VERBS shì AND xìng

Verbs such as shì and xìng are called equative verbs. These verbs connect or equate two nominal expressions on either side of the verb, like the English "is" in the sentence "She is a teacher." In this sentence, "is" equates "she" with "teacher."

S	EV	N
Tā	shì	lǎoshī.
She is a teacher.		

1.	Wǒ shì xuésheng.	I am a student.
2.	Tā xìng Mǎ.	His family name is Ma.
3.	Tā shì wǒ mèimei.	She is my younger sister.
4.	Tā shì wǒ māma.	She is my mother.

1.2 QUESTIONS USING ma

One way to form a question in Chinese is to add the question particle ma at the end of a statement.

S	EV	N	QP?
Nǐ	shì	lǎoshī	ma?
Are you a teacher?			

1.	Nǐ shì xuésheng ma?	Are you a student?
2.	Tā shì lǎoshī ma?	Is she a teacher?
3.	Nǐ xìng Wáng ma?	Is your family name Wang?
4.	Zhè shì biǎo ma?	Is this a watch?

1.3 QUESTIONS USING shénme

Another way to form a question in Chinese is to add the question word shénme at the end of a statement. Shénme can also be used to modify persons, things, times, and places.

S	EV	QW ?
Nǐ	xìng	shénme?
What is your family name?		

1. A: Nǐmen lǎoshī xìng shénme?   What is your teacher's family name?

    B: Tā xìng Wáng.   His family name is Wang.

2. A: Tā shì shénme rén?   Who is he?

    B: Tā shì wǒ gēge.   He is my elder brother.

3. A: Nǐ yào shénme?   What do you want?

    B: Wǒ yào qián.   I want money.

1.4 THE ADVERB yě

Yě "also, too" is a nonmovable adverb. Nonmovable adverbs must precede the verb or stative verb in a sentence.

S	Adv	V / SV	QP
Nǐ	yě	lěng	ma?
Are you cold too?			

1. A: Nǐ shì xuésheng, tā yě shì   You are a student. Is he also a student?
       xuésheng ma?

    B: Shì, tā yě shì xuésheng.   Yes, he is also a student.

2. A: Tā ài hē qìshuǐ, nǐ yě ài hē   She likes to have soft drinks. Do you
       qìshuǐ ma?   like to have soft drinks too?

    B: Wǒ yě ài hē qìshuǐ.   I like to have soft drinks too.

3. A: Wǒ hěn lèi, nǐ lèi ma?   I am very tired. How about you?

    B: Wǒ yě hěn lèi.   I am also very tired.

1.5 THE QUESTION PARTICLE ne

<u>Ne</u> has many uses. In the question "What about (that person or thing)?", <u>ne</u> is used as a question particle. In discourse, both the speaker and the listener know what the question refers to either from the previous conversation or from the context. A new question can be made by adding <u>ne</u> to a new subject. <u>Ne</u> can also be added after a noun or pronoun to create a question.

S	EV	N	S	QP?
Nǐ	shì	xuésheng.	Tā	ne?

You are a student. What about him?

1. A: Wǒ xìng Qián. Nǐ ne?   My family name is Qian. And you?

   B: Wǒ xìng Mǎ.   My family name is Ma.

2. A: Tā shì Rìběnrén. Nǐ ne?   He is Japanese. What about you?

   B: Wǒ yě shì Rìběnrén.   I am also Japanese.

3. A: Xuésheng hěn máng. Lǎoshī ne? Students are very busy. How about teachers?

   B: Lǎoshī yě hěn máng.   Teachers are very busy too.

1.6 THE WORD yào

<u>Yào</u> "want, want to" can function either as a verb or an auxiliary verb. When <u>yào</u> appears in a sentence with a simple direct object, it functions as a verb.

1.6.1 <u>Yào</u> "want" as a verb

S	V	O
Wǒ	yào	biǎo.

I want a watch.

1. A: Nǐ yào shénme?   What do you want?

   B: Wǒ yào qián.   I want money.

2. A: Nǐ de xuésheng yào shénme?   What do your students want?

    B: Tāmen yào qiānbǐ.   They want pencils.

1.6.2 Yào "want to" as an auxiliary verb

When yào occurs in a sentence with another verb, it functions as an auxiliary verb.

S	AV	V	O
Wǒ	yào	hē	jiǔ.
I want to drink wine.			

1. A: Nǐ māma yào hē shénme?   What does your mother want to drink?

    B: Tā yào hē chá.   She wants to drink tea.

2. A: Nǐ yào shuō shénme huà?   What language do you want to speak?

    B: Wǒ yào shuō Rìběnhuà.   I want to speak Japanese.

1.7 THE CONJUNCTION hé

Hé "and" is a conjunction that can connect two or more nouns or pronouns.

1.7.1 Hé joins two nouns or two pronouns as the subject of a sentence

When using hé to join two nouns or two pronouns as the **subject** of a sentence, the subject is often followed by the adverb dōu "all" to indicate plurality.

S	Conj	S	Adv	EV	N
Wǒ	hé	tā	dōu	shì	lǎoshī.
Both she and I are teachers.					

1. Wǒ mèimei hé jiějie dōu shì   My elder sister and younger sister are
    xuésheng.   both students.

2. Wáng lǎoshī hé Jīn lǎoshī dōu shì   Both Professor Wang and Professor
    wǒmen lǎoshī.   Jin are our teachers.

1.7.2 Hé joins two nouns or two pronouns as the object of a sentence

When using hé to join two nouns or two pronouns as the **object** of a sentence, do **not** add the adverb dōu "all" to the sentence.

S	V	O	Conj	O
Wǒ	yǒu	qiānbǐ	hé	zhǐ.
I have a pencil and paper.				

1. Tā yǒu gēge hé mèimei.   He has elder brothers and younger
                                                sisters.

2. Wǒmen yào hē qìshuǐ hé chá.   We want to have soft drinks and tea.

1.8 THE AUXILIARY VERB děi

Děi "have to, must, ought to" is an auxiliary verb which always follows the subject and comes before a verb in a sentence.

S	AV	V	O
Wǒ	děi	hē	shuǐ.
I have to drink water.			

1. Tā děi qù Rìběn.   He has to go to Japan.

2. Wǒmen dōu děi jìnqù.   All of us have to go in.

1.8.1 The pattern yàoshì ... děi ...

Yàoshì ... děi ... "if, suppose, in case ... have to, must" creates a conditional sentence.

```
Yàoshì   S    AV   V    O      S    děi   V    O
Yàoshì   nǐ   yào  xué  Rìwén, nǐ   děi   qù   Rìběn.
If you want to learn Japanese, you have to go to Japan.
```

1. Yàoshì nǐ míngtiān lái, wǒ děi   If you're coming tomorrow, I have to
   děng nǐ.   wait for you.

2. Yàoshì nǐ qù, wǒ yě děi qù.   If you go, I have to go too.

1.9 THE NEGATIVE ADVERB bù/bú

In Chinese, all verbs (except the verb yǒu) can be negated by placing the adverb bù/bú "not, no" before them. Bù is pronounced in its fourth tone when it is used alone or is followed by a word with the first, second or third tone. When it is followed by a word with the fourth tone, bú is pronounced in its second tone.

```
S           bú        V/SV      O
Tā          bú        shì       xuésheng.
He is not a student.
```

1. A: Nǐ shì lǎoshī ma?   Are you a teacher?
   B: Wǒ bú shì.   I am not.

2. A: Nǐ lèi ma?   Are you tired?
   B: Wǒ bú lèi.   I am not tired.

3. A: Nǐ māma máng ma?   Is your mother busy?
   B: Tā bù máng.   She is not busy.

4. A: Jīntiān hěn lěng ma?   Is it very cold today?
   B: Jīntiān bù hěn lěng.   It's not very cold today.

1.9.1　The choice-type question V-<u>bu</u>-V

Choice-type questions are formed by stating affirmative and negative forms of a verb in rapid succession. <u>Bu</u> is pronounced in a neutral tone in choice-type questions.

S	*V*-<u>*bu*</u>-*V*	*O*?
Tā	shì-bu-shì	nǐ jiějie?
Is she your elder sister?		

1. A: Nǐ jīntiān qù-bu-qù zhǎo Wáng lǎoshī?

   B: Wǒ jīntiān bú qù, míngtiān qù.

2. A: Nǐ yào-bu-yào xué Rìwén?

   B: Wǒ bú yào xué Rìwén.

Are you going to see Professor Wang today?

I am not going today, (I) am going tomorrow.

Do you want to study Japanese?

I don't want to study Japanese.

1.9.2　The split choice-type question V O <u>bu</u>-V

Split choice-type questions are formed by placing the negative form of a verb at the end of a sentence. <u>Bu</u> is pronounced in a neutral tone in split choice-type questions.

S	*V*	*O*	<u>*bu*</u>-*V*?
Tā	shì	nǐ jiějie	bu-shì?
Is she your elder sister?			

1. A: Nǐ jīntiān qù zhǎo Wáng lǎoshī bu-qù?

   B: Wǒ jīntiān bú qù, míngtiān qù.

2. A: Nǐ yào xué Rìwén bu-yào?

   B: Wǒ bú yào xué Rìwén.

Are you going to see Professor Wang today?

I am not going today, (I) am going tomorrow.

Do you want to study Japanese?

I don't want to study Japanese.

1.10 THE ADVERBS zhème AND nàme

Zhème "so, such, this way, like this" and nàme "like that, in that way; then, in that case" are adverbs. They always come before a verb or a stative verb in a sentence.

S	AV	Adv	V/SV
Nǐ	děi	zhème/nàme	shuō!

You must say it this/that way!

1. Xuéshēng dōu zhème kuàilè.   The students are all so happy.

2. Nǐ děi zhème dǎ qiú.   You have to play ball this way.

3. Jīntiān zhème lěng!   It is so cold today!

4. Tā tiāntiān dōu nàme xiǎoxīn.   He is so careful every day.

❀ Sentence Building

1.
Shénme?
Shì shénme?
Zhè shì shénme?
Zhè shì Rìběn zhǐ.

2.
Shì
Shì shéi?
Nǐ shì shéi?
Wǒ shì Wáng lǎoshī.

3.
Xìng
Xìng shénme?
Tā xìng shénme?
Tā xìng Mǎ.

❀ Questions and Responses

1. Nǐ xìng shénme?
   What is your family name?

   Wǒ xìng Mǎ.
   My family name is Ma.

2. Tā xìng shénme?
   What is his family name?

   Tā xìng Lín.
   His family name is Lin.

3. Nǐmen lǎoshī xìng shénme?
   What is your teacher's family name?

   Wǒmen lǎoshī xìng Wáng.
   Our teacher's family name is Wang.

4. Shéi xìng Mǎ?
   Whose family name is Ma?

   Tā xìng Mǎ.
   His family name is Ma.

5. Shéi xìng Wáng?
   Whose family name is Wang?

   Wǒ xìng Wáng. Tā yě xìng Wáng.
   My family name is Wang. His family name is also Wang.

6. Zhè shì shénme?
   What is this?

   Zhè shì bǐ.
   This is a pen.

7. Nà shì shénme?
   What is that?

   Nà shì jiǔ.
   That is wine.

8. Nà shì shénme zhǐ?
   What kind of paper is that?

   Nà shì Rìběn zhǐ.
   That is Japanese paper.

9. Nà shì shénme biǎo?
   What kind of watch is that?

   Nà shì jīnbiǎo.
   That is a gold watch.

10. Zhè shì shénme bǐ?
    What kind of writing tool is this?

    Zhè shì qiānbǐ.
    This is a pencil.

11. Nà shì shénme jiǔ?
    What kind of wine is that?

    Nà shì Rìběn jiǔ.
    That is Japanese wine.

Fun Activity

Cheer for Your Team

Dé Dì-Yī	
To Be Number One	
Yī èr sān	One two three
Sān èr yī	Three two one
Yī èr sān sì wǔ liù qī	One two three four five six seven
Qī liù wǔ sì sān èr yī	Seven six five four three two one
Wǒmen yào dé dì-yī	We want to be number one

Tones 2 ⌐
      3 ⌐
      4 ⌐

① Two 3rd tones in succession becomes 2+3 tones
   nǐ hǎo → ní hǎo
② bù + another 4th tone, bù becomes bú
   eg bú shì I'm not

第一課
漢字本

· ·

內容

🌸 課 文

你姓甚麼？

老師　：同學早！我姓王，我是你們老師。

　　　　你姓甚麼？

學生 1：我姓許。

老師　：你姓甚麼？

學生 2：我姓馬。

老師　：你呢？

學生 3：我也姓馬。

老師　：你是他姐姐嗎？

學生 3：不是，我是他妹妹。

老師　：你姓甚麼？

學生 4：我姓 Linden。

老師　：你姓林，好嗎？

學生 4：好。

🐾 生詞及例句

1. **同**　　**same, similar, be the same as** (SV)

☞ 同學　　be in the same school, fellow student, schoolmate; a form of address used in speaking to a student (N)

(1) 他和我是同學。

(2) A: 同學們，你們好嗎？

　　B: 我們好，老師。

2. **學**　　**study, learn; imitate, mimic; knowledge, subject of study** (V)

(1) 你要學甚麼？

(2) 他學我說話。

☞ 學問　　learning, knowledge, scholarship (N)

(1) 他很有學問。

(2) 要是你想有學問，你得"學"也得"問"。

3. **生**　　**give birth to; unfamiliar, unacquainted** (V)

☞ 生日　　birthday (N)

A: 明天是你生日嗎？

B: 是。明天是我生日。

☞ 學生　　student, pupil, disciple, follower (N)

(1) 他是好學生。

(2) 今天老師給學生紙和筆。

4. **是**　　**be, am, is, are; correct, right, yes** (EV)

(1) A: 他是王老師嗎？

　　B: 是。

(2) A: 馬老師是日本人嗎？

　　B: 他也許是日本人。

5. 老　　**old, aged** (SV); **always (doing something)** (AV)

(1) 他是我老同學。

(2) 我小妹妹老愛喝汽水。

☞ 老人　　old people (N)

老人都很愛說話嗎？

6. 師　　**teacher, master** (N)

☞ 老師　　teacher (N)

(1) A: 你的老師姓甚麼？

B: 他姓金。

(2) 我們老師很愛我們。

7. 甚　　**very, extremely, more than** (AV)

8. 麼　　(suffix for shénme, zhème, nàme, zěnme and duóme)

☞ 甚麼　　what (thing)? (QW)

(1) A: 這是甚麼？

B: 這是錢。

(2) A: 那是甚麼？

B: 那是鉛筆。

(3) A: 你說甚麼？

B: 我說我要喝汽水。

☞ 這麼　　so, such, this way, like this (Adv)

(1) 媽媽今天這麼快樂。

(2) 你們今天都這麼忙嗎？

☞ 那麼　　like that, in that way; then, in that case (Adv)

A: 你那麼愛你姐姐嗎？

B: 是。我很愛我姐姐。她也很愛我。

9. 不   **no, not** (Neg/Adv)

(1) 我不愛喝酒。

(2) 我不想去日本。

(3) A: 你今天來不來我家？

B: 我今天不去，明天去。

☞ 不大   not very, not too (AV)

(1) 我姐姐最近不大快樂。

(2) 他哥哥不大愛說話。

☞ 不過   but, however (Conj)

A: 他愛你嗎？

B: 他愛我，不過我不愛他。

10. 馬   **a surname; horse** (N)

我媽媽姓馬。她也有馬。

❀ 句型練習

1.1 THE EQUATIVE VERBS 是 AND 姓

Verbs such as 是 and 姓 are called equative verbs. These verbs connect or equate two nominal expressions on either side of the verb, like the English "is" in the sentence "She is a teacher." In this sentence, "is" equates "she" with "teacher."

S	EV	N
她	是	老師。
She is a teacher.		

1. 我是學生。

2. 他姓馬。

3. 她是我妹妹。

4. 她是我媽媽。

1.2 QUESTIONS USING 嗎

One way to form a question in Chinese is to add a question particle 嗎 at the end of a statement.

S	EV	N	QP?
你	是	老師	嗎?
Are you a teacher?			

1. 你是學生嗎?

2. 她是老師嗎?

3. 你姓王嗎?

4. 這是錶嗎?

1.3 QUESTIONS USING 甚麼

Another way to form a question in Chinese is to add the question word 甚麼 at the end of a statement. 甚麼 can also be used to modify persons, things, times, and places.

S	EV	QW?
你	姓	甚麼?
What is your family name?		

1. A: 你們老師姓甚麼?

   B: 他姓王。

2. A: 他是甚麼人?

   B: 他是我哥哥。

3. A: 你要甚麼?

   B: 我要錢。

1.4 THE ADVERB 也

也 "also, too" is a nonmovable adverb. Nonmovable adverbs must precede the verb or stative verb in a sentence.

S	Adv	V/SV	QP?
你	也	冷	嗎？
Are you cold too?			

1. A: 你是學生，他也是學生嗎？

    B: 是，他也是學生。

2. A: 他愛喝汽水，你也愛喝汽水嗎？

    B: 我也愛喝汽水。

3. A: 我很累，你累嗎？

    B: 我也很累。

1.5 THE QUESTION PARTICLE 呢

呢 has many uses. In the question "What about (that person or thing)?", 呢 is used as a question particle. In discourse, both the speaker and the listener know what the question refers to either from the previous conversation or from the context. A new question can be made by adding 呢 to a new subject. 呢 can also be added after a noun or pronoun to create a question.

S	EV	N	S	QP?
你	是	學生。	他	呢？
You are a student. What about him?				

1. A: 我姓錢。你呢？

    B: 我姓馬。

2. A: 他是日本人。你呢？

    B: 我也是日本人。

3. A: 學生很忙。老師呢？

    B: 老師也很忙。

1.6 THE WORD 要

要 "want, want to" can function either as a verb or an auxiliary verb. When 要 appears in a sentence with a simple direct object, it functions as a verb.

1.6.1 要 "want" as a verb

S	V	O
我	要	錶。
I want a watch.		

1. A: 你要甚麼？

   B: 我要錢。

2. A: 你的學生要甚麼？

   B: 他們要鉛筆。

1.6.2 要 "want to" as an auxiliary verb

When 要 occurs in a sentence with another verb, it functions as an auxiliary verb.

S	AV	V	O
我	要	喝	酒。
I want to drink wine.			

1. A: 你媽媽要喝甚麼？

   B: 她要喝茶。

2. A: 你要説甚麼話？

   B: 我要説日本話。

1.7 THE CONJUNCTION 和

和 "and" is a conjunction that can connect two or more nouns or pronouns.

1.7.1 和 joins two nouns or two pronouns as the subject of a sentence

When using 和 to join two nouns or two pronouns as the **subject** of a sentence, the subject is often followed by the adverb 都 "all" to indicate plurality.

S	Conj	S	Adv	EV	N
我	和	他	都	是	老師。
Both she and I are teachers.					

1. 我妹妹和姐姐都是學生。

2. 王老師和金老師都是我們老師。

1.7.2 和 joins two nouns or two pronouns as the object of a sentence

When using 和 to join two nouns or two pronouns as the **object** of a sentence, do **not** add the adverb 都 "all" to the sentence.

S	V	O	Conj	O
我	有	鉛筆	和	紙。
I have a pencil and paper.				

1. 他有哥哥和妹妹。

2. 我們要喝汽水和茶。

1.8 THE AUXILIARY VERB 得

得 "have to, must, ought to" is an auxiliary verb which always follows the subject and comes before a verb in a sentence.

S	AV	V	O
我	得	喝	水。
I have to drink water.			

1. 他得去日本。

2. 我們都得進去。

1.8.1 The Pattern 要是 ⋯⋯ 得 ⋯⋯

要是 ⋯⋯ 得 ⋯⋯ "if, suppose, in case ... have to, must" creates a conditional sentence.

要是	S	AV	V	O	S	得	V	O
要是	你	要	學	日文，	你	得	去	日本。

If you want to learn Japanese, you have to go to Japan.

1. 要是你明天來，我得等你。

2. 要是你去，我也得去。

1.9 THE NEGATIVE ADVERB 不

In Chinese, all verbs (except the verb 有) can be negated by placing the adverb 不 "not, no" before them. 不 is pronounced in its fourth tone when it is used alone or is followed by a word with the first, second or third tone. When it is followed by a word with the fourth tone, 不 is pronounced in its second tone.

S	不	V / SV	O
他	不	是	學生。

He is not a student.

1. A: 你是老師嗎？

   B: 我不是。

2. A: 你累嗎？

   B: 我不累。

3. A: 你媽媽忙嗎？

   B: 她不忙。

4. A: 今天很冷嗎？

   B: 今天不很冷。

1.9.1 The choice-type question V-不-V

Choice-type questions are formed by stating affirmative and negative forms of a verb in rapid succession. 不 is pronounced in a neutral tone in choice-type questions.

S	V-不-V	O?
她	是不是	你姐姐？
Is she your elder sister?		

1. A: 你今天去不去找王老師？

   B: 我今天不去，明天去。

2. A: 你要不要學日文？

   B: 我不要學日文。

1.9.2 The split choice-type question V O 不-V

Split choice-type questions are formed by placing the negative form of a verb at the end of a sentence. 不 is pronounced in a neutral tone in split choice-type questions.

S	V	O	不-V?
她	是	你姐姐	不是？
Is she your elder sister?			

1. A: 你今天去找王老師不去？

   B: 我今天不去，明天去。

2. A: 你要學日文不要？

   B: 我不學日文。

1.10 THE ADVERBS 這麼 AND 那麼

這麼 "so, such, this way, like this" and 那麼 "like that, in that way; then, in that case" are adverbs. They always come before a verb or a stative verb in a sentence.

S	AV	Adv	V/SV
你	得	這麼/那麼	説!

You must say it this/that way!

1. 學生都這麼快樂。

2. 你得這麼打球。

3. 今天這麼冷!

4. 他天天都那麼小心。

造句

1.	2.	3.
甚麼?	是	姓
是甚麼?	是誰?	姓甚麼?
這是甚麼?	你是誰?	他姓甚麼?
這是日本紙。	我是王老師。	他姓馬。

問答

1. 你姓甚麼?	我姓馬。
2. 他姓甚麼?	他姓林。
3. 你們老師姓甚麼?	我們老師姓王。
4. 誰姓馬?	他姓馬。
5. 誰姓王?	我姓王,他也姓王。
6. 這是甚麼?	這是筆。
7. 那是甚麼?	那是酒。
8. 那是甚麼紙?	那是日本紙。
9. 那是甚麼錶?	那是金錶。
10. 這是甚麼筆?	這是鉛筆。
11. 那是甚麼酒?	那是日本酒。

閱 讀

王老師

　　我們老師姓王。我們同學，有人姓馬、有人姓許。

　　王老師問我姓甚麼。我說："我姓 Linden。"他說："你姓林，好嗎？"我說："好。"他也問我是不是日本人。我說："我不是日本人，我媽媽是日本人。"王老師問我們累不累？我們說："我們今天很累。"

　　王老師很好，他也很有學問。他說，要是我們想要有學問，我們得"學"，不要怕"問"。

第二課　你叫甚麼名字？
Lesson 2　What is your given name?

Lesson 2
Pinyin Text

· ·

CONTENTS

🌸 Text

Nǐ jiào shénme míngzi?

What is your given name?

Lǎoshī	: Tóngxuémen zǎo.	Good morning, students.
Xuéshengmen:	Zǎo!	Good morning!
Lǎoshī	: Nǐmen hǎo ma?	How are you?
Xuéshengmen:	Hěn hǎo.	(We) are very well.
Lǎoshī	: Nǐ jiào shénme míngzi?	What is your given name?
Xuésheng 1	: Wǒ jiào Xiǎoměi.	My given name is Xiaomei.
Lǎoshī	: Nǐ de míngzi jiào shénme?	What is your given name?
Xuésheng 2	: Wǒ jiào Sīwén.	My given name is Siwen.
Lǎoshī	: Nǐ mèimei jiào shénme míngzi?	What is your younger sister called?
Xuésheng 2	: Tā jiào Àiwén.	Her given name is Aiwen.
Lǎoshī	: Nǐ de míngzi jiào shénme ne?	What is your given name?
Xuésheng 3	: Wǒ jiào Helen.	My name is Helen.
Lǎoshī	: Nǐ de Zhōngguó míngzi jiào Hǎiyīng, hǎo ma?	Your Chinese given name will be Haiying, okay?
Xuésheng 3	: Hǎo. Wǒ xìng Lín, jiào Hǎiyīng.	Okay, my family name is Lin and my given name is Haiying.
Lǎoshī	: Hěn hǎo. Nǐmen de míngzi de yìsi dōu hěn hǎo.	Very good. The meanings of your names are all very nice.

. . . .

🐾 Vocabulary and Illustrative Sentences

1. **jiào**   **call** (V/EV)

    (1) Māma jiào nǐ lái.   Mama asked you to come.

    (2) "Qiānbǐ" Yīngwén jiào   What is "qianbi" called in
        shénme?   English?

    (3) Àiwén, tā jiào shénme   Aiwen, what is his given name?
        míngzi?

2. **míng**   **name** (N)

☞ yǒumíng   well-known, famous, celebrated (SV)

    (1) Nà běn xiǎoshuō hěn yǒumíng.   That novel is quite famous.

    (2) Zhè shì hěn yǒumíng de   This is a well-known brand of
        shǒubiǎo.   watch.

☞ míngrén   famous person, celebrity (N)

    A: Nǐmen de lǎoshī yǒumíng ma?   Is your teacher well known?

    B: Tā hěn yǒumíng, tā shì   He is very well known. He is a
       míngrén.   famous person.

3. **zì**   **word, character, writing** (N)

☞ míngzi   given name, first name, name (N)

    A: Nǐ jiào shénme míngzi?   What is your given name?

    B: Wǒ jiào Měiyīng.   My given name is Meiying.

☞ wénzì   characters, script, writing, written language (N)

    (1) Wǒ guó de wénzì hěn měi.   My country's written language
                                          is very beautiful.

    (2) Zhè shì Rìběn de wénzì.   That is Japanese writing.

4. **měi**   **beautiful, pretty; short form of "American"** (SV)

☞ měirén   beautiful woman, beauty (N)

A: Wǒ de tóngxué dōu shuō nǐ jiějie shì měirén.
All my classmates say your elder sister is a beauty.

B: Shì ma!
Really!

☞ Měiguó — The United States of America (PW)

A: Shéi shì Měiguórén?
Who is American?

B: Lín Hǎiyīng shì Měiguórén.
Lin Haiying is American.

5. **de** — (subordinating particle)

A: Zhè shì shéi de shǒubiǎo?
Whose watch is this?

B: Zhè shì Xǔ Xiǎoměi de shǒubiǎo.
This is Xu Xiaomei's watch.

☞ yǒude — some (+ N/Adj)

A: Rénrén dōu ài hē rè tāng, shì ma?
Everybody loves (to drink) hot soup, right?

B: Wǒ xiǎng yǒude rén ài hē rè tāng, yǒude rén ài hē lěng tāng.
I think some people like (to drink) hot soup and some like (to drink) cold soup.

☞ shìde — yes, right (IE)

A: Tā shì nǐ de lǎoshī ma?
Is he your teacher?

B: Shìde.
Yes.

6. **guó** — **country, state, nation** (N)

A: Nǐ shì Yīngguórén ma?
Are you English?

B: Shì, wǒ shì Yīngguórén.
Yes, I am English.

☞ guówáng — king (N)

A: "Guówáng" shì shénme yìsi?
What does "guowang" mean?

B: "Guówáng" shì yì guó de "wáng" de yìsi.
"Guowang" means the king of a country.

7. **yì** — **meaning, idea, intention** (N)

☞ dàyì   careless (SV); general idea (S); main point(s) (N)

(1) Nǐ shuōhuà tài dàyì, děi   You speak too carelessly. Be
    xiǎoxīn.   careful (when you speak).

(2) Jīntiān lǎoshī shuō de huà,   What are the main ideas of the
    dàyì shì shénme?   teacher's lecture today?

☞ tóngyì   agree, consent, approve (V)

A: Nǐ tóngyì nǐ bàba māma   Do you agree with what your
   shuō de huà ma?   father and mother say?

B: Yǒude wǒ tóngyì.   I agree with some of what they
                                    say.

☞ shēngyi   business, trade (N)

Tā bàba de shēngyi hěn dà.   His father's business is very
                                    large.

8. sī   **think, consider; think of; long for** (V)

☞ yìsi   meaning, idea, opinion (N)

A: Nǐ de yìsi shì wǒmen míngtiān   Do you mean we will go to the
   qù yínháng ma?   bank tomorrow?

B: Shì.   Yes.

☞ yǒuyìsi   interesting, significant, meaningful (SV)

A: Tā jīntiān shuō de huà   Was what he said today
   yǒuyìsi ma?   interesting?

B: Hěn yǒuyìsi.   Very interesting.

A: Tā yě shì hěn yǒuyìsi de rén.   He is also a very interesting
                                    person.

☞ xiǎoyìsi   small token of kindly feelings (IE)

A: Zhè shì Yīngguó hěn yǒumíng   This is a celebrated English
   de hóngchá, sòng gěi nǐ.   black tea. I'd like to give it to
                                    you.

B: Nǐ zhème hǎo.   That's very kind of you.

A: Méishénme, xiǎoyìsi.   It's nothing, just a small token.

☞ bùhǎoyìsi   feel embarrassed, be ill at ease, find it embarrassing (to do something) (IE)

> A: Wǒ lái wǎn le, bùhǎoyìsi.   I have come late. I am very sorry.
>
> B: Méishénme.   That's alright.

9. **yīng**   **hero** (N)

☞ Yīngguó   Britain, England (PW)

> A: Nǐ ài Yīngguó ma?   Do you love England?
>
> B: Wǒ hěn ài Yīngguó.   I love England very much.

10. **wén**   **character, written script, language (N); literary** (Adj)

☞ Yīngwén   English (language) (N)

> A: Zhè shì shénme guójiā de xiǎoshuō?   What country is this novel from?
>
> B: Zhè shì Yīngwén xiǎoshuō.   This is an English novel.

☞ Rìwén   Japanese (language) (N)

> A: Nǐ xiǎng, xué Rìwén yǒuyìsi ma?   Do you think learning Japanese is interesting?
>
> B: Wǒ xiǎng yǒuyìsi.   I think it's interesting.
>
> A: Nǐ xiǎng xué ma?   Are you thinking of studying it?
>
> B: Xiǎng.   (I) want (to study it).

☞ wénxué   literature (N)

> A: Wǒ hěn xiǎng xué Yīngguó wénxué. Nǐ ne?   I really want to study English literature. What about you?
>
> B: Wǒ yě xiǎng xué Yīngguó wénxué.   I also want to study English literature.
>
> A: Nà, wǒmen dōu xué Yīngguó wénxué, hǎo ma?   Then, we'll both study English literature, okay?
>
> B: Hǎo.   Okay.

🐾 Pattern Drills

2.1 THE EQUATIVE VERB jiào

Jiào "be called, be named" is an equative verb. It is used to ask people's given names or the names of objects.

S	EV	QW	N
Nǐ	jiào	shénme	míngzi?
What is your given name?			

1. A: Nǐ jiào shénme míngzi?   What is your given name?

    B: Wǒ jiào Xiǎoměi.   My name is Xiaomei.

2. Nà běn xiǎoshuō jiào shénme míngzi?   What is the title of that novel?

3. Wǒ jiào Yè Míng, nǐ ne?   My name is Ye Ming, and yours?

2.2 THE VERB jiào

S	V	N
Lǎoshī	jiào	nǐ.
The teacher is calling you.		

1. Mèimei, bàba jiào nǐ.   Little sister, father is calling you.

2. Jiějie jiào nǐ děng tā.   Elder sister asked you to wait for her.

3. Māma jiào wǒmen hē tāng.   Mother asked us to have some soup.

2.3 THE SUBORDINATING PARTICLE de

The subordinating particle de in an "A-de-B" phrase functions as follows: the "A" element modifies and is subordinate to the "B" element. The "A" element may be a noun, a pronoun, a stative verb, a time word or a more complicated expression. Following are some examples of subordination with de.

2.3.1 The subordinating particle <u>de</u> with a noun

N	<u>de</u>	N
Gēge	de	shǒubiǎo
Elder brother's watch		

1. Měiguó de xiǎoshuō hěn hǎo. American novels are very good.

2. Wáng lǎoshī de míngzi shì Guóyīng. Professor Wang's given name is Guoying.

3. Rìběn de cháyè hěn hǎo. Japanese tea is very good.

2.3.2 The subordinating particle <u>de</u> with a pronoun

The subordinating particle <u>de</u> with a pronoun is used to indicate the ownership of the modified noun.

Pron	<u>de</u>	N
Wǒ	de	qián
My money		

1. Wǒ de qián zài yínháng. My money is in the bank.

2. Wǒmen de tǔdì hěn dà. We have a lot of land.

3. Nǐ de biǎo hǎo ma? Is your watch good?

2.3.3 The subordinating particle <u>de</u> with a stative verb

The subordinating particle <u>de</u> with a stative verb serves as an adjective to describe the modified noun.

SV	<u>de</u>	N
Yǒumíng	de	rén
Famous person		

1. Tā shì yǒumíng de rén. He is a well-known person.

2. Shéi shì rèxīn de rén? Who is an enthusiastic person?

3.　Tā yǒu hěn měi de tàitai.   He has a beautiful wife.

4.　Tā shì hěn kuàilè de rěn.   He is a very happy person.

2.3.4 The subordinating particle <u>de</u> with time words

When the subordinating particle <u>de</u> is used with time words, the time word modifies the noun which follows.

TW	<u>de</u>	*N*
Jīntiān	de	bào
Today's newspaper		

1.　A: Zhè shì jīntiān de bào ma?   Is this today's newspaper?

　　B: Zhè shì jīntiān de bào.   This is today's newspaper.

2.　A: Jīntiān de cài hǎo chī ma?   Is today's food good?

　　B: Jīntiān de cài hěn hǎo chī.   Today's food is delicious.

2.3.5 The subordinating particle <u>de</u> with a verb

When the subordinating particle <u>de</u> is used with a verb, it modifies the noun which follows, and forms a noun phrase.

V	<u>de</u>	*N*
Shuō	de	huà
What (one) said		

1.　Māma hē de tāng hěn rè.   The soup mother is drinking is very hot.

2.　Tā hē de jiǔ hěn hǎo.   The wine she is drinking is very good.

3.　Wǒ tóngxué shuō de huà hěn   What my classmate said was very
　　yǒuyìsi.   interesting.

2.3.6 Omitting the subordinating particle <u>de</u>

The particle <u>de</u> is often omitted when a pronoun is subordinated to a noun expressing personal relationship or after a noun in certain patterns.

	Pron	*(<u>de</u>)*	*N*
(1)	Wǒ		māma
	My mother		
(2)	Mǎ		jiā
	The Ma's home		

If more than one <u>de</u> appears in a sentence, the first <u>de</u> after the pronoun is usually omitted.

Pron	*(<u>de</u>)*	*N*	*<u>de</u>*	*N*
Wǒ	(de)	péngyou	de	shēngrì
My friend's birthday				

1. Zhè shǐ wǒ (de) péngyou de bǐ.   This is my friend's pen.
2. Wǒ (de) māma de qián zài yínháng.   My mother's money is in the bank.

2.4 THE PATTERN <u>yǒude</u> … <u>yǒude</u>

The <u>yǒude</u> … <u>yǒude</u> "some of … some of" pattern is used to describe the various components of an aggregation, or a collective or plural noun designating a whole at the beginning of a sentence, after which the parts follow.

Whole	<u>youde</u>-*Part …*	<u>youde</u>-*Part …*
Wǒ de péngyou,	yǒude shì Měiguórén,	yǒude shì Yīngguórén.
As for my friends, some of them are American and some are English.		

1. Tā de xiǎoshuō, yǒude shì Rìwén de, yǒude shì Yīngwén de.

   As for her novels, some are in Japanese and some are in English.

2. Wǒ de tóngxué dōu ài hē tāng. Yǒude ài hē rè tāng, yǒude ài hē lěng tāng.

   All my classmates love (to drink) soup; some of them love hot soup and some love cold soup.

2.5 THE VERB g<u>ěi</u>

G<u>ěi</u> "give" has several uses. When it is used in the following pattern, it functions as a verb.

S	V	IO	DO
Māma	gěi	wǒ	qián.
Mother gave me (some) money.			

1. Qǐng nǐ gěi wǒ qiānbǐ.   Please give me a pencil.

2. Lǎoshī gěi xuésheng zhǐ.   The teacher gave the students paper.

3. Wǒ gēge gěi wǒ shǒubiǎo.   My elder brother gave me a watch.

4. A: Nǐ bàba gěi nǐ qián ma?   Does your father give you money?
   B: Wǒ bàba gěi wǒ qián.   My father gives me money.

2.5.1 G<u>ěi</u> after a verb

When g<u>ěi</u> comes after a verb, it functions as the preposition "to."

S	(AV)	V	<u>gei</u>	IO	DO
Wǒ	yào	sòng	gěi	māma	huā.
I'd like to send some flowers to my mother.					

1. Wǒ xiǎng sònggěi tā zhè běn xiǎoshuō.   I'd like to give him this novel as a present.

2. Bàba sònggěi māma hěn hǎo de shǒubiǎo.   Father gave mother a very good watch.

3. Tā sònggěi wǒ de nà běn xiǎoshuō hěn yǒumíng.   The novel he gave me is very famous.

🌸 Sentence Building

1.

Jiào

Jiào shénme?

Jiào shénme míngzi?

Nǐ jiào shénme míngzi?

Wǒ jiào Wáng Sān.

2.

De

Shéi de?

Shéi de zhǐ?

Shì shéi de zhǐ?

Zhè shì shéi de zhǐ?

3.

Xìng

Xìng Wáng

Shénme rén xìng Wáng?

Nàge rén xìng Wáng.

4.

Wénxué

Yīngguó wénxué

Xué Yīngguó wénxué

Wǒ xiǎng xué Yīngguó wénxué.

🌸 Questions and Responses

1. Nǐ jiào shénme míngzi?
   What is your given name?

   Wǒ jiào Xiǎoměi.
   My given name is Xiaomei.

2. Tā jiào shénme míngzi?
   What is his given name?

   Tā jiào Sīwén.
   His given name is Siwen.

3. Nǐ mèimei jiào shénme míngzi?
   What is your younger sister's given name?

   Wǒ mèimei jiào Àiwén.
   My younger sister's given name is Aiwen.

4. Nǐ jiějie jiào shénme míngzi?
   What is your elder sister's given name?

   Wǒ jiějie jiào Guóyīng.
   My elder sister's given name is Guoying.

5. Zhè shì shéi de qiānbǐ?
   Whose pencil is this?

   Zhè shì wǒ gēge de qiānbǐ.
   This is my elder brother's pencil.

6. Zhè shì shéi de shǒubiǎo?
   Whose watch is this?

   Zhè shì wǒ māma de shǒubiǎo.
   This is my mother's watch.

7. Shéi hěn yǒumíng?
   Who is very famous?

   Tā bàba hěn yǒumíng.
   His father is very famous.

8. Nǐmen dōu shì Měiguórén ma?

   Are all of you American?

   Wǒmen yǒude shì Měiguórén, yǒude shì Yīngguórén.
   Some of us are American and some of us are English.

9. Nǐmen dōu xué Rìběn wénxué ma?

   Are all of you studying Japanese
   literature?

   Wǒmen yǒude xué Rìběn wénxué,
   yǒude xué Yīnguó wénxué.
   Some of us are studying Japanese
   literature and some of us are
   studying English literature.

10. Nǐmen dōu ài hē jiǔ ma?

    Do all of you like to drink wine?

    Wǒmen yǒude ài hē jiǔ, yǒude ài
    hē qìshuǐ.
    Some of us like to drink wine and
    some of us like to have soft drinks.

Pronunciation Review

Contrasting Retroflexes and Palatals

(a)	zhā	jiā	(d)	zhào	jiào	(g)	zhàn	jiàn
(b)	chà	qià	(e)	chǎo	qiǎo	(h)	chán	qián
(c)	shā	xiā	(f)	shào	xiào	(i)	shān	xiān

Fun Activity

Play a Name Game

Qǐng Kāi Mén Please Open the Door	
A: Pēng, pēng, pēng. 　　Qǐng kāi mén.	A: Knock, knock, knock. 　　Please open the door.
B: Nǐ shì shéi?	B: Who are you?
A: Wǒ shì nǐ tóngxué.	A: I am your classmate.
B: Nǐ xìng shénme?	B: What is your family name?
A: Wǒ xìng Léi.	A: My family name is Lei.
B: Léi shénme?	B: Lei what?
A: Léi Dàmíng.	A: Lei Daming.
B: Nǐ shì Léi Dàmíng. 　　Qǐng jìn, qǐng jìn. 　　Qǐng zuò, qǐng hē chá.	B: You are Lei Daming. 　　Please come in, come in. 　　Please sit down and have some tea.

🌸 Cultural Notes

1. In Chinese, the family name (last name) is the first element in a person's name. Given name (first name), usually one or two syllables, follows the family name. For example:

	Xìng Family name (Last name)	Míng Given name (First name)	Chēngwèi Title
Liping Huang	Huáng	Lǐpíng	
Miss Weina Mao	Máo	Wéinà	Xiǎojiě
Chairman Mao	Máo		Zhǔxī

2. A married woman in the People's Republic of China now usually does not take her husband's family name. The Chinese include family names in addressing one another more than Americans do. In China and Taiwan, teachers address a student by his or her full name (family name and given name). Students address their teachers by family name with the title Lǎoshī, to show respect.

第二課
漢字本

內容

✿✿ 課 文

你叫甚麼名字？

老師 ：同學們早！

學生們：早！

老師 ：你們好嗎？

學生們：很好。

老師 ：你叫甚麼名字？

學生 1 ：我叫小美。

老師 ：你的名字叫甚麼？

學生 2 ：我叫思文。

老師 ：你妹妹叫甚麼名字？

學生 2 ：她叫愛文。

老師 ：你的名字叫甚麼呢？

學生 3 ：我叫Helen。

老師 ：你的中國名字叫海英，好嗎？

學生 3 ：好，我姓林，叫海英。

老師 ：很好。你們的名字的意思都很好。

🌸 生詞及例句

1. 叫　　**call** (V/EV)

　　(1) 媽媽叫你來。

　　(2) "鉛筆"英文叫甚麼？

　　(3) 愛文，他叫甚麼名字？

2. 名　　**name** (N)

☞ 有名　well-known, famous, celebrated (SV)

　　(1) 那本小説很有名。

　　(2) 這是很有名的手錶。

☞ 名人　famous person, celebrity (N)

　　A: 你們的老師有名嗎？

　　B: 他很有名，他是名人。

3. 字　　**word, character, writing** (N)

☞ 名字　given name, first name, name (N)

　　A: 你叫甚麼名字？

　　B: 我叫美英。

☞ 文字　characters, script, writing, written language (N)

　　(1) 我國的文字很美。

　　(2) 這是日本的文字。

4. 美　　**beautiful, pretty; short form of "American"** (SV)

☞ 美人　beautiful woman, beauty (N)

　　A: 我的同學都説你姐姐是美人。

　　B: 是嗎！

☞ 美國　　The United States of America (PW)

A: 誰是<u>美國</u>人？

B: <u>林海英</u>是<u>美國</u>人。

5. 的　　(subordinating particle)

A: 這是誰的手錶？

B: 這是<u>許小美</u>的手錶。

☞ 有的　　some (+ N/Adj)

A: 人人都愛喝熱湯，是嗎？

B: 我想有的人愛喝熱湯，有的人愛喝冷湯。

☞ 是的　　yes, right (IE)

A: 他是你的老師嗎？

B: 是的。

6. 國　　**country, state, nation** (N)

A: 你是<u>英國</u>人嗎？

B: 是，我是<u>英國</u>人。

☞ 國王　　king (N)

A: "國王"是甚麼意思？

B: "國王"是一國的"王"的意思。

7. 意　　**meaning, idea, intention** (N)

☞ 大意　　careless (SV); general idea (S); main point(s) (N)

(1) 你說話太大意，得小心。

(2) 今天老師說的話，大意是甚麼？

☞ 同意　　agree, consent, approve (V)

A: 你同意你爸爸媽媽說的話嗎？

B: 有的我同意。

☞ 生意　　　　　business, trade (N)

他爸爸的生意很大。

8. **思**　　　　　**think, consider; think of; long for** (V)

☞ 意思　　　　　meaning, idea, opinion (N)

A: 你的意思是我們明天去銀行嗎？

B: 是。

☞ 有意思　　　　interesting, significant, meaningful (SV)

A: 他今天說的話有意思嗎？

B: 很有意思。

A: 他也是很有意思的人。

☞ 小意思　　　　small token of kindly feelings (IE)

A: 這是英國很有名的紅茶，送給你。

B: 你這麼好。

A: 沒甚麼，小意思。

☞ 不好意思　　　feel embarrassed, be ill at ease, find it embarrassing (to do something) (IE)

A: 我來晚了，不好意思。

B: 沒甚麼。

9. **英**　　　　　**hero** (N)

☞ 英國　　　　　Britain, England (PW)

A: 你愛英國嗎？

B: 我很愛英國。

10. **文**　　　　　**character, written script, language (N); literary** (Adj)

☞ 英文　　　　　English (language) (N)

A: 這是甚麼國家的小說？

B: 這是英文小說。

☞ 日文　　　Japanese (language) (N)

　　　　　　A: 你想，學日文有意思嗎？

　　　　　　B: 我想有意思。

　　　　　　A: 你想學嗎？

　　　　　　B: 想。

☞ 文學　　　literature (N)

　　　　　　A: 我很想學英國文學。你呢？

　　　　　　B: 我也想學英國文學。

　　　　　　A: 那，我們都學英國文學，好嗎？

　　　　　　B: 好。

句型練習

2.1 THE EQUATIVE VERB 叫

叫 "be called, be named" is an equative verb. It is used to ask people's given names or the names of objects.

S	EV	QW	N
你	叫	甚麼	名字？

What is your given name?

1. A: 你叫甚麼名字？
   B: 我叫小美。

2. 那本小說叫甚麼名字？

3. 我叫葉名，你呢？

2.2 THE VERB 叫

S	V	N
老師	叫	你。
The teacher is calling you.		

1. 妹妹，爸爸叫你。

2. 姐姐叫你等她。

3. 媽媽叫我們喝湯。

2.3 THE SUBORDINATING PARTICLE 的

The subordinating particle 的 in an "A-的-B" phrase functions as follows: the "A" element modifies and is subordinate to the "B" element. The "A" element may be a noun, a pronoun, a stative verb, a time word or a more complicated expression. Following are some examples of subordination with 的.

2.3.1 The subordinating particle 的 with a noun

N	的	N
哥哥	的	手錶
Elder brother's watch		

1. 美國的小說很好。

2. 王老師的名字是國英。

3. 日本的茶葉很好。

2.3.2 The subordinating particle 的 with a pronoun

The subordinating particle 的 with a pronoun is used to indicate the ownership of the modified noun.

Pron	的	N
我	的	錢
My money		

1. 我的錢在銀行。

2. 我們的土地很大。

3. 你的錶好嗎？

2.3.3 The subordinating particle 的 with a stative verb

The subordinating particle 的 with a stative verb serves as an adjective to describe the modified noun.

SV	的	N
有名	的	人
Famous person		

1. 他是有名的人。

2. 誰是熱心的人？

3. 他有很美的太太。

4. 他是很快樂的人。

2.3.4 The subordinating particle 的 with time words

When the subordinating particle 的 is used with time words, the time word modifies the noun which follows.

TW	的	N
今天	的	報
Today's newspaper		

1. A: 這是今天的報嗎？

   B: 這是今天的報。

2. A: 今天的菜好吃嗎？

   B: 今天的菜很好吃。

2.3.5 The subordinating particle 的 with a verb

When the subordinating particle 的 is used with a verb, it modifies the noun which follows, and forms a noun phrase.

V	的	N
說	的	話
What (one) said		

1. 媽媽喝的湯很熱。

2. 他喝的酒很好。

3. 我同學說的話很有意思。

2.3.6 Omitting the subordinating particle 的

The particle 的 is often omitted when a pronoun is subordinated to a noun expressing personal relationship or after a noun in certain patterns.

	Pron	(的)	N
(1)	我		媽媽
	My mother		
(2)	馬		家
	The Ma's home		

If more than one 的 appears in a sentence, the first 的 after the pronoun is usually omitted.

Pron	(的)	N	的	N
我	(的)	朋友	的	生日
My friend's birthday				

1. 這是我 (的) 朋友的筆。

2. 我 (的) 媽媽的錢在銀行。

2.4 THE PATTERN 有的……有的

The 有的……有的 "some of … some of" pattern is used to describe the various components of an aggregation, or a collective or plural noun designating a whole at the beginning of a sentence, after which the parts follow.

Whole	有的-*Part* …	有的-*Part* …
我的朋友，	有的是美國人，	有的是英國人。
As for my friends, some of them are American and some are English.		

1. 他的小説，有的是日文的，有的是英文的。

2. 我的同學都愛喝湯，有的愛喝熱湯，有的愛喝冷湯。

2.5 THE VERB 給

給 "give" has several uses; when it is used in the following pattern, it functions as a verb.

S	*V*	*IO*	*DO*
媽媽	給	我	錢。
Mother gave me (some) money.			

1. 請你給我鉛筆。

2. 老師給學生紙。

3. 我哥哥給我手錶。

4. A: 你爸爸給你錢嗎？

   B: 我爸爸給我錢。

2.5.1 給 after a verb

When 給 comes after a verb, it functions as the preposition "to."

S	*(AV)*	*V*	給	*IO*	*DO*
我	(要)	送	給	媽媽	花。
I'd like to send some flowers to my mother.					

1. 我想送給他這本小説。

2. 爸爸送給媽媽很好的手錶。

3. 他送給我的那本小説很有名。

🐾 造句

1.
叫

叫甚麼？

叫甚麼名字？

你叫甚麼名字？

我叫王三。

2.
的

誰的？

誰的紙？

是誰的紙？

這是誰的紙？

3.
姓

姓王

甚麼人姓王？

那個人姓王。

4.
文學

英國文學

學英國文學

我想學英國文學。

🐾 問答

1. 你叫甚麼名字？　　　　　　我叫小美。
2. 他叫甚麼名字？　　　　　　他叫思文。
3. 你妹妹叫甚麼名字？　　　　我妹妹叫愛文。
4. 你姐姐叫甚麼名字？　　　　我姐姐叫國英。
5. 這是誰的鉛筆？　　　　　　這是我哥哥的鉛筆。
6. 這是誰的手錶？　　　　　　這是我媽媽的手錶。
7. 誰很有名？　　　　　　　　他爸爸很有名。
8. 你們都是美國人嗎？　　　　我們有的是美國人，有的是英國人。
9. 你們都學日本文學嗎？　　　我們有的學日本文學，有的學英國文學。
10. 你們都愛喝酒嗎？　　　　　我們有的愛喝酒，有的愛喝汽水。

🐾 閱 讀

海英的生日

明天是林海英的生日，我們送她甚麼呢？愛文說，她要送海英鉛筆，思文說，他要送她茶葉，許小美想送她花，王老師也送她花。我送她甚麼呢？我也許送她英文小說。

海英生日那天，她媽媽送她金錶跟錢。有很多同學來給她過生日。同學們，有的送她鉛筆、有的送她茶葉、有的送她花跟英文小說。她很快樂。海英請我們喝汽水、紅茶。她請老師和她媽媽喝酒。我們也吃中國菜和日本菜。那天大家都很快樂。

第三課　介紹我的家人
Lesson 3　Introducing my family

Lesson 3
Pinyin Text

. . . .

CONTENTS

✿ Text

Jièshào wǒ de jiārén
Introducing my family

| Lǎoshī: | Jīntiān qǐng nǐmen jièshào jièshào nǐmen de jiārén. | Today, please introduce your family. |

| Xǔ Xiǎoměi: | Zǎo! Wǒ xìng Xǔ, míngzi jiào Xiǎoměi. Wǒ jiā yǒu wǔ ge rén: bàba, māma, liǎng ge dìdi gēn wǒ. Wǒmen shì Yīngguórén. | Good morning! My family name is Xu, my given name is Xiaomei. There are five people in my family: my father, my mother, two younger brothers and I. We are English. |

| Mǎ Sīwén: | Nǐmen hǎo! Wǒ xìng Mǎ, wǒ de míngzi shì Sīwén. Wǒmen jiā yǒu qī ge rén: bàba, māma, yí ge gēge, yí ge dìdi, yí ge jiějie, yí ge mèimei gēn wǒ. | Hello, everyone! My family name is Ma, my given name is Siwen. There are seven people in my family: my father, my mother, an elder brother, a younger brother, an elder sister, a younger sister and I. |

| Mǎ Àiwén: | Wǒ yě xìng Mǎ, wǒ jiào Àiwén. Mǎ Sīwén shì wǒ gēge. | My family name is also Ma. My given name is Aiwen. Ma Siwen is my elder brother. |

| Lín Hǎiyīng: | Zǎo! Wǒ yě jièshào wǒ de jiārén. Wǒ xìng Lín, jiào Hǎiyīng. Wǒ jiā yǒu wǔ ge rén: bàba, māma, yí ge mèimei, yí ge jiějie gēn wǒ. Wǒ méiyǒu gēge, yě méiyǒu dìdi. Wǒ bàba shì Měiguórén, māma shì Rìběnrén. Wǒ gēn wǒ jiějie, mèimei shì Měiguórén. | Good morning! I will introduce my family too. My family name is Lin. I'm called Haiying. There are five people in my family: my father, my mother, one younger sister, one elder sister and I. I don't have an elder brother or a younger brother. My father is American, my mother is Japanese. My elder sister, my younger sister and I are Americans. |

🎴 Vocabulary and Illustrative Sentences

1. jiā   **family, household, home; a specialist in a certain field; a school of thought** (N)

☞ guójiā   country, state, nation (N)

> A: Nǐ qùguo shénme guójiā?

> What countries have you visited before?

> B: Wǒ qùguo Rìběn, Yīngguó gēn Měiguó.

> I've visited Japan, England and the United States.

☞ dàjiā   everybody, everyone (N)

> (1) A: Nǐmen dàjiā dōu yǒu qiānbǐ hé zhǐ ma?

> Does everyone have pencil and paper?

> B: Wǒmen dōu yǒu.

> We all do.

> (2) A: Dàjiā gēn wǒ shuō: "Zǎo!"

> Everybody repeats after me: "Zao!"

> B: "Zǎo!"

> "Zao!"

☞ lǎojiā   native place; hometown (PW)

> A: Wǒ hěn xiǎng wǒ de lǎojiā.

> I miss my hometown.

> B: Nǐ lǎojiā yǒu shénme rén?

> Who lives at your hometown?

> A: Wǒ bàba de bàba hé māma dōu zài wǒmen lǎojiā.

> My father's father and mother are both at our hometown.

2. jiè   **be situated between** (V)

3. shào   **carry on, continue** (V)

☞ jièshào   introduce, present; recommend (V)

> (1) A: Qǐng nǐ gěi wǒmen jièshào jièshào.

> Please introduce us.

> B: Hǎo, zhè shì wǒ gēge Sīwén. Zhè shì wǒ tóngxué Xǔ Xiǎoměi. Dàjiā dōu jiào tā Xiǎo Xǔ.

> Okay, this is my elder brother Siwen. This is my classmate Xu Xiaomei. Everyone calls her Xiao Xu.

C:	Nǐ hǎo, Mǎ Sīwén!	Hello, Ma Siwen!
A:	Nǐ hǎo, Xǔ Xiǎoměi.	Hi, Xu Xiaomei!
(2)	Qǐng nǐ gěi wǒmén jièshào jièshào nǐ de guójiā.	Please tell us something about your country.
(3)	Wǒ děi xué Yīngwén, qǐng nǐ gěi wǒ jièshào yí ge Yīngwén lǎoshī.	I have to learn English. Please recommend an English teacher to me.

4. **gè** **individual** (N); (MW for person or thing)

☞ gèrén individual (person) (N)

A:	Zhè shì guójiā de tǔdì.	This land belongs to the nation.
B:	Shéi shuō de? Zhè shì wǒ gèrén de.	Says who? This is my own land.

☞ nàge/ nèige that (Det)

A:	Nàge rén shì hǎorén ma?	Is that person a good person?
B:	Wǒ xiǎng tā shì hǎorén. Tā hěn rèxīn.	I think that he is a good person. He is very warm-hearted.

☞ zhège/ zhèige this one; this (Det)

(1)	Zhège guójiā de rénkǒu hěn duō.	This is a populous country.
(2)	Qǐngwèn, zhège zì shì shénme yìsi?	Excuse me, what does this word mean?

5. **dì** **younger brother** (N)

☞ dìdi younger brother (N)

A:	Wǒ yǒu yí ge dìdi.	I have one younger brother.
B:	Nǐ dìdi jiào shénme míngzi?	What is your brother's given name?
A:	Tā jiào Lètiān.	His given name is Letian.

6. liǎng   **two; both; either; a few; some** (Nu)

(1) Nǐmen liǎng ge rén de qián dōu zài yínháng ma? — Do both of you put your money in the bank?

(2) Wǒ māma zhè yìliǎng tiān yào qù Rìběn. — My mother is going to Japan in a couple of days.

7. bà   **pa, dad, father** (N)

A: Dìdi, bà ne? — Little brother, where is Dad?

B: Tā zài hē chá. — He is drinking tea.

☞ bàba   papa, dad, father (N)

A: Nǐ bàba jìnlái hǎo ma? — How has your father been lately?

B: Tā hěn hǎo. Nǐ bàba ne? — He is fine. What about your father?

A: Tā yě hěn hǎo. Nǐ bàba zài jiā ma? — He is also fine. Is your father home?

B: Zài. Qǐng jìn. — Yes, please come in.

8. wǔ   **five** (Nu)

A: Shéi jiā yǒu wǔ ge rén? — Whose family has five people?

B: Lín Hǎiyīng jiā yǒu wǔ ge rén. — Lin Haiying's family has five people.

9. qī   **seven** (Nu)

A: Wǒ yǒu qīshí ge tóngxué. Nǐ ne? — I have seventy classmates. How about you?

B: Wǒ yǒu shíqī ge tóngxué. — I have seventeen classmates.

☞ Qīxǐ   Seven-up (N)

A: Nǐ yào hē shénme qìshuǐ? — Which soft drink do you like to have?

B: Qīxǐ. — Seven-up.

10. **méi**   **not** (Neg/Adv)

☞ méi(yǒu)   does not have, there is not (V)

        (1) Wǒ méi(yǒu) gěi tā   I didn't give him much money.
            duōshǎo qián.

        (2) Wǒ yǒu liǎng ge mèimei,   I have two younger sisters, no
            méi(yǒu) dìdi.   younger brothers.

☞ méishénme   it doesn't matter, it's nothing; that's all right (IE)

        A: Wǒ jīntiān méiyǒu qián   I don't have any money for you
           gěi nǐ.   today.

        B: Méishénme.   That's all right.

☞ yǒu-méiyǒu?   have or have not? (QW)

        A: Nǐ yǒu-méiyǒu qiānbǐ?   Do you have a pencil?

        B: Méiyǒu.   No, I don't.

🌸 Pattern Drills

3.1 THE VERB jièshào

The verb jièshào can be used to introduce people, books, and places. It can be translated as "introduce, recommend, present, brief," depending on the context of the sentence. Jièshào often has to be duplicated or requires some other complement, such as yíxià "a bit," after it.

S	gěi	*N*	jièshào	jièshào
Wǒ	gěi	nǐmen	jièshào	jièshào.

Let me introduce you to each other.

1. Qǐng nǐ gěi wǒmen jièshào yíxià.   Would you please introduce us?

2. Wǒ gěi nǐmen jièshào yì běn hǎo   I'll recommend a good novel to you.
   xiǎoshūo.

3. Wǒ jièshào jièshào wǒ jiārén.   I'll tell you about my family.

4. Qǐng nǐ gěi wǒmen jièshào yíxià nǐ   Please give us a brief introduction
   de guójiā.   to your country.

3.2 THE NEGATIVE PREFIX méi

The negative prefix <u>méi</u> is used with the verb <u>yǒu</u> "have." The <u>yǒu</u> is optional except when it is at the end of a sentence.

S	méi(yǒu)	N
Wǒ	méi(yǒu)	qián.
I don't have any money.		

1. Wǒ méi(yǒu) qiānbǐ. I don't have any pencils.

2. Yǒude xuésheng yǒu shǒubiǎo, yǒude xuésheng méiyǒu. Some students have watches and some don't.

3. Wǒ méi(yǒu) jīnbiǎo. I don't have a gold watch.

3.3 <u>Méi(yǒu)</u> WITH AN ACTION VERB

When an action is negated by <u>méi(yǒu)</u>, it indicates that the action or event in the sentence did not take place.

S	méi(yǒu)	V	O
Wǒ	méi(yǒu)	hē	jiǔ.
I didn't drink wine.			

1. A: Nǐ jīntiān méi(yǒu) qù zhǎo tā ma? Did you go looking for him today?

   B: Wǒ jīntiān méi(yǒu) qù zhǎo tā. I didn't go looking for him today.

2. A: Nǐ qùnián qù Zhōngguó le ma? Did you go to China last year?

   B: Wǒ qùnián méi(yǒu) qù, wǒ jīnnián qù le. I didn't go last year. I went (there) this year.

3.4 THE CHOICE-TYPE QUESTION yǒu-méiyǒu

S	yǒu-méiyǒu	N?
Nǐ	yǒu-méiyǒu	mèimei?
Do you have a younger sister?		

1. A: Nǐ yǒu-méiyǒu jiějie?   Do you have an elder sister?

   B: Wǒ méiyǒu jiějie.   I don't have any elder sisters.

2. A: Nǐmen guójiā yǒu-méiyǒu guówáng?   Does your country have a king?

   B: Méiyǒu.   (We) don't have (a king).

3. A: Nǐ yǒu-méiyǒu Yīngwén xiǎoshuō?   Do you have an English novel?

   B: Wǒ méiyǒu Yīngwén xiǎoshuō,   I don't have any English novels, (but)
      wǒ yǒu Rìwén xiǎoshuō.   I have Japanese novels.

3.5 THE CONJUNCTION gēn

Gēn "and" and hé "and" are conjunctions. They can connect two or more nouns/pronouns. When they connect two or more elements and serve as the subject of a sentence, the subject is often followed by the adverb dōu "all" for plurality.

3.5.1 N gēn N as a subject

N	gēn	N	dōu	EV	O
Wǒ	gēn	tā	dōu	shì	xuésheng.
He and I are both students.					

1. A: Nǐ gēn tā dōu yào hē chá ma?   Do both of you want to drink tea?

   B: Wǒ gēn tā dōu yào hē chá.   He and I both want to drink tea.

2. A: Nǐ gēn tā dōu yào xué Yīngguó   Do both of you want to study
      wénxué ma?   English literature?

   B: Wǒ gēn tā dōu yào xué Yīngguó   Both of us want to study English
      wénxué.   literature.

3. Wǒ gēn tā de shēngrì dōu shì jīntiān. Today is our birthday.

3.5.2 N gēn N as an object

S	V	N	gēn	N
Wǒ	yǒu	zhǐ	gēn	bǐ.
I have paper and pen.				

1. A: Nǐ yǒu shénme?   What have you got?

   B: Wǒ yǒu qián gēn qiānbǐ.   I've got money and a pencil.

2. A: Nǐ yào hē shénme?   What do you want to drink?

   B: Wǒ yào hē chá gēn qìshuǐ.   I'd like to have tea and soft drinks.

3.6 THE DETERMINATIVES zhè/zhèi AND nà/nèi

Zhè/zhèi "this" and nà/nèi "that" are determinatives. They precede a number before a measure word. The number yī "one" is optional after zhè/zhèi or nà/nèi.

	Det	Nu	MW	N
(1)	Zhè/zhèi	sān	ge	xuésheng
	These three students			
(2)	Nà/nèi	bā	běn	xiǎoshuō
	Those eight (volumes of) novels			
(3)	Zhè/nà	(yì)	běn	xiǎoshuō
	This/that (volume of) novel			

1. A: Zhè běn xiǎoshuō shì shéi de?   Whose novel is this?

   B: Zhè běn xiǎoshuō shì wǒ de.   This novel is mine.

2. A: Nàge rén xìng shénme?   What is that person's last name?

   B: Tā xìng Wáng.   Her last name is Wang.

3. A: Zhèi sān ge biǎo dōu shì nǐ de ma?   Are these three watches all yours?

   B: Zhèi sān ge biǎo dōu bú shì wǒ de.   None of these watches are mine.

4. A: Nǐ ài nèi ge rén ma?   Do you love that person?

   B: Wǒ hěn ài tā.   Yes, I love him very much.

3.7 THE GENERAL MEASURE WORD ge

A measure word is a grammatical element that follows a number: in yí ge rén "one person," ge is a measure word. A measure word must be used between a number and a noun. A number cannot precede a noun directly. When the word ge is used as a measure word, it is pronounced in its neutral tone.

S	V	Nu	MW	N
Wǒ	yǒu	sān	ge	tóngxué.
I have three classmates.				

1. A: Wǒ yǒu liǎng ge mèimei, nǐ ne?   I have two younger sisters. How about you?

   B: Wǒ yǒu yí ge mèimei.   I have one younger sister.

2. A: Zhège biǎo shì shéi de?   Whose watch is this?

   B: Zhège biǎo shì wǒmen lǎoshī de.   This watch is our teacher's.

3. A: Nàge rén shì shéi?   Who is that person?

   B: Nàge rén shì wǒ māma.   That person is my mother.

3.8 THE NUMBER "TWO" èr AND liǎng

There are two forms for the number "two" in Mandarin Chinese, èr and liǎng. Sometimes either form can be used. Sometimes one cannot correctly replace the other.

3.8.1 Before a measure word

When the number "two" appears before a measure word, liǎng is most often used.

Nu	MW	N
Liǎng	běn	shū
Two (volumes of) books		

Wǒ yǒu liǎng běn xiǎoshuō.   I have two (volumes of) novels.

3.8.2 As the last digit of a numerical expression

When "two" is the last digit of a numerical expression, èr is used.

Nu	MW	N
Shíèr	ge	rén
Twelve people		

Wǒ yǒu èrshíèr ge tóngxué.   I have twenty-two classmates.

3.8.3 As cardinal numbers

When counting numbers, or when the number "two" appears before shí "ten," èr is used.

1. yī, èr, sān ...   one, two, three …

2. shíèr   twelve

3. èrshíèr   twenty-two

3.8.4 As ordinal numbers

Èr is used as ordinal number.

1. dì-èr ge rén   the second person

2. xingqī èr   Tuesday (i.e. the second day of a week)

3. èr yuè   February (i.e. the second month of a year)

4. A: Nǎge rén shì nǐ mèimei?   Which one is your little sister?
    B: Dì-èr ge rén shì wǒ mèimei.   The second one is my sister.

3.9 THE VERB SUFFIX -guo

When the word guò "pass" is used as a verb suffix, it is pronounced in its neutral tone. The verb suffix -guo indicates that some action or event has taken place in the past. The meaning of -guo is determined by the time expression in the sentence.

3.9.1 -guo with a time expression

In a sentence where a specific time is mentioned or understood, -guo indicates that an event or action has already been completed during that time.

S	TW	V-guo	O
Tā	qùnián	xuéguo	Yīngwén.

He studied English last year.

3.9.2 -guo with no time expression

In a sentence where no specific time is mentioned, -guo indicates that the event has happened at least once in the past.

S	V-guo	O
Wǒ	qùguo	Rìběn.

I have been to Japan (at some time in the past).

3.9.3 The negative form of V-guo

Sentences that contain a verb and the suffix -guo are always negated by using the expression méiyǒu.

S	méiyǒu	V-guo	O
Tā	méiyǒu	hēguo	qìshuǐ.

He has never had soft drinks (before).

3.9.4 An interrogative sentence with -guo

There are three ways to form an interrogative sentence with a verb plus -guo:

3.9.4.1	S	V-guo	O	ma?
	Nǐ	hēguo	Rìběn jiǔ	ma?

Have you ever had Japanese wine?

> 3.9.4.2   *S*   y<u>ǒu-méiyǒu</u>   *V*-<u>guo</u>   *O*
>   Nǐ   yǒu-méiyǒu   hēguo   Rìběn jiǔ?
> Have you ever had (or not) Japanese wine?
>
> 3.9.4.3   *S*   *V*-<u>guo</u>   *O*   <u>méiyǒu</u>?
>   Nǐ   hēguo   Rìběn jiǔ   méiyǒu?
> Have you ever had Japanese wine or not?

1. A: Nǐ qùguo Yīngguó ma?   Have you ever been to England?

    B: Wǒ méi(yǒu) qùguo Yīngguó.   I have never been to England.

2. A: Nǐ xuéguo Rìwén méiyǒu?   Have you ever studied Japanese?

    B: Wǒ xuéguo.   (Yes,) I have.

3. A: Nǐ jīntiān qùguo yínháng méiyǒu?   Have you been to the bank today?

    B: Wǒ méi(yǒu) qùguo.   I haven't been to the bank today.

3.10 <u>Zài</u> AS A VERB

<u>Zài</u> has many uses. When it is used to indicate a location, it means "in, at or on."

> *N*   <u>zài</u>   *PW*
> Bào   zài   tā jiā.
> The newspaper is at his house.

1. A: Nǐ de qián zài jiā ma?   Is your money at home?

    B: Wǒ de qián bú zài jiā, zài yínháng.   My money is not at home. (It is) in the bank.

2. A: Nǐ bàba zài jiā ma?   Is your dad at home?

    B: Tā zài jiā.   Yes, he is (at home).

3. A: Nǐ gēge gēn jiějie yě zài jiā ma?   Are your elder brother and sister at home too?

    B: Tāmen yě dōu zài jiā.   Yes, they are also at home.

ing se.

3.10.1 <u>Zài</u> as a durative marker

When <u>zài</u> comes before an action verb, it functions as a durative marker and indicates an ongoing activity.

S	<u>zài</u>	V	O
Māma	zài	hē	chá.
Mother is drinking tea.			

1. Wǒ māma **zài** gēn bàba shuōhuà. — My mother is talking with my father.
2. Xuésheng dōu **zài** dǎ qiú. — The students are all playing ball.
3. Wǒmen dōu **zài** xué Yīngwén. — We are all studying English.

Sentence Building

1.
Shénme
Shénme rén?
Shì shénme rén?
Tā shì shénme rén?
Tā shì wǒ dìdi.

2.
Liǎng ge
Liǎng ge guójiā
Qùguo liǎng ge guójiā.
Shéi qùguo liǎng ge guójiā?
Wǒ qùguo liǎng ge guójiā.

3.
Méi
Méiyǒu.
Méi(yǒu) qián.
Nǐ yǒu-méiyǒu qián?
Wǒ méi(yǒu) qián.

4.
-guo
Qùguo.
Méi qùguo.
Méi qùguo Yīngguó.
Tā méi qùguo Yīngguó.

Questions and Responses

1. Nǐ qùguo shénme guójiā?
   To which countries have you been?

   Wǒ qùguò Yīngguó, yě qùguò Měiguó.
   I have been to England and America.

2. Zhè liǎng ge biǎo shì shéi de?
   To whom do these two watches belong?

   Yí ge shì wǒ de, yí ge shì wǒ jiějie de.
   One is mine and one is my elder sister's.

3. Nǐ yǒu-méiyǒu qùguo Rìběn?
    Have you ever been to Japan?

    Wǒ méi qùguo Rìběn, wǒ bàba qùguo.
    I have never been to Japan, but my father has been there.

4. Nà liǎng běn xiǎoshuō yǒu yìsi ma?
    Are those two novels interesting?

    Nà liǎng běn xiǎoshuō méiyǒuyìsi.
    No, they are not interesting.

5. Qǐng nǐ gěi wǒ jièshào jièshào, hǎo ma?
    Would you please introduce me?

    Hǎo, zhè shì Wáng lǎoshī, zhè shì wǒ tóngxué Hǎiyīng.
    Sure, this is Professor Wang. This is my classmate Haiying.

6. Nǐ jìnlái máng ma?
    Have you been busy lately?

    Wǒ jìnlái hěn máng.
    Yes, I have been very busy lately.

7. Nǐ yào hē shénme?
    What would you like to drink?

    Chá.
    Tea.

8. Zhōng-Měi liǎng guó dōu hěn dà ma?
    Are China and America both large countries?

    Shìde. Zhè liǎng ge guójiā dōu hěn dà.
    Yes. They are both large countries.

9. Nǐmen liǎng ge rén dōu yào xué Yīngguó wénxué ma?
    Do both of you want to study English literature?

    Wǒ yào xué Yīngguó wénxué, Àiwén yào xué Rìběn wénxué.
    I want to study English literature, (but) Aiwen wants to study Japanese literature.

10. Guóyīng shuō xué Rìwén méiyǒuyìsi. Nǐ tóngyì ma?
    Guoying says Japanese is not interesting to study. Do you agree?

    Wǒ tóngyì.

    Yes, I agree.

❧ Pronunciation Review

Differentiating i-ü and ie-üe

(a) nǐ   nǔ   (d) qī   qū   (g) jié   jué
(b) lí   lú   (e) xì   xù   (h) xié   xué
(c) jī   jū   (f) liè   lüè   (i) qiē   quē

🌺 Fun Activity

Let's Sing a Song

Liǎng Zhī Lǎohǔ Two Tigers	
Liǎng zhī lǎohǔ, liǎng zhī lǎohǔ,	Two tigers, two tigers,
Pǎo de kuài, pǎo de kuài.	Running very fast, running very fast.
Yì zhī méiyǒu ěrduo, yì zhī méiyǒu yǐba.	One has no ears, one has no tail.
Zhēn qíguài, zhēn qíguài.	Really strange, really strange.

🌺 Supplementary Vocabulary

Kinship terms are always used as terms of address in family. Kinship terms are usually used with close acquaintances, they may be used with a family name or used alone. Children often use kinship terms as a polite and friendly way to address strangers who are senior to them.

Some Chinese Kinship Terms

yéye/zǔfù	grandfather (father's father)
nǎinai/zǔmǔ	grandmother (father's mother)
wàigōng/wàizǔfù	grandfather (mother's father)
wàipó/wàizǔmǔ	grandmother (mother's mother)
bóbo/bófù	uncle (father's elder brother)
shěnshen/bómǔ	aunt (the wife of father's elder brother)
shūshu/shūfù	uncle (father's younger brother)
jiùjiu/ jiùfù	uncle (mother's brother)
jiùmā/ jiùmǔ	aunt (the wife of mother's brother)
jiěfù	brother-in-law (the husband of elder sister)
mèifù	brother-in-law (the husband of younger sister)
sǎosao	sister-in-law (the wife of elder brother)
dìmèi	sister-in-law (the wife of younger brother)

第三課
漢字本

内容

🐾 課文

介紹我的家人

老　　師：今天請你們介紹介紹你們的家人。

許小美：早，我姓許，名字叫小美。我家有五個人：爸爸、媽媽、兩個弟弟跟我。我們是英國人。

馬思文：你們好！我姓馬，我的名字是思文。我們家有七個人：爸爸、媽媽、一個哥哥、一個弟弟、一個姐姐、一個妹妹跟我。

馬愛文：我也姓馬，我叫愛文。馬思文是我哥哥。

林海英：早！我也介紹我的家人。我姓林，叫海英。我家有五個人：爸爸、媽媽、一個妹妹、一個姐姐跟我。我沒有哥哥，也沒有弟弟。我爸爸是美國人，媽媽是日本人。我跟我姐姐、妹妹是美國人。

🌸 生詞及例句

1. **家**   **family, household, home; a specialist in a certain field; a school of thought** (N)

☞ 國家   country, state, nation (N)

  A: 你去過甚麼國家？

  B: 我去過日本、英國跟美國。

☞ 大家   everybody, everyone (N)

  (1) A: 你們大家都有鉛筆和紙嗎？

    B: 我們都有。

  (2) A: 大家跟我說："早！"

    B: "早！"

☞ 老家   native place; hometown (PW)

  A: 我很想我的老家。

  B: 你老家有甚麼人？

  A: 我爸爸的爸爸和媽媽都在我們老家。

2. **介**   **be situated between** (V)

3. **紹**   **carry on, continue** (V)

☞ 介紹   introduce, present; recommend (V)

  (1) A: 請你給我們介紹介紹。

    B: 好，這是我哥哥思文。這是我同學許小美。大家都叫他小許。

    C: 你好，馬思文！

    A: 你好，許小美。

  (2) 請你給我們介紹介紹你的國家。

  (3) 我得學英文，請你給我介紹一個英文老師。

4. **個**　**individual** (N); (MW for person and things)

☞ 個人　individual (person) (N)

　　A: 這是國家的土地。

　　B: 誰説的？這是我個人的。

☞ 那個　that (Det)

　　A: 那個人是好人嗎？

　　B: 我想他是好人。他很熱心。

☞ 這個　this one; this (Det)

　　(1) 這個國家的人口很多。

　　(2) 請問，這個字是甚麼意思？

5. **弟**　**younger brother** (N)

☞ 弟弟　younger brother (N)

　　A: 我有一個弟弟。

　　B: 你弟弟叫甚麼名字？

　　A: 他叫樂天。

6. **兩**　**two; both; either; a few; some** (Nu)

　　(1) 你們兩個人的錢都在銀行嗎？

　　(2) 我媽媽這一兩天要去日本。

7. **爸**　**pa, dad, father** (N)

　　A: 弟弟，爸呢？

　　B: 他在喝茶。

☞ 爸爸　papa, dad, father (N)

　　A: 你爸爸近來好嗎？

　　B: 他很好。你爸爸呢？

A: 他也很好。你爸爸在家嗎？

B: 在。請進。

8. 五   **five** (Nu)

A: 誰家有五個人？

B: 林海英家有五個人。

9. 七   **seven** (Nu)

A: 我有七十個同學。你呢？

B: 我有十七個同學。

☞ 七喜   Seven-up (N)

A: 你要喝甚麼汽水？

B: 七喜。

10. 沒   **not** (Neg/Adv)

☞ 沒(有)   does not have, there is not (V)

(1) 我沒(有)給他多少錢。

(2) 我有兩個妹妹，沒(有)弟弟。

☞ 沒甚麼   it doesn't matter, it's nothing; that's all right (IE)

A: 我今天沒有錢給你。

B: 沒甚麼。

☞ 有沒有？ have or have not? (QW)

A: 你有沒有鉛筆？

B: 沒有。

❀ 句型練習

3.1 THE VERB 介紹

The verb 介紹 can be used to introduce people, books, and places. It can be translated as "introduce, recommend, present, brief," depending on the context of the sentence. 介紹 often has to be duplicated or requires some other complement, such as 一下 "a bit," after it.

S	給	N	介紹介紹
我	給	你們	介紹介紹。

Let me introduce you to each other.

1. 請你給我們介紹一下。

2. 我給你們介紹一本好小說。

3. 我介紹介紹我家人。

4. 請你給我們介紹一下你的國家。

3.2 THE NEGATIVE PREFIX 沒

The negative prefix 沒 is used with the verb 有 "have." The 有 is optional except when it is at the end of a sentence.

S	沒(有)	N
我	沒(有)	錢。

I don't have any money.

1. 我沒(有)鉛筆。

2. 有的學生有手錶，有的學生沒有。

3. 我沒(有)金錶。

3.3 沒有 WITH AN ACTION VERB

When an action is negated by 沒(有), it indicates that the action or event in the sentence did not take place.

S	沒(有)	V	O
我	沒有	喝	酒。
I didn't drink wine.			

1. A: 你今天沒(有)去找他嗎？

   B: 我今天沒(有)去找他。

2. A: 你去年去中國了嗎？

   B: 我去年沒(有)去，我今年去了。

3.4 THE CHOICE-TYPE QUESTION 有沒有

S	有沒有	N?
你	有沒有	妹妹？
Do you have a younger sister?		

1. A: 你有沒有姐姐？

   B: 我沒有姐姐。

2. A: 你們國家有沒有國王？

   B: 沒有。

3. A: 你有沒有英文小說？

   B: 我沒有英文小說，我有日文小說。

3.5 THE CONJUNCTION 跟

跟 "and" and 和 "and" are conjunctions. They can connect two or more nouns/pronouns. When they connect two or more elements and serve as the subject of a sentence, the subject is often followed by the adverb 都 "all" for plurality.

3.5.1 N 跟 N as a subject

N	跟	N	都	EV	O
我	跟	他	都	是	學生。

He and I are both students.

1. A: 你跟他都要喝茶嗎？

   B: 我跟他都要喝茶。

2. A: 你跟他都要學英國文學嗎？

   B: 我跟他都要學英國文學。

3. 我跟他的生日都是今天。

3.5.2 N 跟 N as an object

S	V	N	跟	N
我	有	紙	跟	筆。

I have paper and pen.

1. A: 你有甚麼？

   B: 我有錢跟鉛筆。

2. A: 你要喝甚麼？

   B: 我要喝茶跟汽水。

3.6 THE DETERMINATIVES 這 AND 那

這 "this" and 那 "that" are determinatives. They precede a number before a measure word. The number 一 "one" is optional after zhè/zhèi or nà/nèi.

	Det	Nu	MW	N
(1)	這	三	個	學生
	These three students			
(2)	那	八	本	小説
	Those eight (volumes of) novels			
(3)	這／那	(一)	本	小説
	This/that (volums of) novel			

1. A: 這本小説是誰的？

   B: 這本小説是我的。

2. A: 那個人姓甚麼？

   B: 他姓王。

3. A: 這三個錶都是你的嗎？

   B: 這三個錶都不是我的。

4. A: 你愛那個人嗎？

   B: 我很愛他。

3.7 THE GENERAL MEASURE WORD 個

A measure word is a grammatical element that follows a number: in 一個人 "one person," 個 is a measure word. A measure word must be used between a number and a noun. A number cannot precede a noun directly. When the word 個 is used as a measure word, it is pronounced in its neutral tone.

S	有	Nu	MW	N
我	有	三	個	同學。

I have three classmates.

1. A: 我有兩個妹妹。你呢？

   B: 我有一個妹妹。

2. A: 這個錶是誰的？

   B: 這個錶是我們老師的。

3. A: 那個人是誰？

   B: 那個人是我媽媽。

3.8 THE NUMBER "TWO" 二 AND 兩

There are two forms for the number "two" in Mandarin Chinese, 二 and 兩. Sometimes either form can be used. Sometimes one cannot correctly replace the other.

3.8.1 Before a measure word

When the number "two" appears before a measure word, 兩 is most often used.

Nu	MW	N
兩	本	書
Two (volumes of) books		

我有兩本小說。

3.8.2 As the last digit of a numerical expression

When "two" is the last digit of a numerical expression, 二 is used.

Nu	MW	N
十二	個	人
Twelve people		

我有二十二個同學。

3.8.3 As cardinal numbers

When counting numbers, or when the number "two" appears before 十 "ten," 二 is used.

1. 一、二、三……

2. 十二

3. 二十二

3.8.4 As ordinal numbers

二 is used as ordinal number.

1. 第二個人

2. 星期二

3. 二月

4. A: 哪個人是你妹妹？

   B: 第二個人是我妹妹。

3.9 THE VERB SUFFIX -過

When the word -過 "pass" is used as a verb suffix, it is pronounced in its neutral tone. The verb suffix -過 indicates that some action or event has taken place in the past. The meaning of -過 is determined by the time expression in the sentence.

3.9.1 -過 with a time expression

In a sentence where a specific time is mentioned or understood, -過 indicates that an event or action has already been completed during that time.

S	TW	V-過	O
他	去年	學過	英文。
He studied English last year.			

3.9.2 -過 with no time expression

In a sentence where no specific time is mentioned, -過 indicates that the event has happened at least once in the past.

S	V-過	O
我	去過	日本。
I have been to Japan (at some time in the past).		

3.9.3 The negative form of V-過

Sentences that contain a verb and the suffix -過 are always negated by using the expression 沒有.

S	沒有	V-過	O
他	沒有	喝過	汽水。
He has never had soft drink (before).			

3.9.4 An interrogative sentence with -過

There are three ways to form an interrogative sentence with a verb plus -過:

3.9.4.1	*S*	*V*-過	*O*	嗎?
	你	喝過	日本酒	嗎?

Have you ever had Japanese wine?

3.9.4.2	*S*	有沒有	*V*-過	*O*
	你	有沒有	喝過	日本酒?

Have you ever had (or not) Japanese wine?

3.9.4.3	*S*	*V*-過	*O*	沒有?
	你	喝過	日本酒	沒有?

Have you ever had Japanese wine or not?

1. A: 你去過英國嗎？

   B: 我沒(有)去過英國。

2. A: 你學過日文沒有？

   B: 我學過。

3. A: 你今天去過銀行沒有？

   B: 我沒(有)去過。

3.10 在 AS A VERB

在 has many uses. When it is used to indicate a location, it means "in, at or on."

N	在	*PW*
報	在	他家。

The newspaper is at his house.

1. A: 你的錢在家嗎？

   B: 我的錢不在家，在銀行。

2. A: 你爸爸在家嗎？

   B: 他在家。

3. A: 你哥哥跟姐姐也在家嗎？

    B: 他們也都在家。

3.10.1 在 as a durative marker

When 在 comes before an action verb, it functions as a durative marker and indicates an ongoing activity.

S	在	V	O
媽媽	在	喝	茶。
Mother is drinking tea.			

1. 我媽媽在跟爸爸說話。

2. 學生都在打球。

3. 我們都在學英文。

造 句

1.
甚麼
甚麼人？
是甚麼人？
他是甚麼人？
他是我弟弟。

2.
兩個
兩個國家
去過兩個國家。
誰去過兩個國家？
我去過兩個國家。

3.
沒
沒有。
沒(有)錢。
你有沒有錢？
我沒(有)錢。

4.
-過
去過。
沒去過。
沒去過英國。
他沒去過英國。

問答

1. 你去過甚麼國家？　　　　　　　　我去過英國，也去過美國。
2. 這兩個錶是誰的？　　　　　　　　一個是我的，一個是我姐姐的。
3. 你有沒有去過日本？　　　　　　　我沒去過日本，我爸爸去過。
4. 那兩本小說有意思嗎？　　　　　　那兩本小說沒有意思。
5. 請你給我介紹介紹，好嗎？　　　　好，這是王老師，這是我同學海英。
6. 你近來忙嗎？　　　　　　　　　　我近來很忙。
7. 你要喝甚麼？　　　　　　　　　　茶。
8. 中美兩國都很大嗎？　　　　　　　是的，這兩個國家都很大。
9. 你們兩個人都要學英國文學嗎？　　我要學英國文學，愛文要學日本文學。
10. 國英說學日文沒有意思。　　　　　我同意。
　　 你同意嗎？

閱讀

馬愛文的生日

　　今天是馬愛文的生日。我們同學有的送她花、有的送她筆、有的送她中文小說。我送她花茶。她爸爸跟媽媽送她很好看的手錶，她姐姐送她英文小說，她哥哥送她鉛筆。

　　馬愛文問我們喝甚麼。她說："我們有花茶、紅茶、汽水也有酒。"我說："我喝茶和汽水，不喝酒。"馬太太請我們吃中國菜、喝日本湯。中國菜很好吃，日本湯也很好喝。

　　馬思文是馬愛文的哥哥，他也是我們的同學。他很熱心、跟他說話很有意思。馬愛文今天很美、也很快樂。我們也都很快樂。

第四課　你要選幾門課？
Lesson 4　How many courses are you going to take?

Lesson 4
Pinyin Text

· ·

CONTENTS

🐾 Text

Nǐ yào xuǎn jǐ mén kè?

How many courses are you going to take?

Lín Hǎiyīng:	Mǎ Àiwén, nǐ hǎo ma?	Ma Aiwen, how are you?
Mǎ Àiwén:	Wǒ hěn hǎo. Nǐ ne?	I am fine. And you?
Lín Hǎiyīng:	Wǒ yě hěn hǎo. Mǎ Àiwén, nǐ zhè xuéqī yào xuǎn jǐ mén kè?	I am fine too. Ma Aiwen, how many courses are you taking this semester?
Mǎ Àiwén:	Wǒ xiǎng xuǎn wǔ mén kè. Nǐ ne?	I want to take five courses. And you?
Lín Hǎiyīng:	Wǒ xiǎng xuǎn sì mén kè. Nǐ xiǎng xuǎn shénme kè?	I want to take four courses. What courses are you thinking of taking?
Mǎ Àiwén:	Wǒ xiǎng xuǎn yì mén Zhōngwén, yì mén Rìwén, yì mén Yīngwén, yì mén shùxué gēn yì mén Yīngguó wénxué. Nǐ ne?	I want to take courses in Chinese, Japanese, English, math and English literature. And you?
Lín Hǎiyīng:	Wǒ xiǎng xuǎn yì mén Zhōngwén, yì mén shùxué, yì mén Rìběn wénxué gēn yì mén Yīngwén.	I want to take Chinese, math, Japanese literature and English.
Mǎ Àiwén:	Nǐ xiǎng Rìběn wénxué kè yǒuyìsi ma?	Do you think the Japanese literature course is interesting?
Lín Hǎiyīng:	Wǒ tóngxué shuō zhè mén kè hěn yǒuyìsi, lǎoshī yě hěn hǎo. Nǐ míngnián yào xuǎn nǎ jǐ mén kè?	My classmate told me that this course is very interesting and the teacher is great too. What courses are you going to take next year?
Mǎ Àiwén:	Wǒ xiǎng wènwen wǒ tóngxué de yìsi.	I'd like to ask my classmates' opinions.

✿ Vocabulary and Illustrative Sentences

1. **qī**　　　　　**a period of time, phase, scheduled time** (N)

☞ xuéqī　　　school term, semester (N)

　　　A: Nǐ zhè xuéqī máng-bu-máng?　　Are you busy this semester?

　　　B: Hěn máng. Nǐ ne?　　　　　　Very busy. And you?

　　　A: Yě hěn máng.　　　　　　　　(I am) very busy too.

☞ rìqī　　　　date (N)

　　　A: Zhè shì shénme rìqī de bào?　　What is the date of this
　　　　　　　　　　　　　　　　　　　　newspaper?

　　　B: Shì liùyuè bárì de.　　　　　　It was the paper of 8 June.

☞ zǎo qī　　　early stage; early phase (TW)

　　　A: Nǐ xiǎng xué Zhōngguó zǎo　　Do you want to study ancient
　　　　 qī de wénxué ma?　　　　　　Chinese literature?

　　　B: Zhōngguó zǎo qī de　　　　　Is ancient Chinese literature
　　　　 wénxué yǒuyìsi ma?　　　　　interesting?

　　　A: Wáng lǎoshī shuō hěn　　　　Professor Wang says it's very
　　　　 yǒuyìsi.　　　　　　　　　　interesting.

2. **xuǎn**　　　　**select, choose, pick, elect** (V)

☞ xuǎn kè　　　select courses (VO)

　　　A: Zhè xuéqī nǐ yào xuǎn　　　How many courses are you
　　　　 jǐ mén kè?　　　　　　　　going to take this semester?

　　　B: Wǒ xiǎng xuǎn sì mén kè.　　I want to take four courses.

　　　A: Nǐ nǎ tiān qù xuǎn kè?　　　When are you going to register?

　　　B: Míngtiān.　　　　　　　　　Tomorrow.

☞ dàxuǎn　　　general election (N)

　　　A: Jīnnián dàxuǎn, nǐ xuǎn　　In this year's election, who will
　　　　 shéi?　　　　　　　　　　you vote for?

　　　B: Wǒ děi xiǎngxiang.　　　　I have to think about it.

3. **jǐ**   **how many (QW); a few; several; some (Nu)**

   A: Nǐ qùguo jǐ ge guójiā?   How many countries have you visited?

   B: Wǒ qùguo shí jǐ ge guójiā.   I have visited more than ten countries.

4. **mén**   **entrance, door, gate (N); (MW for courses)**

   (1) A: Qǐng nǐ zài nǐ jiā ménkǒu děng wǒ.   Please wait for me at the entrance to your house.

   B: Hǎo.   Okay.

   (2) A: Nǐ zhè xuéqī xuǎn jǐ mén kè?   How many courses are you taking this semester?

   B: Sì mén.   Four.

5. **kè**   **subject, course, class (N); (MW for lessons)**

   (1) A: Nǐ xuǎn de nà mén kè yǒuyìsi ma?   Is the course you picked interesting?

   B: Méiyìsi.   It is not interesting.

   (2) A: Wǒmen jīntiān xué dì jǐ kè?   Which lesson are we going to study today?

   B: Dì-shí kè.   Lesson ten.

☞ **kèběn**   textbook (N)

   A: Wǒmen de kèběn yǒu Yīngwén méiyǒu?   Does our textbook have an English (edition)?

   B: Wǒmen de kèběn Zhōng-Yīngwén dōu yǒu.   Our textbook has both Chinese and English editions.

☞ **kèwén**   text (N)

   A: Zhè kè de kèwén hěn méiyìsi.   The text for this lesson is very boring.

   B: Wǒ xiǎng hěn yǒuyìsi.   I think it is very interesting.

☞ kèbiǎo   class schedule (N)

A: Lǎoshī shuō míngtiān
gěi wǒmen kèbiǎo.

The teacher says (she will) give
us the class schedule tomorrow.

B: Shì zhège yuè de kèbiǎo, shì
zhè xuéqī de kèbiǎo?

Is it the schedule for this month
or this semester?

A: Shì zhège yuè de.

It is the schedule for this month.

6. sì   **four** (Nu)

☞ sìyuè   April (N)

A: Wǒ sìyuè qù Zhōngguó.

I'm going to China in April.

B: Wǒ gēn nǐ qù, hǎo ma?

Is it okay if I go with you?

7. zhōng   **center, middle, among** (PW)

☞ Zhōngwén   Chinese (language) (N)

A: Wǒ jīnnián yào xué
Zhōngwén, nǐ ne?

I'm going to learn Chinese this
year. What about you?

B: Wǒ māma shuō wǒ jīnnián
děi xué Zhōngwén.

My mother says that I have to
take Chinese this year.

☞ Zhōngguó   China (PW)

A: Shì Zhōngguó dà, shì
Měiguó dà?

Is China bigger or is America
bigger?

B: Zhōng-Měi liǎng guó dōu dà.

China and America are both
large countries.

☞ zhōngxué   middle school (N)

A: Měiyīng, wǒ gěi nǐ jièshào
jièshào, tā shì wǒ zhōngxué
de tóngxué. Tā jiào Àilè.

Meiying, let me introduce you
to my classmate from middle
school. Her name is Aile.

B: Àilè, nǐ hǎo!

Hello, Aile.

C: Nǐ hǎo, Měiyīng!

Hello, Meiying.

☞ zhōngxīn   center, core, hub (N)

> A: Wǒmen qù Xuésheng   Let's go to the Student Center,
> Zhōngxīn, hǎo ma?   okay?
>
> B: Hǎo, wǒ gēn nǐ qù.   Okay, I will go with you.

8. shù   **number** (N)

☞ shùxué   mathematics (N)

> A: Wǒ gēge de shùxué hěn hǎo.   My brother is very good at math.
>
> B: Tā yǒu-méiyǒu xuǎn   Has he taken a math class?
> shùxué kè?
>
> A: Méiyǒu.   No, he has not.

9. nián   **year** (TW)

> A: Yì nián yǒu jǐ ge yuè?   How many months are there in a
>   year?
>
> B: Yì nián yǒu shí'èr ge yuè.   A year has twelve months.

☞ nǎ nián/   which year (QW)
  něi nián

> A: Nǐ shì nǎ nián/něi nián   In which year were you born?
> shēng de?
>
> B: Yījiǔqīsì nián.   1974.

☞ jīnnián   this year (TW)

> Jīnnián Měiguó de dàxuǎn hěn   The general election in the
> yǒuyìsi.   United States this year was very
>   interesting.

☞ míngnián   next year (TW)

> A: Míngnián nǐ yào xuǎn nǎ   What courses are you going to
> jǐ mén kè?   take next year?
>
> B: Wǒ yào xuǎn nǐ jīnnián   I'd like to take those courses that
> xuǎn de kè.   you're taking this year.

☞ hòunián   the year after the next (TW)

> A: Nǐ něi nián qù Yīngguó?   When are you going to England?

B: Wǒ xiǎng hòunián qù.　　　　I am thinking of going (to England) the year after the next.

☞ dàhòunián　three years from now (TW)

Wǒ dàhòunián qù Zhōngguó xué Zhōngwén.　　　　I am going to China to study Chinese three years from now.

☞ qùnián　last year (TW)

A: Qùnián wǒ shì zhōngxué-sheng, nǐ ne?　　　　Last year, I was a middle school student. (What about) you?

B: Wǒ shì dàxuésheng.　　　　I was a college student.

☞ niánnián　every year (TW)

Zhè jǐ nián, niánnián dōu yǒu huǒzāi.　　　　For the past few years, there have been (disastrous) fires every year.

☞ xuénián　school (or academic) year (N)

Wǒmen yì xuénián yǒu liǎng ge xuéqī.　　　　We have two semesters each academic year.

10. nǎ/něi　**which; what** (QW)

A: Nǐ yào xuǎn nǎ/něi mén kè?　　　　Which courses will you take?

B: Nǎ/něi mén kè yǒuyìsi, wǒ xuǎn nǎ/něi mén.　　　　I will pick whichever is the most interesting.

🌸 Pattern Drills

4.1 THE QUESTION WORD nǎ/něi

S	V	nǎ/něi	MW	O
Nǐ	xuǎn	nǎ/něi	mén	kè?
Which courses are you going to take?				

1. A: Nǐ yào hē nǎ guó jiǔ?　　　　Which country's wine would you like to drink?

   B: Wǒ yào hē Zhōngguó jiǔ.　　　　I'd like to drink Chinese wine.

2. A: Nǐ nǎ tiān qù xuǎn kè?   When are you going to register?

    B: Wǒ hòutiān qù xuǎn kè.   I'll register the day after tomorrow.

3. A: Nǎge rén shì nǐ de lǎoshī?   Who is your teacher?

    B: Nǎge Zhōngguórén shì wǒ   That Chinese is my teacher.
       de lǎoshī.

4. A: Nǎ běn xiǎoshuō yǒuyìsi?   Which novel is interesting?

    B: Nǎ běn Yīngwén xiǎoshuō yǒuyìsi,   That English novel is interesting, this
       zhè běn Rìwén xiǎoshuō méiyìsi.   Japanese novel is not interesting.

4.2 THE PATTERN xiǎng

Xiǎng can function as a verb or as an auxiliary verb.

4.2.1 Xiǎng as a verb

When Xiǎng is followed by a direct object, it functions as a verb and means "miss."

S	V	O
Wǒ	xiǎng	jiā.
I miss home.		

1. A: Nǐ xiǎng nǐ māma ma?   Do you miss your mother?

    B: Wǒ hěn xiǎng wǒ māma.   I miss my mother very much.

2. A: Nǐ xiǎng nǐ de guójiā ma?   Do you miss your country?

    B: Wǒ hěn xiǎng wǒ de guójiā.   I miss my country very much.

When xiǎng is followed by an event as its direct object, it means "to think."

S	V	O	Adv	SV
Wǒ	xiǎng	tā	hěn	měi.
I think she is very beautiful.				

1. A: Nǐ xiǎng tā shì Rìběnrén ma?   Do you think she is Japanese?

    B: Wǒ xiǎng tā búshì Rìběnrén.   I don't think she is Japanese.

2.　A: Nǐ xiǎng shùxué yǒuyìsi ma?   Do you think math is interesting?

　　B: Wǒ xiǎng shùxué méi(yǒu)yìsi.   I don't think math is interesting.

4.2.2 Xiǎng as an auxiliary verb

When xiǎng is followed by another verb, it functions as an auxiliary verb.

S	AV	V	O
Wǒ	xiǎng	hē	jiǔ.

I'd like to drink some wine.

1.　A: Wǒ xiǎng hòunián qù Zhōngguó.   I'd like to go to China the year after
　　　Nǐ ne?   next. How about you?

　　B: Wǒ xiǎng jīnnián qù.   I think I will go this year.

2.　A: Wǒ xiǎng qù mànpǎo, nǐ yào   I want to go for a jog. Do you want to
　　　qù ma?   go?

　　B: Hǎo. Wǒ yě qù.   Okay, I'll go too.

4.3 THE QUESTION WORD jǐ

Jǐ "how many, how much" is a question word. It is usually used to ask about
a small quantity of objects (less than ten). To ask about the price of a car, the
appropriate question word is duōshǎo, not jǐ. A measure word must be used
between the question word jǐ and a noun. The correct translation of the
question "How many books do you have?" is "Nǐ yǒu jǐ běn shū?" not "Nǐ yǒu
jǐ shū?"

Jǐ	MW	N?
Jǐ	ge	rén?

How many people?

1.　A: Nǐ jiā yǒu jǐ ge rén?   How many people are there in your
　　　　　　　　　　　　　　　　　　　　　　family?

　　B: Wǒ jiā yǒu qī ge rén.   There are seven people in my family.

2. A: Nǐ xiǎng xuǎn jǐ mén kè?   How many courses are you going to take?

   B: Wǒ xiǎng xuǎn sì mén kè.   I am thinking of taking four courses.

3. A: Nǐ yǒu jǐ běn Zhōngwén shū?   How many Chinese books do you have?

   B: Wǒ yǒu yì běn Zhōngwén shū.   I have one Chinese book.

4. A: Nǐ yǒu jǐ ge nǚtóngxué?   How many female schoolmates do you have?

   B: Wǒ yǒu bá ge nǚtóngxué.   I have eight female schoolmates.

4.4 THE CHOICE-TYPE QUESTION shì ... shì

The choice-type question shì ... shì is used to ask the listener to make a choice between two options ("A" and "B").

S	shì	*"A"*	shì	*"B"*?
Nǐ	shì	Zhōngguórén,	shì	Rìběnrén?
Are you Chinese or Japanese?				

1. A: Nǐ shì jīntiān qù xuǎn kè, shì míngtiān qù xuǎn kè?   Are you going to register today or tomorrow?

   B: Wǒ xiǎng míngtiān qù xuǎn kè.   I am going to register tomorrow.

2. A: Nǐ shì míngnián qù Zhōngguó, shì hòunián qù Zhōngguó?   Are you going to China next year or the year after the next?

   B: Wǒ yěxǔ hòunián qù.   I may be going there the year after the next.

3. A: Tā shì nǐ jiějie, shì nǐ mèimei?   Is she your elder sister or younger sister?

   B: Tā shì wǒ mèimei.   She is my younger sister.

4. A: Qǐngwèn, nǐ shì tā gēge, shì ta dìdi?   May I ask, are you his elder brother or younger brother?

   B: Wǒ shì tā gēge.   I am his elder brother.

4.5 THE MOVABLE ADVERB yěxǔ

Yěxǔ "perhaps, probably, maybe" is a movable adverb. It can come either
before or after a subject in a sentence.

(1)	S	yěxǔ	EV	O
	Tā	yěxǔ	shì	Rìběnrén.

Maybe he is Japanese.

(2)	Yěxǔ	S	EV	O
	Yěxǔ	tā	shì	Rìběnrén.

Maybe he is Japanese.

1. A: Tā shì hǎo xuésheng ma?   Is she a good student?

   B: Tā yěxǔ shì hǎo xuésheng.   Maybe she is a good student.

2. A: Shéi míngtiān qù Rìběn?   Who is going to Japan tomorrow?

   B: Yěxǔ tā qù.   Maybe he is going.

4.5.1 The pattern yěxǔ ... yěxǔ

The yěxǔ ... yěxǔ "maybe, either ... or" pattern is used to link two clauses in a
sentence.

S	yěxǔ	(TW)	V,	yěxǔ	(TW)	V
Wǒ	yěxǔ	jīntiān	qù,	yěxǔ	míngtiān	qù.

I may go today or (I may go) tomorrow.

1. A: Nǐ jiějie ài hē shénme?   What does your elder sister like to
                                       drink?

   B: Tā yěxǔ ài hē jiǔ, yěxǔ ài hē chá.   She likes to drink either wine or tea.

2. A: Jīntiān shéi qù yínháng?   Who is going to the bank today?

   B: Yěxǔ wǒ qù, yěxǔ wǒ mèimei qù.   Maybe I'll go, maybe my younger
                                       sister will go.

4.6 THE QUESTION WORD <u>nǎr</u>

The question word <u>nǎr</u> "where?" is used to ask about the location of people or things.

S	V	nǎr ?
Nǐ de qián	zài	nǎr?
Where is your money?		

1. A: Nǐ bàba zài nǎr?   Where is your father?

    B: Tā zài jiā.   He is at home.

2. A: Nǐ qù nǎr?   Where are you going?

    B: Wǒ qù Wáng lǎoshī jiā.   I'm going to Professor Wang's house.

3. A: Wǒmen qù nǎr yuǎnzú?   Where are we going for hiking?

    B: Wǒmen lǎoshī méi shuō wǒmen   Our teacher hasn't said where we are
       qù nǎr.   going.

4. A: Xuésheng Zhōngxīn zài nǎr?   Where is the Student Center?

    B: Zài nàr.   Over there.

4.7 THE DUPLICATION OF MEASURE WORDS AND NOUNS

Some Chinese measure words and nouns can be duplicated. The meaning of the duplicated form is "every."

1. Wǒ niánnián qù Zhōngguó.   I go to China every year.

2. Tā tiāntiān hē jiǔ.   He drinks wine every day.

3. Rénrén dōu yào xué Zhōngwén ma?   Does everybody want to learn
                                         Chinese?

4. Wǒmen de xuésheng, gègè dōu   Every student of ours is very busy.
    hěn máng.

5. Wǒ zhè xuéqī xuǎn de kè, ménmén   All the courses I am taking this
    dōu hěn yǒuyìsi.   semester are interesting.

4.8 THE ADVERB cónglái

Cónglái "from the beginning" together with the negative méi stresses that an activity or event has never taken place before.

S	cónglái	méi	V-guo	N / PW
Wǒ	cónglái	méi	qùguo	Zhōngguó.

I have never been to China.

1. A: Nǐ chīguo Rìběnfàn ma?   Have you ever had Japanese food?

    B: Wǒ cónglái méi chīguo Rìběnfàn.   I've never had Japanese food.

2. A: Nǐ māma dǎguo nǐ ma?   Did your mother ever spanked you?

    B: Wǒ māma cónglái méi dǎguo wǒ.   My mother has never spanked me.

3. A: Nǐ yǒu-méiyǒu àiguo tā?   Have you ever loved him?

    B: Wǒ cónglái méi àiguo tā.   I've never loved him.

4. A: Sīwén shuō nǐ xuǎnguo Wáng   Siwen said that you had taken
        lǎoshī de kè.   Professor Wang's course.

    B: Méiyǒu. Wǒ cónglái méi xuǎnguo   No. I've never taken Professor Wang's
        Wáng lǎoshī de kè.   class.

🐾 Sentence Building

1.
Xuǎn
Xuǎn Zhōngwén.
Xuǎn Zhōngwén kè.
Xuǎn yì mén Zhōngwén kè.
Wǒ xiǎng xuǎn yì mén Zhōngwén kè.

2.
Jǐ
Jǐ ge?
Jǐ ge tóngxué?
Jǐ ge Zhōngguó tóngxué?
Nǐ yǒu jǐ ge Zhōngguó tóngxué?

3.
Shùxué
Xué shùxué.
Shéi xué shùxué?
Shéi yào xué shùxué?
Wǒ yào xué shùxué.

4.
Mén
Jǐ mén?
Jǐ mén kè?
Xuǎn jǐ mén kè?
Nǐ xiǎng xuǎn jǐ mén kè?

❧ Questions and Responses

1. Nǐ de shēngrì shì nǎ tiān?
   When is your birthday?

   Wǒ de shēngrì shì shíèryuè èrrì.
   My birthday is 2 December.

2. Nǐ nǎ nián yào qù Zhōngguó?
   In which year are you going to China?

   Wǒ xiǎng míngnián qù Zhōngguó.
   I'd like to go to China next year.

3. Nǐ yào xuǎn nǎ mén kè?
   Which course would you like to take?

   Wǒ yào xuǎn Zhōngwén kè.
   I'd like to take Chinese.

4. Tā shì nǎ guó rén?
   What is his nationality?

   Wǒ xiǎng tā shì Zhōngguórén.
   I think he is Chinese.

5. Zhè shì shénme?
   What is this?

   Zhè shì wǒmen Zhōngwén kè de kèbiǎo.
   This is the schedule for our Chinese class.

6. Qǐngwèn, Xuéshēng Zhōngxīn zài nǎr?
   May I ask where the Student Center is?

   Xuéshēng Zhōngxīn zài nàr.
   The Student Center is over there.

7. Nǐ qùguo Xuéshēng Zhōngxīn ma?

   Have you been to the Student Center before?

   Wǒ cónglái méi qùguo Xuéshēng Zhōngxīn.
   No, I have never been to the Student Center.

8. Lín Hǎiyīng shì Měiguórén, shì Rìběnrén?
   Is Lin Haiying American or Japanese?

   Tā shì Měiguórén.

   She is American.

9. Zhè shì nǐ de kèbiǎo, shì tā de kèbiǎo?
   Is this your class schedule or his?

   Zhè shì tā de kèbiǎo.
   This is his class schedule.

10. Nǐmen yì xuénián yǒu jǐ ge xuéqī?
    How many semesters do you have in an academic year?

    Wǒmen yì xuénián yǒu liǎng ge xuéqī.
    We have two semesters in an academic year.

🐾 Pronunciation Review

(1) Differentiating u-ü and un-ün

(a) nǔ	nǚ	(d) zhū	jū	(g) wén	yún
(b) lú	lǘ	(e) chú	qú	(h) zhūn	jūn
(c) wū	yū	(f) shù	xù	(i) shùn	xùn

(2) Intonation

(a) Tā yě hǎo.   He is also well.

(b) Tā yě hǎo ma?   Is he also well?

(c) Tāmen hěn gāo.   They are very tall.

(d) Tāmen hěn gāo ma?   Are they very tall?

🐾 Fun Activity

Try a Chinese Tongue Twister

Chī Pútao Eat Grapes	
Chī pútao, bù tǔ pútao pí.	When you eat grapes, don't spit out the peel.
Bù chī pútao, dào tǔ pútao pí.	When you don't eat grapes, spit out the peel.

(Be assured, this tongue twister makes no more sense in Chinese than it does in English. It is just another way to practice Chinese pronunciation.)

🌸 Supplementary Vocabulary

Some Names of Courses

rénlèixué	Anthropology
yìshù	Arts
shēngwùxué	Biology
huàxué	Chemistry
bǐjiào wénxué	Comparative Literature
diànnǎo	Computer Science
wǔdǎo	Dance
dōngyǎ yánjiū	East Asian Studies
jīngjìxué	Economics
jiàoyù	Education
dìlǐ	Geography
lìshǐ	History
guójì màoyì	International Business
guójì guānxì	International Relations
xīnwénxué	Journalism
fǎlù	Law
yǔyánxué	Linguistics
dàzhòng chuánbō	Mass Communication
shùxué	Mathematics
yīxué	Medical Science
yīnyuè	Music
zhéxué	Philosophy
tǐyù	Physical Education
wùlǐ	Physics
zhèngzhìxué	Political Science
xīnlǐxué	Psychology
zōngjiào	Religion

第四課
漢字本

內容

✿ 課文

你要選幾門課？

林海英：馬愛文，你好嗎？

馬愛文：我很好。你呢？

林海英：我也很好。馬愛文，你這學期要選幾門課？

馬愛文：我想選五門課。你呢？

林海英：我想選四門課。你想選甚麼課？

馬愛文：我想選一門中文，一門日文、一門英文、一門數
學跟一門英國文學。你呢？

林海英：我想選一門中文、一門數學、一門日本文學跟一
門英文。

馬愛文：你想日本文學課有意思嗎？

林海英：我同學說這門課很有意思，老師也很好。

你明年要選哪幾門課？

馬愛文：我想問問我同學的意思。

🌼 生詞及例句

1. **期**   **a period of time, phase, scheduled time** (N)

☞ 學期   school term, semester (N)

A: 你這學期忙不忙？

B: 很忙。你呢？

A: 也很忙。

☞ 日期   date (N)

A: 這是甚麼日期的報？

B: 是六月八日的。

☞ 早期   early stage; early phase (TW)

A: 你想學中國早期的文學嗎？

B: 中國早期的文學有意思嗎？

A: 王老師說很有意思。

2. **選**   **select, choose, pick, elect** (V)

☞ 選課   select courses (VO)

A: 這學期你要選幾門課？

B: 我想選四門課。

A: 你哪天去選課？

B: 明天。

☞ 大選   general election (N)

A: 今年大選，你選誰？

B: 我得想想。

3. **幾**   **how many** (QW); **a few; several; some** (Nu)

A: 你去過幾個國家？

B: 我去過十幾個國家。

4. **門**　　**entrance, door, gate** (N); (MW for courses)

(1) A: 請你在你家門口等我。

B: 好。

(2) A: 你這學期選幾門課？

B: 四門。

5. **課**　　**subject, course, class** (N); (MW for lessons)

(1) A: 你選的那門課有意思嗎？

B: 沒意思。

(2) A: 我們今天學第幾課？

B: 第十課。

☞ 課本　　textbook (N)

A: 我們的課本有英文沒有？

B: 我們的課本中英文都有。

☞ 課文　　text (N)

A: 這課的課文很沒意思。

B: 我想很有意思。

☞ 課表　　class schedule (N)

A: 老師說明天給我們課表。

B: 是這個月的課表，是這學期的課表？

A: 是這個月的。

6. **四**　　**four** (Nu)

☞ 四月　　April (N)

A: 我四月去<u>中國</u>。

B: 我跟你去好嗎？

7. **中**   **center, middle, among** (PW)

☞ 中文   Chinese (language) (N)

A: 我今年要學中文，你呢？

B: 我媽媽說我今年得學中文。

☞ 中國   China (PW)

A: 是中國大，是美國大？

B: 中美兩國都大。

☞ 中學   middle school (N)

A: 美英，我給你介紹介紹，他是我中學的同學。他叫愛樂。

B: 愛樂，你好！

C: 你好，美英。

☞ 中心   center, core, hub (N)

A: 我們去學生中心，好嗎？

B: 好，我跟你去。

8. **數**   **number** (N)

☞ 數學   mathematics (N)

A: 我哥哥的數學很好。

B: 他有沒有選數學課？

A: 沒有。

9. **年**   **year** (TW)

A: 一年有幾個月？

B: 一年有十二個月。

☞ 哪年   which year (QW)

A: 你是哪年生的？

B: 一九七四年。

☞ 今年　　　this year (TW)

今年美國的大選很有意思。

☞ 明年　　　next year (TW)

A: 明年你要選哪幾門課？

B: 我要選你今年選的課。

☞ 後年　　　the year after the next (TW)

A: 你哪年去英國？

B: 我想後年去。

☞ 大後年　　three years from now (TW)

我大後年去中國學中文。

☞ 去年　　　last year (TW)

A: 去年我是中學生。你呢？

B: 我是大學生。

☞ 年年　　　every year (TW)

這幾年，年年都有火災。

☞ 學年　　　school (or academic) year (N)

我們一學年有兩個學期。

10. **哪**　　　**which; what (QW)**

A: 你要選哪門課？

B: 哪門課有意思，我選哪門。

🐾 句型練習

4.1 THE QUESTION WORD 哪

S	V	哪	MW	O
你	選	哪	門	課？

Which courses are you going to take?

1. A: 你要喝哪國酒？
   B: 我要喝中國酒。

2. A: 你哪天去選課？
   B: 我後天去選課。

3. A: 哪個人是你的老師？
   B: 那個中國人是我的老師。

4. A: 哪本小說有意思？
   B: 那本英文小說有意思，這本日文小說沒意思。

4.2 THE PATTERN 想

想 can function as a verb or as an auxiliary verb.

4.2.1 想 as a verb

When 想 is followed by a direct object, it functions as a verb and means "miss."

S	V	O
我	想	家。

I miss home.

1. A: 你想你媽媽嗎？
   B: 我很想我媽媽。

2. A: 你想你的國家嗎？
   B: 我很想我的國家。

When 想 is followed by an event as its direct object, it means "to think."

S	V	O	Adv	SV
我	想	她	很	美。
I think she is very beautiful.				

1. A: 你想他是日本人嗎？

   B: 我想他不是日本人。

2. A: 你想數學有意思嗎？

   B: 我想數學沒 (有) 意思。

4.2.2 想 as an auxiliary verb

When 想 is followed by another verb, it functions as an auxiliary verb.

S	AV	V	O
我	想	喝	酒。
I'd like to drink some wine.			

1. A: 我想後年去中國。你呢？

   B: 我想今年去。

2. A: 我想去慢跑，你要去嗎？

   B: 好。我也去。

4.3 THE QUESTION WORD 幾

幾 "how many, how much" is a question word. It is usually used to ask about a small quantity of objects (less than ten). To ask the price of a car, the appropriate question word is 多少, not 幾. A measure word must be used between the question word 幾 and a noun. The correct translation of the question "How many books do you have?" is "你有幾本書？" **not** "你有幾書？"

幾	MW	N ?
幾	個	人 ？
How many people?		

1. A: 你家有<u>幾</u>個人？

    B: 我家有七個人。

2. A: 你想選<u>幾</u>門課？

    B: 我想選四門課。

3. A: 你有<u>幾</u>本中文書？

    B: 我有一本中文書。

4. A: 你有<u>幾</u>個女同學？

    B: 我有八個女同學。

4.4 THE CHOICE-TYPE QUESTION 是……是

The choice-type question 是……是 is used to ask the listener to make a choice between two options ("A" and "B").

S	是	"A"	是	"B" ?
你	是	<u>中國</u>人，	是	<u>日本</u>人？
Are you Chinese or Japanese?				

1. A: 你<u>是</u>今天去選課，<u>是</u>明天去選課？

    B: 我想明天去選課。

2. A: 你<u>是</u>明年去<u>中國</u>，是後年去<u>中國</u>？

    B: 我也許後年去。

3. A: 她<u>是</u>你姐姐，<u>是</u>你妹妹？

    B: 她是我妹妹。

4. A: 請問，你<u>是</u>他哥哥，<u>是</u>他弟弟？

    B: 我是他哥哥。

4.5 THE MOVABLE ADVERB 也許

<u>也許</u> "perhaps, probably, maybe" is a movable adverb. It can come either before or after a subject in a sentence.

(1)	S	也許	EV	O
	他	也許	是	日本人。
	Maybe he is Japanese.			
(2)	也許	S	EV	O
	也許	他	是	日本人。
	Maybe he is Japanese.			

1. A: 他是好學生嗎？

    B: 他也許是好學生。

2. A: 誰明天去日本？

    B: 也許他去。

4.5.1 The pattern 也許……也許

The 也許……也許 "maybe, either … or" pattern is used to link two clauses in a sentence.

S	也許	(TW)	V,	也許	(TW)	V
我	也許	今天	去，	也許	明天	去。
I may go today or (I may go) tomorrow.						

1. A: 你姐姐愛喝甚麼？

    B: 她也許愛喝酒，也許愛喝茶。

2. A: 今天誰去銀行？

    B: 也許我去，也許我妹妹去。

4.6 THE QUESTION WORD 哪兒

The question word 哪兒 "where" is used to ask about the location of people or things.

S	V	哪兒？
你的錢	在	哪兒？
Where is your money?		

1. A: 你爸爸在哪兒？

   B: 他在家。

2. A: 你去哪兒？

   B: 我去王老師家。

3. A: 我們去哪兒遠足？

   B: 我們老師沒說我們去哪兒。

4. A: 學生中心在哪兒？

   B: 在那兒。

4.7 THE DUPLICATION OF MEASURE WORDS AND NOUNS

Some Chinese measure words and nouns can be duplicated. The meaning of the duplicated form is "every."

1. 我年年去中國。

2. 他天天喝酒。

3. 人人都要學中文嗎？

4. 我們的學生，個個都很忙。

5. 我這學期選的課，門門都很有意思。

4.8 THE ADVERB 從來

從來 "from the beginning" together with the negative 沒 stresses that an activity or event has never taken place before.

S	從來	沒	V-過	N / PW
我	從來	沒	去過	中國。

I have never been to China.

1. A: 你吃過日本飯嗎？

   B: 我從來沒吃過日本飯。

2. A: 你媽媽打過你嗎？

   B: 我媽媽從來沒打過我。

3. A: 你有沒有愛過他？

   B: 我從來沒愛過他。

4. A: 思文說你選過王老師的課。

   B: 沒有。我從來沒選過王老師的課。

🌸 造 句

1.

選

選中文。

選中文課。

選一門中文課。

我想選一門中文課。

2.

幾

幾個？

幾個同學？

幾個中國同學？

你有幾個中國同學？

3.

數學

學數學。

誰學數學？

誰要學數學？

我要學數學。

4.

門

幾門？

幾門課？

選幾門課？

你想選幾門課？

🌸 問 答

1. 你的生日是哪天？　　　　我的生日是十二月二日。

2. 你哪年要去中國？　　　　我想明年去中國。

3. 你要選哪門課？　　　　　我要選中文課。

4. 他是哪國人？　　　　　　我想他是中國人。

5. 這是甚麼？   這是我們中文課的課表。

6. 請問，學生中心在哪兒？   學生中心在那兒。

7. 你去過學生中心嗎？   我從來沒去過學生中心。

8. 林海英是美國人，是日本人？   他是美國人。

9. 這是你的課表，是他的課表？   這是他的課表。

10. 你們一學年有幾個學期？   我們一學年有兩個學期。

🐾 閱讀練習

馬愛文的日記

　　我想找林海英問她這學期要選甚麼課。我去她家找她。海英的媽媽說她不在家，也許她在學生中心。

　　我去學生中心找海英。海英在跟許小美說話。她們也在說要選甚麼課。我問她們這學期要選幾門課。她們都說要選四門課。我說我想選五門課。她們想五門課也許太難。我也問她們選甚麼課好。她們說數學課都得選。她們兩個人都要選一門英國文學、一門中文跟一門日文。我問她們是學中文難，是學日文難。海英說，也許日文不太難。她在中學沒有學過中文，他們中學沒有中文課，不過她在家跟媽媽說日本話。小美說，她在中學沒學過日文，也沒有學過中文，不過她在家跟爸爸媽媽說中國話，也許學中文不太難。我在中學日文、中文都沒學過，不過我媽媽說我在大學得學中文，我也想日文、中文都很有意思。我不怕難。我都要學。

註釋：難 (nàn) means "difficult" in English.

問 題

1. 馬愛文為甚麼要去找海英？

2. 馬愛文在哪兒找到了海英？

3. 海英跟小美要選幾門課？為甚麼？

4. 馬愛文要選甚麼課？

5. 馬愛文在中學有沒有學過中文？

6. 為甚麼她們都要選數學課？

7. 你想在同一個學期學中文也學日文好不好？為甚麼？

第五課　你選了甚麼課？
Lesson 5　What courses did you take?

Lesson 5
Pinyin Text

•••

CONTENTS

🌸 Text

Nǐ xuǎn le shénme kè?

What courses did you take?

Xǔ Xiǎoměi:	Mǎ Àiwén, nǐ jīntiān qù xuǎn kè le ma?	Ma Aiwen, have you gone to register for your classes today?
Mǎ Àiwén:	Qù le. Nǐ ne?	(I) have already gone. And you?
Xǔ Xiǎoměi:	Wǒ míngtiān qù. Nǐ xuǎn le shénme kè?	I will go tomorrow. What classes did you pick?
Mǎ Àiwén:	Yì mén Zhōngguó wénxué, yì mén shùxué, yì mén Rìběn wénxué, hái yǒu yì mén Zhōngwén. Nǐ xiǎng xuǎn shénme kè?	Chinese literature, math, Japanese literature and Chinese. What classes do you want to take?
Xǔ Xiǎoměi:	Zhè xuéqī, wǒ xiǎng xuǎn wǔ mén kè: Zhōngwén, Yīngwén, shùxué, Zhōngguó wénxué gēn Rìběn wénxué.	This semester, I want to take five classes: Chinese, English, math, Chinese literature and Japanese literature.
Mǎ Àiwén:	Wèishénme xuǎn wǔ mén kè?	Why are you taking five classes?
Xǔ Xiǎoměi:	Yīnwèi zhè jǐ mén kè wǒ dōu hěn xǐhuan.	Because I really like all the classes.
Mǎ Àiwén:	Wǔ mén kè shì-bu-shì tài nán?	Isn't taking five classes too hard?
Xǔ Xiǎoměi:	Wǒ hái bù zhīdào, yěxǔ bú tài nán.	I don't really know yet. Maybe it won't be too hard.
Mǎ Àiwén:	Nǐ zhīdào wǒmen xuéxiào de xuésheng xǐhuan xuǎn wǔ mén kè ma?	Do you know whether students in our school like to take five courses?
Xǔ Xiǎoměi:	Wǒ bù zhīdào.	I don't know.

🐾 Vocabulary and Illustrative Sentences

1. **le**　　　(As)

   A: Nǐ dìdi lái le ma?　　　　Has your little brother come yet?

   B: Lái le.　　　　　　　　　(Yes, he) has come.

   A: Tā xuǎn kè le ma?　　　　Has he chosen his classes yet?

   B: Xuǎn le.　　　　　　　　(Yes, he) has.

2. **zhī**　　　**know, realize, be aware of** (V)

   ☞ zhīzú　　be content with one's lot (SV)

   A: Wǒ māma shì yí ge hěn
   zhīzú de rén.

   My mother is a very contented
   person.

   B: Nà hěn hǎo. Zhōngguórén shuō, zhīzú de rén
   lǎo hěn kuàilè.

   That's great. The Chinese say
   that people who are contented
   are always very happy.

3. **dào**　　　**road, way, path; channel** (N)

   ☞ zhīdào　　know, realize, be aware of (V)

   (1) A: Nǐ zhīdào-bu-zhīdào
   xuǎn nǎ mén kè hǎo?

   Do you know which courses are
   good choices?

   B: Wǒ bù zhīdào.　　　　　I don't know.

   (2) A: Nǐ zhīdào shéi shì wǒmen
   de lǎoshī ma?

   Do you know who our teacher is?

   B: Zhīdào.　　　　　　　　(Yes, I) know.

   (3) A: Nǐ zhīdào zhè ge zì shì
   shénme yìsi ma?

   Do you know the meaning of
   this word?

   B: Wǒ yě bù zhīdào.　　　　I don't know either.

   (4) Wǒ bù zhīdào xué Rìwén
   zhème nán.

   I didn't know that learning
   Japanese was going to be so hard.

4. **nán**   **difficult, hard, troublesome** (SV)

A: Dàjiā dōu shuō Zhōngwén hěn **nán** xué, nǐ shuō ne?

Everyone says that Chinese is very hard to learn. What do you say to that?

B: Wǒ xiǎng bú tài **nán**.

I don't think it's too hard.

☞ **nánguò**   have a hard time (SV); feel sorry; hard to endure (V)

A: Bàba shuō wǒmen jiā jīnnián méiyǒu qián gěi wǒ qù Zhōngguó xué Zhōngwén. Wǒ hěn **nánguò**.

Father says that this year our family does not have the money for me to go to China to study Chinese. I am very sad.

B: Bú yào **nánguò**, jīnnián bú qù, míngnián qù.

Don't be upset! (If you) don't go this year, (you can) go next year.

☞ **nándào**   do you mean to say? are you not aware? (rhetorical questions)

A: Nǐ **nándào** bù zhīdào nǐ bàba māma hěn ài nǐ ma?

Are you not aware that your father and mother love you very much?

B: Yàoshì tāmen ài wǒ, wèishénme bù gěi wǒ qián qù Zhōngguó?

If they love me, why don't they give me the money to go to China?

5. **xiào**   **school** (N)

☞ **xiàozhǎng**   headmaster, principal, president, chancellor (N)

A: Nǐmen **xiàozhǎng** xìng shénme?

What is the family name of your principal?

B: Tā xìng Walsh.

Her family name is Walsh.

☞ **xuéxiào**   school, educational institution (N)

A: Nǐmen **xuéxiào** yǒu duōshǎo xuésheng?

How many students are there in your school?

B: Wǒ hái bù zhīdào ne.

I haven't got any idea yet.

6. **hái**　　**still, yet; even more, also, too, in addition** (Adv)

(1) A: Nǐ **hái** yǒu shénme huà yào shuō ma?

Do you have anything else to say?

B: Méiyǒu le.

(I) don't have anything else to say.

(2) Wǒ qùnián qùguo Zhōngguó, wǒ jīnnián **hái** xiǎng qù.

I went to China last year. I want to go there again this year.

☞ **háihǎo**　　not bad, fortunately (IE)

(1) A: Lǎoshī, wǒ mèimei de Zhōngguó huà shuō de hěn bù hǎo, shì ma?

Teacher, my younger sister's spoken Chinese is really bad, isn't it?

B: **Háihǎo.**

(No, it's) not too bad.

(2) Yīngguó wénxué nàme nán, **háihǎo**, wǒ méiyǒu xuǎn.

English literature is so hard, it's a good thing that I didn't take the course.

☞ **háishì**　　still, nevertheless, had better (Adv); or (Conj)

(1) Bàba bú yào wǒ qù, wǒ **háishì** yào qù.

Father doesn't want me to go, but I still want to go.

(2) Nǐ bú ài wǒ, wǒ **háishì** ài nǐ.

Even though you don't love me, I still love you.

(3) A: Nǐ xiǎng xué Zhōngwén hǎo **háishì** xué Rìwén hǎo?

Do you think it is better to study Chinese or Japanese?

B: Wǒ xiǎng **háishì** xué Zhōngwén hǎo.

I think it is better to study Chinese.

7. **yīn**　　**because of, as a result of** (MA)

8. **wèi**　　**act as; serve as** (V)

☞ **yīnwèi**　　because, for, on account of (MA)

(1) Wǒ dìdi jìnlái hěn fán, **yīnwèi** tā nǚpéngyou bù xǐhuan tā le.

Recently, my younger brother has been extremely annoyed because his girlfriend does not like him anymore.

(2) Yīnwèi nǐ tiāntiān hē jiǔ, māma hěn nánguò.

Mother has been very upset because you drink wine every day.

☞ wèishénme why, why (or how) is it that? (QW)

(1) A: Nǐ wèishénme bù xuǎn shùxué kè?

Why didn't you take math?

B: Yīnwèi shùxué tài nán le.

Because math is too hard.

(2) A: Nǐ zhīdào bàba wèishénme bú yào nǐ qù Zhōngguó ma?

Do you know why father doesn't want you to go to China?

B: Bù zhīdào.

(I) don't know.

A: Yīnwèi tā méiyǒu qián.

Because he doesn't have the money.

9. xǐ **happy, delighted, pleased** (V)

10. huān **joyous, merry, jubilant** (V)

☞ xǐhuan like, love, be fond of (V/AV)

(1) A: Nǐ xǐhuan gēn shéi shuōhuà?

Whom do you like to talk to?

B: Wǒ xǐhuan gēn yǒuyìsi de rén shuōhuà.

I like to talk to interesting people.

(2) A: Nǐ xǐhuan hē chá háishì hē qìshuǐ?

Do you like to have tea or soft drinks?

B: Wǒ dōu xǐhuan.

I like both.

☞ huānsòng see off, send off (V)

A: Jīntiān wǒmen de tóngxué qù Yīngguó. Nǐ yào-bu-yào qù huānsòng tāmen?

Our classmates are going to England today. Do you want to see them off?

B: Yào.

Yes.

🌸 Pattern Drills

5.1 THE PARTICLE le

The particle le appears in a great variety of speech situations. It carries many semantic implications. The meaning of le is determined by its position in the sentence, the nature of the main verb, adverb, or auxiliary verb, and the structure of the sentence. To gain an accurate understanding of le, one must focus on the entire sentence structure rather than the particle le alone.

5.1.1 The intransitive verb with le

When le comes at the end of a sentence and is preceded by an action verb, le indicates the completion of an action.

S	IV	le
Tā	lái	le.
He/she has come.		

1. A: Shéi lái le?   Who has come/is here?

   B: Wǒ tóngxué lái le.   My classmates are here.

2. A: Hǎiyīng zài jiā ma?   Is Haiying at home?

   B: Tā bú zài, tā qù péngyou jiā le.   She is not here. She has gone to her friend's house.

5.1.2 Bù / bú V (O) le

When a verb and le are negated by bù / bú, it means "no longer, not anymore."

S	bù / bú	V(O)	le
Wǒ	bù	hē jiǔ	le.
I am not drinking wine anymore.			

1. Tā bú shì wǒ de tàitai le.   She is no longer my wife.

2. Jīntiān wǒ bú qù nǐ jiā le.   I am not going to your house anymore today.

3. Wǒ bú ài tā le.   I don't love him anymore.

4. Wǒ jīntiān bú qù shàng kè le.   I am not going to class anymore today.

5.1.3 Méi(yǒu) (O) le

S	méi(yǒu)	(O)	le
Wǒ	méi(yǒu)	qián	le.
I don't have money anymore.			

1. A: Nǐ hái yǒu-méiyǒu Zhōngwén kè?   Do you have any more Chinese
                                             classes?

    B: Méiyǒu le.   (I) don't have anymore.

2. A: Wáng lǎoshī de kè yǒu-méiyǒu   Is Professor Wang's class interesting?
       yìsi?

    B: Tā de kè méiyìsi le. Wǒ bù xǐhuan le. His class is no longer interesting.
                                              I don't like it anymore.

3. A: Nǐ wèishénme bú qù Zhōngguó le?   Why aren't you going to China
                                             anymore?

    B: Wǒmen jiā méiyǒu qián le.   Our family no longer has any money.

5.1.4 The pattern tài ... le

When le comes at the end of a sentence along with the adverb tài "too much" or is preceded by such words as jí "extremely" and sǐ "die," it indicates an exaggeration or extreme degree.

S	tài	SV	le
Jīntiān	tài	lěng	le.
It's too cold today.			

1. Wáng tàitai tài měi le.   Mrs. Wang is extremely beautiful.

2. Wǒ jīntiān tài kuàilè le.   I am extremely happy today.

3. Xuésheng dōu tài máng le.   The students are all very busy.

5.2 THE ADVERB <u>hái</u>

The adverb <u>hái</u> "still, again" has many uses: when <u>hái</u> is followed by a negative <u>bù</u> or <u>méi</u>, it means "not yet, have not." The particle <u>ne</u> often comes at the end of the sentence.

1. A: Nǐ qùnián qù Rìběn le, jīnnián hái qù ma?

   B: Wǒ jīnnián hái qù.

   You went to Japan last year. Are you going there again this year?

   (Yes,) I am going again this year.

2. A: Zhè yuè nǐ māma gěi nǐ qián le ma?

   B: Tā hái méi gěi ne.

   Has your mother given you any money this month?

   She hasn't given (me any money) yet.

3. A: Nǐ dìdi yǒu nǚpéngyou le ma?

   B: Tā hái méiyǒu nǚpéngyou ne.

   Does your younger brother have a girlfriend yet?

   He does not have a girlfriend yet.

5.3 ALTERNATIVE QUESTIONS USING <u>shì</u> ... <u>háishì</u>

The alternative question pattern <u>shì</u> ... <u>háishì</u> presents an either-or choice to the respondent. <u>Shì</u> ... <u>háishì</u> is optional in some structures. The various sentence patterns are discussed below.

5.3.1 <u>Shì</u> ... <u>háishì</u> when <u>shì</u> is the main verb

When <u>shì</u> is the main verb in the sentence, <u>shì</u> ... <u>háishì</u> must be used.

S	shì	V1	O	háishì	V2	O?
Nǐ	shì	xué	Zhōngwén	háishì	xué	Rìwén?

Are you going to learn Chinese or Japanese?

1. A: Tā shì Zhōngwén lǎoshī háishì Yīngwén lǎoshī?

   B: Tā shì Yīngwén lǎoshī.

   Is she a Chinese teacher or an English teacher?

   She is an English teacher.

2. A: Tā shì nǐ jiějie háishì nǐ mèimei?　　Is she your elder sister or your younger sister?

   B: Tā shì wǒ jiějie.　　She is my elder sister.

5.3.2 <u>Shì</u> ... <u>háishì</u> when <u>shì</u> is used with action verbs

<u>Shì</u> is optional when <u>shì</u> ... <u>háishì</u> is used with action verbs in a sentence.

S	(shì)	V/SV	O	háishì	V/SV	O
Nǐ	(shì)	qù	yínháng	háishì	qù	péngyou jiā?

Are you going to the bank or to your friend's house?

1. A: Wǒmen (shì) qù chī Zhōngguófàn háishì qù chī Měiguófàn?　　Should we have Chinese food or American food?

   B: Wǒ xiǎng wǒmen qù chī Zhōngguófàn.　　I think we should go to have Chinese food.

2. A: Nǐ míngnián yào xué Rìběn wénxué háishì Yīngguó wénxué?　　Are you going to take Japanese literature or English literature?

   B: Wǒ yào xué Rìběn wénxué.　　I'm going to take Japanese literature.

5.3.3 <u>Shì</u> ... <u>háishì</u> to compare two items

When <u>shì</u> ... <u>háishì</u> is used in a sentence to compare two items ("A" and "B"), <u>shì</u> is placed at the beginning of the sentence.

<u>Shì</u>	"A"	(Adj)	háishì	"B"	Adj
Shì	Zhōngwén	nán	háishì	Rìwén	nán?

Is Chinese or Japanese more difficult?

1. A: Shì Zhōngguó jiǔ hǎo háishì Měiguó jiǔ hǎo?　　Is Chinese wine or American wine better?

   B: Wǒ xiǎng Měiguó jiǔ hǎo.　　I think American wine is better.

2. A: Shì Sīwén hǎokàn háishì Àiwén hǎokàn?　　Is Siwen or Aiwen prettier?

   B: Tāmen liǎng ge rén dōu hěn hǎokàn.　　Both of them are pretty.

5.4 ALTERNATIVE QUESTIONS USING (shì) ... hǎo ... háishì ... hǎo

The (shì) ... hǎo ... háishì ... hǎo "is A better or B better" construction is used in an interrogative sentence to seek suggestions from the respondent.

S	(shì)	V	O	hǎo,	háishì	V	O	hǎo?
Wǒ		xuǎn	shùxué	hǎo,	háishì	xuǎn	wénxué	hǎo?

Is it better for me to take math or literature?

1. A: Wǒ jīntiān qù xuǎn kè hǎo, háishì míngtiān qù xuǎn kè hǎo?

   Is it better for me to register today or tomorrow?

   B: Wǒ xiǎng nǐ jīntiān qù hǎo.

   I think it's better for you to go today.

2. A: Nǐ xiǎng wǒ qǐng tā hǎo, háishì bù qǐng tā hǎo?

   Do you think it's better for me to invite him or not to invite him?

   B: Wǒ xiǎng nǐ bù qǐng tā hǎo.

   I think it's better for you not to invite him.

3. A: Nǐ xiǎng wǒmen qù huānsòng tā hǎo, háishì bú qù huānsòng tā hǎo?

   Do you think we should see him off or not?

   B: Wǒ xiǎng wǒmen qù huānsòng tā hǎo.

   I think it is better for us to see him off.

5.5 THE LINKING ADVERBS wèishénme AND yīnwèi

Wèishénme "why" and yīnwèi "because" are movable adverbs. Yīnwèi is often used to answer the question wèishénme.

1. A: Nǐ wèishénme bù gěi tā qián?

   Why don't you give him the money?

   B: Yīnwèi wǒ méiyǒu qián.

   Because I don't have any money.

2. A: Nǐ wèishénme bù xǐhuan tā?

   Why don't you like him?

   B: Yīnwèi tā bú shì hǎorén.

   Because he is not a good person.

3. A: Nǐ wèishénme bú qù shàng kè?

   Why don't you attend class?

   B: Yīnwèi nà mén kè méiyǒuyìsi le.

   Because that class isn't interesting anymore.

5.6 RHETORICAL QUESTIONS USING nándào

Nándào "do you mean to say" is used in a rhetorical question for emphasis. The question particle ma often comes at the end of the sentence.

1. Rénrén dōu xǐhuan hē qìshuǐ, nándào nǐ bù xǐhuan ma?

   Everyone likes to have soft drinks. Do you mean to say you don't like soda?

2. Tā nàme ài nǐ, nándào nǐ bú ài tā ma?

   He loves you so much. Do you mean to say you don't love him at all?

3. Nǐ nándào bù zhīdào wǔ mén kè tài nán ma?

   Do you mean to say that you didn't know taking five classes was too difficult?

4. Rénrén dōu xiǎng qù Zhōngguó. Nándào nǐ bù xiǎng qù ma?

   Everybody wants to go to China. Do you mean to say you don't want to go?

5.7 THE QUESTION WORD shénme WITH dōu OR yě

When question words such as shénme "what," nǎr "where," and shéi "who" are followed by the quantifier dōu "all" or yě "also," they mean "all." When shénme dōu and shénme yě are used in negative contexts, they mean "any." (Dōu and yě are interchangeable in these contexts.)

1. A: Nǐ xǐhuan kàn shénme xiǎoshuō?

   What kind of novels do you like to read?

   B: Wǒ shénme xiǎoshuō dōu xǐhuan kàn. Nǐ ne?

   I like to read all kinds of novels. How about you?

   A: Wǒ shénme xiǎoshuō dōu bù xǐhuan kàn.

   I don't like to read any kind of novel.

2. A: Nǐ xǐhuan shéi?

   Whom do you like?

   B: Wǒ shéi dōu xǐhuan. Nǐ ne?

   I like everyone. How about you?

   A: Wǒ shéi dōu bù xǐhuan.

   I don't like anyone.

🌸 Sentence Building

1.
Yào

Yào qù.

Yào qù Měiguó.

Jīnnián yào qù Měiguó.

Lǎoshī jīnnián yào qù Měiguó.

2.
Zhǎo

Zhǎo shénme?

Zhǎo shénme kèběn?

Zhǎo Zhōngwén kèběn.

Wǒ zhǎo Zhōngwén kèběn.

3.
Xǐhuan

Bù xǐhuan.

Bù xǐhuan hē jiǔ.

Wèishénme bù xǐhuan hē jiǔ?

Nǐ wèishénme bù xǐhuan hē jiǔ?

4.
Yìsi

Méi(yǒu)yìsi.

Hē jiǔ méi(yǒu)yìsi.

Yīnwèi hē jiǔ méi(yǒu)yìsi.

Tā shuō yīnwèi hē jiǔ méi(yǒu)yìsi.

🌸 Questions and Responses

1. Nǐ xiǎng xuǎn wǔ mén kè duō-bu-duō?
   Do you think taking five courses is too much to handle?

   Yěxǔ bú tài duō.
   Maybe not.

2. Nǐ zhè xuéqī xuǎn de kè, nǎ mén kè bù nán?
   Among the courses that you picked this semester, which course is not difficult?

   Yīngwén kè bù nán.

   The English course is not that difficult.

3. Tā zhīdào nǐ jīntiān yào lái ma?
   Does he know that you are coming today?

   Tā hái bù zhīdào ne.
   He does not know yet.

4. Nǐ wèishénme bù shuō Zhōngguóhuà?

   Why don't you speak Chinese?

   Yīnwèi wǒ de Zhōngguóhuà bù hǎo, bùhǎoyìsi shuō.
   Because my Chinese is not very good, I find it embarrassing to speak Chinese.

5. Zuìjìn nǐ bàba de shēngyi hǎo-bu-hǎo?
   How has your father's business been lately?

   Zuìjìn tā de shēngyi hěn bù hǎo.
   His business has been pretty bad lately.

6. Nǐ xǐhuan kàn shénme xiǎoshuō?
   What kind of novels do you like
   to read?

   Wǒ shénme xiǎoshuō dōu xǐhuan kàn.
   I like to read any kind of novel.

7. Nǐ jīnnián de shēngrì yào qǐng
   shénme rén?
   Who would you like to invite to your
   birthday party this year?

   Wǒ hái bù zhīdào ne.

   I don't know yet.

8. Nǐ māma yào qù Měiguó yì nián,
   nǐ nánguò ma?
   Since your mother is going to
   America for a year, are you sad?

   Wǒ bù nánguò.

   I am not sad.

9. Míngtiān shéi qù huānsòng Xǔ Xiǎoměi?
   Who is going to see Xu Xiaomei off
   tomorrow?

   Tā de tóngxué dōu qù huānsòng tā.
   All her classmates are going to see her
   off.

10. Nǐ yínháng de qián dōu méiyǒu le,
    nǐ nándào bù zhīdào ma?
    You don't have any money in the
    bank, (and) you mean to say you
    didn't know about it?

    Wǒ bù zhīdào.

    I didn't know.

🐾 Pronunciation Review

Differentiating i̠ after Retroflexes and i̠ After Sibilants

(a)	zhī	zī	(d)	zhì	jì	(g)	zī	jī
(b)	chí	cí	(e)	chì	qì	(h)	cí	qí
(c)	shǐ	sǐ	(f)	shì	xì	(i)	sì	xì

🐾 Fun Activity

Read a Chinese Poem

This is a very famous poem by Li Bo (Lǐ Bó) (701–762). This poem has four lines, each containing five characters, with a strict tonal pattern and rhyme scheme. This type of poem is called *"wu yan lushi"* (wǔ yán lǜshī). Can you determine the tonal pattern and rhyme in this poem? There are many English translations for this poem. We will give two here. Can you come up with your own translation?

		Jìngyèsī		
		Thought on a Quiet Night		
		Lǐ Bó (701–762)		
		Li Bo		
Chuáng	qián	míng	yuè	guāng
Bed	*front*	*bright*	*moon*	*shine*
床	前	明	月，	光，
Yí	shì	dì	shàng	shuāng
Suspect	*is*	*earth*	*on*	*shine*
疑	是	地	上	霜；
Jǔ	tóu	wàng	míng	yuè
Raise	*head*	*gaze*	*bright*	*moon*
舉	頭	望	明	月，
Dī	tóu	sī	gù	xiāng
Lower	*head*	*think*	*old*	*home (village)*
低	頭	思	故	鄉。

English Translation (1):

I saw the moonlight before my couch,

And wondered if it were not the frost on the ground.

I raised my head and looked out on the mountain moon;

I bowed my head and thought of my far-off home.   (Obata)

English Translation (2):

So bright a gleam at the foot of my bed —

Could there have been a frost already?

Lifting myself to look, I found that it was moonlight.

Sinking back again, I thought suddenly of home.   (Witter Bynner)

第五課
漢字本

內容

課 文

你選了甚麼課？

許小美：馬愛文，你今天去選課了嗎？

馬愛文：去了。你呢？

許小美：我明天去。你選了甚麼課？

馬愛文：一門中國文學、一門數學、一門日本文學，還有
一門中文。你想選甚麼課？

許小美：這學期，我想選五門課：中文、英文、數學、中
國文學跟日本文學。

馬愛文：為甚麼選五門課？

許小美：因為這幾門課我都很喜歡。

馬愛文：五門課是不是太難？

許小美：我還不知道，也許不太難。

馬愛文：你知道我們學校的學生喜歡選五門課嗎？

許小美：我不知道。

❀❀ 生詞及例句

1. 了　　　　　(As)

   A: 你弟弟來了嗎？

   B: 來了。

   A: 他選課了嗎？

   B: 選了。

2. 知　　　　　**know, realize, be aware of** (V)

☞ 知足　　　be content with one's lot (SV)

   A: 我媽媽是一個很知足的人。

   B: 那很好，中國人説，知足的人老很快樂。

3. 道　　　　　**road, way, path; channel** (N)

☞ 知道　　　know, realize, be aware of (V)

   (1) A: 你知道不知道選哪門課好？

   　　 B: 我不知道。

   (2) A: 你知道誰是我們的老師嗎？

   　　 B: 知道。

   (3) A: 你知道這個字是甚麼意思嗎？

   　　 B: 我也不知道。

   (4) 我不知道學日文這麼難。

4. 難　　　　　**difficult, hard, troublesome** (SV)

   A: 大家都説中文很難學，你説呢？

   B: 我想不太難。

☞ 難過　　　have a hard time (SV); feel sorry, hard to endure (V)

   A: 爸爸説我們家今年沒有錢給我去中國學中文，我很難過。

   B: 不要難過，今年不去，明年去。

☞ 難道　　　do you mean to say? are you not aware? (rhetorical questions)

　　　　　　A: 你難道不知道你爸爸媽媽很愛你嗎？

　　　　　　B: 要是他們愛我，為甚麼不給我錢去中國？

5. **校**　　　**school** (N)

☞ 校長　　　headmaster, principal, president, chancellor (N)

　　　　　　A: 你們校長姓甚麼？

　　　　　　B: 她姓 Walsh。

☞ 學校　　　school, educational institution (N)

　　　　　　A: 你們學校有多少學生？

　　　　　　B: 我還不知道呢。

6. **還**　　　**still, yet; even more, also, too, in addition** (Adv)

　　　　　　(1) A: 你還有甚麼話要說嗎？

　　　　　　　　 B: 沒有了。

　　　　　　(2) 我去年去過中國，我今年還想去。

☞ 還好　　　not bad, fortunately (IE)

　　　　　　(1) A: 老師，我妹妹的中國話說得很不好，是嗎？

　　　　　　　　 B: 還好。

　　　　　　(2) 英國文學那麼難，還好，我沒有選。

☞ 還是　　　still, nevertheless, had better (Adv); or (Conj)

　　　　　　(1) 爸爸不要我去，我還是要去。

　　　　　　(2) 你不愛我，我還是愛你。

　　　　　　(3) A: 你想學中文好還是學日文好？

　　　　　　　　 B: 我想還是學中文好。

7. 因　　**because of, as a result of** (MA)

8. 為　　**act as; serve as** (V)

☞ 因為　　because, for, on account of (MA)

(1) 我弟弟近來很煩，因為他女朋友不喜歡他了。

(2) 因為你天天喝酒，媽媽很難過。

☞ 為甚麼　　why, why (or how) is it that? (QW)

(1) A: 你為甚麼不選數學課？

　　B: 因為數學太難了。

(2) A: 你知道爸爸為甚麼不要你去中國嗎？

　　B: 不知道。

　　A: 因為他沒有錢。

9. 喜　　**happy, delighted, pleased** (V)

10. 歡　　**joyous, merry, jubilant** (V)

☞ 喜歡　　like, love, be fond of (V/AV)

(1) A: 你喜歡跟誰說話？

　　B: 我喜歡跟有意思的人說話。

(2) A: 你喜歡喝茶還是喝汽水？

　　B: 我都喜歡。

☞ 歡送　　see off, send off (V)

　　A: 今天我們的同學去英國。你要不要去歡送他們？

　　B: 要。

🐾❀ 句型練習

5.1 THE PARTICLE 了

The particle 了 appears in a great variety of speech situations. It carries many semantic implications. The meaning of 了 is determined by its position in the sentence, the nature of the main verb, adverb, or auxiliary verb, and the structure of the sentence. To gain an accurate understanding of 了, one must focus on the entire sentence structure rather than the particle 了 alone.

5.1.1 The intransitive verb with 了

When 了 comes at the end of a sentence and is preceded by an action verb, 了 indicates the completion of an action.

S	IV	了
他	來	了。
He/she has come.		

1. A: 誰來了？

   B: 我同學來了。

2. A: 海英在家嗎？

   B: 她不在。她去朋友家了。

5.1.2 不 V (O) 了

When a verb and 了 are negated by 不, it means "no longer, not anymore."

S	不	V(O)	了
我	不	喝酒	了。
I am not drinking wine anymore.			

1. 她不是我的太太了。

2. 今天我不去你家了。

3. 我不愛他了。

4. 我今天不去上課了。

5.1.3 沒(有) (O) 了

S	沒(有)	(O)	了
我	沒有	錢	了。
I don't have money anymore.			

1. A: 你還有沒有中文課？
   B: 沒有了。

2. A: 王老師的課有沒有意思？
   B: 他的課沒意思了。我不喜歡了。

3. A: 你為甚麼不去中國了？
   B: 我們家沒有錢了。

5.1.4 The pattern 太……了

When 了 comes at the end of a sentence along with the adverb 太 "too much" or is preceded by such words as 極 "extremely" and 死 "die," it indicates an exaggeration or extreme degree.

S	太	SV	了
今天	太	冷	了。
It's too cold today.			

1. 王太太太美了。

2. 我今天太快樂了。

3. 學生都太忙了。

5.2 THE ADVERB 還

The adverb 還 "still, again" has many uses: when 還 is followed by a negative 不 or 沒, it means "not yet, have not." The particle 呢 often comes at the end of the sentence.

1. A: 你去年去<u>日本</u>了，今年還去嗎？

    B: 我今年還去。

2. A: 這月你媽媽給你錢了嗎？

    B: 她還沒給呢。

3. A: 你弟弟有女朋友了嗎？

    B: 他還沒有女朋友呢。

5.3 ALTERNATIVE QUESTIONS USING 是……還是

The alternative question pattern 是……還是 presents an either-or choice to the respondent. 是……還是 is optional in some structures. The various sentence patterns are discussed below.

5.3.1 是……還是 when 是 is the main verb

When 是 is the main verb in the sentence, 是……還是 must be used.

S	是	V1	O	還是	V2	O ?
你	是	學	中文	還是	學	日文？
Are you going to learn Chinese or Japanese?						

1. A: 他是中文老師還是英文老師？

    B: 他是英文老師。

2. A: 她是你姐姐還是你妹妹？

    B: 她是我姐姐。

5.3.2 是……還是 when 是 is used with action verbs

是 is optional when 是……還是 is used with action verbs in a sentence.

S	(是)	V/SV	O	還是	V/SV	O
你	(是)	去	銀行	還是	去	朋友家？
Are you going to the bank or to your friend's house?						

• •

1. A: 我們 (是) 去吃中國飯還是去吃美國飯?

    B: 我想我們去吃中國飯。

2. A: 你明年要學日本文學還是英國文學?

    B: 我要學日本文學。

5.3.3 是……還是 to compare two items

When 是……還是 is used in a sentence to compare two items ("A" and "B"), 是 is placed at the beginning of the sentence.

是	"A"	(Adj)	還是	"B"	Adj
是	中文	難	還是	日文	難?

Is Chinese or Japanese more difficult?

1. A: 是中國酒好還是美國酒好?

    B: 我想美國酒好。

2. A: 是思文好看還是愛文好看?

    B: 他們兩個人都很好看。

5.4 ALTERNATIVE QUESTIONS USING (是)……好……還是……好

The (是)……好……還是……好 "is A better or B better" construction is used in an interrogative sentence to seek suggestions from the respondent.

S	(是)	V	O	好,	還是	V	O	好?
我		選	數學	好,	還是	選	文學	好?

Is it better for me to take math or literature?

1. A: 我今天去選課好,還是明天去選課好?

    B: 我想你今天去好。

2. A: 你想我請他好,還是不請他好?

    B: 我想你不請他好。

3. A: 你想我們去歡送他好，還是不去歡送他好？

   B: 我想我們去歡送他好。

5.5 THE LINKING ADVERBS 為甚麼 AND 因為

為甚麼 "why" and 因為 "because" are movable adverbs. 因為 is often used to answer the question 為甚麼.

1. A: 你為甚麼不給他錢？

   B: 因為我沒有錢。

2. A: 你為甚麼不喜歡他？

   B: 因為他不是好人。

3. A: 你為甚麼不去上課？

   B: 因為那門課沒有意思了。

5.6 RHETORICAL QUESTIONS USING 難道

難道 "do you mean to say" is used in a rhetorical question for emphasis. The question particle 嗎 often comes at the end of the sentence.

1. 人人都喜歡喝汽水，難道你不喜歡嗎？

2. 他那麼愛你，難道你不愛他嗎？

3. 你難道不知道五門課太難嗎？

4. 人人都想去中國。難道你不想去嗎？

5.7 THE QUESTION WORD 甚麼 WITH 都 OR 也

When question words such as 甚麼 "what," 哪兒 "where," and 誰 "who" are followed by the quantifier 都 "all" or 也 "also," they mean "all." When 甚麼 都 and 甚麼也 are used in negative contexts, they mean "any." (都 and 也 are interchangeable in these contexts.)

1. A: 你喜歡看甚麼小說？

    B: 我甚麼小說都喜歡看。你呢？

    A: 我甚麼小說都不喜歡看。

2. A: 你喜歡誰？

    B: 我誰都喜歡。你呢？

    A: 我誰都不喜歡。

❀ 造 句

1.
要
要去。
要去美國。
今年要去美國。
老師今年要去美國。

2.
找
找甚麼？
找甚麼課本？
找中文課本。
我找中文課本。

3.
喜歡
不喜歡。
不喜歡喝酒。
為甚麼不喜歡喝酒？
你為甚麼不喜歡喝酒？

4.
意思
沒有意思。
喝酒沒有意思。
因為喝酒沒有意思。
他說因為喝酒沒有意思。

❀ 問 答

1. 你想選五門課多不多？   也許不太多。
2. 你這學期選的課，哪門課不難？   英文課不難。
3. 他知道你今天要來嗎？   他還不知道呢。
4. 你為甚麼不說中國話？   因為我的中國話不好，不好意思

                                   說。

5. 最近你爸爸的生意好不好？　　　最近他的生意很不好。
6. 你喜歡看甚麼小説？　　　　　　我甚麼小説都喜歡看。
7. 你今年的生日要請甚麼人？　　　我還不知道呢。
8. 你媽媽要去美國一年，你難過嗎？　我不難過。
9. 明天誰去歡送許小美？　　　　　她的同學都去歡送她。
10. 你銀行的錢都沒有了，你難　　　我不知道。
　　道不知道嗎？

閱讀練習

許小美的日記

　　我弟弟近來很不快樂。他説他很煩，很難過。弟弟難過，我也很難過。我問他為甚麼這麼不快樂。他不説。我説："是不是你選的課太難？"他説："不是。"我説："是不是媽媽沒有給你錢？"他説："也不是。"我説："那是不是你太累了？"他説："不是、不是、都不是。"我説："那，請你跟我説你為甚麼不快樂，好嗎？"他説："我不好意思跟你説。"我説："我是你姐姐，我很愛你，你有難過的事跟姐姐説有甚麼不好意思的。"他説："我有一個女朋友，她不要跟我作朋友了，她説她不愛我了。"我説："那有甚麼，她不愛你，難道你還要愛她？不要因為那個女朋友難過了。我明天給你介紹一個女朋友。你喜歡美國人、日本人、英國人還是中國人？"他沒説話。我想他還在想他從前的那個女朋友呢。

問 題

1. <u>許小美</u>的弟弟近來快樂嗎？

2. <u>許小美</u>的弟弟很難過，但他為甚麼不想告訴 (tell) 他姐姐？

3. <u>許小美</u>的弟弟為甚麼很難過？

4. <u>許小美</u>跟她弟弟說甚麼？

5. 你想<u>許小美</u>的弟弟現在很快樂嗎？為甚麼？

6. 要是你難過的時候，你會跟你的好朋友說嗎？為甚麼？

7. <u>許小美</u>要給她弟弟介紹一個女朋友。你想為甚麼她弟弟沒說話。

第六課　你選的課怎麼樣？
Lesson 6　How are the classes you picked?

Lesson 6
Pinyin Text

• •

CONTENTS

🐾 Text

Nǐ xuǎn de kè zěnmeyàng?
How are the classes you picked?

Xǔ Xiǎoměi:	Àiwén, nǐ xuǎn de kè zěnmeyàng?	Aiwen, how are the classes you picked?
Mǎ Àiwén:	Wǒ xiànzài hái bú tài zhīdào ne. Nǐ ne?	At present, I still don't know yet. How about you?
Xǔ Xiǎoměi:	Wǒ yě hái bù zhīdào. Wǒmen hái méi shàng kè ne.	I don't know either. We haven't started classes yet.
Mǎ Àiwén:	Wǒmen lǎoshī shuō wǒmen zhè xuéqī yǒu hěn duō gōngkè, yě yǒu hěn duō kǎoshì. Yǒu xiǎokǎo, yě yǒu qīzhōngkǎo.	Our teacher says we will have a lot of homework and tests this semester. There will be quizzes and also a midterm exam.
Xǔ Xiǎoměi:	Méiyǒu dàkǎo ma?	No final exam?
Mǎ Àiwén:	Méiyǒu dàkǎo, búguò, děi xiě yí ge cháng bàogào.	No final exam. But we have to write a lengthy paper.
Xǔ Xiǎoměi:	Nǐ xǐhuan xiě bàogào ma?	Do you like writing papers?
Mǎ Àiwén:	Bù xǐhuan. Wǒ hěn pà xiě bàogào. Nǐ ne?	I don't like it. I really dread writing papers. What about you?
Xǔ Xiǎoměi:	Wǒ bù xǐhuan xiě cháng bàogào.	I don't like writing lengthy papers.

🎋 Vocabulary and Illustrative Sentences

1. **zěn**　　**why, how** (QW)

☞　**zěnme**　how, what, why (QW)

> (1) A:　Nǐ jīntiān zǎoshang　Why didn't you show up for class
> 　　zěnme méi lái shàng kè?　this morning?
>
> 　　B:　Wǒ tài lèi le.　I was too tired.
>
> (2) A:　Zhège zì zěnme xiě?　How do you write this character?
>
> 　　B:　Lǎoshī shuō zhème xiě.　The teacher said this is how you
> 　　　　write it.
>
> (3) A:　Nǐ zěnme yǒu zhème　Why do you have so much money?
> 　　duō qián?
>
> 　　B:　Bú tài duō.　It's not that much.

☞　**bù zěnme**　not very, not particularly (IE)

> (1) A:　Jīntiān de kǎoshì　Was today's test difficult?
> 　　nán-bu-nán?
>
> 　　B:　Hái hǎo, bù zěnme nán.　It was all right, not too difficult.
>
> (2) A:　Tā shuō de huà yǒuyìsi　Was what he said interesting?
> 　　ma?
>
> 　　B:　Bù zěnme yǒuyìsi.　Not very interesting.

2. **yàng**　　**appearance, shape, sample, type** (N)

☞　**yàngzi**　appearance, shape, manner, sample, model (N)

> A:　Zhège rén de yàngzi hěn　This person's appearance is very
> 　　yǒuyìsi.　interesting.
>
> B:　Wèishénme?　Why?
>
> A:　Yīnwèi tā gēn wǒmen hěn　Because he is very different from
> 　　bú yíyàng.　us.

☞ zhè yàng   like this, this way (Adv)

(1) Zhège zì, Wáng lǎoshī jiào wǒ zhè yàng xiě, Jīn lǎoshī jiào wǒ nà yàng xiě. Xiànzài wǒ bù zhīdào zěnyàng xiě le.

Professor Wang told me to write this character this way, Professor Jin told me to write it that way. Now I don't know how to write it anymore.

(2) Wǒ bù xǐhuan zhè yàng bù xiǎoxīn de rén.

I don't like such careless people.

☞ nà yàng   of that kind, like that (Adv)

(1) Wǒ bù xǐhuan chī nà yàng de Zhōngguó cài.

I don't like to eat that kind of Chinese food.

(2) Nà yàng nán de kè wǒ bù xuǎn.

I don't take courses as difficult as that one.

☞ yíyàng   the same, equally, alike (SV)

(1) Tāmen jiěmèi liǎng ge rén bù yíyàng. Yí ge ài shuōhuà, yí ge bú ài shuōhuà.

The two sisters are different. One likes to talk, one doesn't like to talk.

(2) Wǒ gēn nǐ yíyàng. Bù xǐhuan hē jiǔ.

You and I are alike. (We) don't like to drink wine.

☞ zěnmeyàng   how, what (QW)

(1) A: Zhège jiǔ zěnmeyàng?

How is this wine?

B: Hěn hǎo, shì nǎ nián de?

It's very good. Which year is it?

(2) A: Nǐ kǎo de zěnmeyàng?

How did you do on your exam?

B: Bú tài hǎo.

Not that well.

☞ bù zěnme- yàng   not much, nothing much (IE)

(1) A: Zhège cài hǎo chī ma?

Does this dish taste good?

B: Bù zěnmeyàng.

It's all right, nothing special.

(2) A: Nǐ xiǎng tā hěn měi ma?

Do you think she's beautiful?

B: Bù zěnmeyàng.

Not really.

3. xiàn   **present, current** (TW)

☞ xiànzài   now, at present (TW)

    (1) A: Nǐ xiànzài yǒu qián ma?   Do you have any money right
                                         now?

        B: Méiyǒu.   (I) don't have any.

    (2) A: Nǐ xiànzài zhīdào tā de   Do you know his name now?
           míngzi le ma?

        B: Zhīdào le.   (I) know now.

☞ xiànqián/   cash (N)
   xiànjīn
        A: Wǒ de qián dōu zài yínháng,   All my money is in the bank. I
           xiànzài méiyǒu xiànqián,   don't have any cash right now.
           míngtiān gěi nǐ, hǎo ma?   I'll give you the money tomorrow,
                                         okay?

        B: Hǎo.   Okay.

4. shàng   **upper, up, upward; preceding; previous** (V)

☞ shànglai   come up (V)

        A: Mèimei, māma jiào nǐ   Little sister, mother asks you to
           xiànzài shànglai.   come up right now.

        B: Wèishénme?   Why?

        A: Wǒ yě bù zhīdào.   I don't know (either).

☞ shàngqu   go up (V)

        A: Māma wèn nǐ shàng-bu-   Mother asks if you're coming up.
           shànglai?

        B: Wǒ xiànzài hěn máng,   I am really busy right now. (I)
           bú yào shàngqu.   don't want to go up.

☞ mǎshàng   at once, immediately, right away (Adv)

        A: Kuài shànglai, māma yào   Come up quickly, mother wants
           gěi nǐ qián.   to give you some money.

        B: Hǎo, wǒ mǎshàng shàngqu.   Okay, I am going up right now.

☞ **shàng kè**   attend class, go to class, conduct a class (VO)

> (1) Tóngxuémen, Wáng lǎoshī jīntiān bù lái shàng kè. Yè lǎoshī gěi nǐmen shàng kè.
>
> Students, Professor Wang will not be teaching today. Professor Ye will teach instead.

> (2) Bù zǎo le, wǒ děi qù shàng kè le.
>
> It's getting late. I have to go to class now.

☞ **shàng bān**   go to work, start work (VO)

> A: Nǐ nǎ tiān qù shàng bān?
>
> When do you start work?

> B: Míngtiān.
>
> Tomorrow.

> A: Zhème kuài! Nǐ zài nǎr shàng bān?
>
> So soon! Where will you work?

> B: Wǒ zài Zhōngguó Yínháng shàng bān.
>
> I will work at the Bank of China.

☞ **zǎoshang**   (early) morning (TW)

> A: Nǐ jīntiān zǎoshang yǒu-méiyǒu kè?
>
> Do you have classes this morning?

> B: Méiyǒu.
>
> (No, I) don't have any.

☞ **wǎnshang**   (in the) evening, (at) night (TW)

> A: Wǒ bù xǐhuan wǎnshang xiě bàogào.
>
> I don't like to write papers at night.

> B: Wèishénme?
>
> Why?

> A: Yīnwèi wǎnshang wǒ tài lèi le, xiě bù hǎo.
>
> Because I am too tired at night, (I) can't write well.

5. **duō**   **many, much, excessive; odd (SV)**

> (1) Lǎoshī gěi wǒmen de gōngkè tài duō le.
>
> The teacher gave us too much homework.

> (2) A: Zhè yí kè yǒu sānshí duō ge shēngzì, tài duō le.
>
> There are more than thirty new words in this lesson. That's too many.

> B: Bù duō, bù duō.
>
> Not too many, not too many.

☞ duōshù   majority, most (Adj)

    (1) Duōshù xuésheng bù   Most students dislike exams.
        xǐhuan kǎoshì.

    (2) Lǎoshī shuō, zhège kǎoshì   The teacher said that most people
        duōshù rén kǎode hěn hǎo.   did well on this exam.

☞ dà duōshù   great majority, vast majority (Adj)

    (1) Dà duōshù de xuésheng   A great majority of the students
        dōu shuō, jīntiān bú yào   say that they don't want to have
        kǎoshì.   a test today.

    (2) Dà duōshù de Zhōngguórén   The vast majority of Chinese
        ài hē chá.   people like to drink tea.

6. gōng   **work, achievement** (N)

☞ gōngkè   schoolwork, homework (N)

    (1) A: Dàxué de gōngkè duō-   Is there a lot of homework in
          bu-duō?   college?

        B: Hái hǎo.   It's reasonable.

    (2) A: Tā de gōngkè   How is his schoolwork?
          zěnmeyàng?

        B: Tā de gōngkè hěn hǎo,   His schoolwork is very good. He
          tā lǎo kǎo dì-yī míng.   always gets the highest score.

7. xiě   **write, compose** (V)

    (1) A: Nǐ zài xiě shénme?   What are you writing?

        B: Wǒ zài xiě jīntiān de   I am doing today's homework.
          gōngkè.

    (2) A: Zhè běn xiǎoshuō shì   Who wrote this novel?
          shéi xiě de?

        B: Shì wǒ yí ge tóngxué   One of my classmates wrote it.
          xiě de.

        A: Xiě de hǎo-bu-hǎo?   Is it well written?

        B: Xiě de hěn hǎo.   It is very well written.

☞ xiě zì   write characters (VO)

> A: Wǒ hěn xǐhuan **xiě zì**.   I really like to write characters.
>
> B: **Xiě** shénme **zì**?   Write what characters?
>
> A: **Xiě** Zhōngguó **zì**.   Write Chinese characters.

8. gào   **tell, inform, notify (V)**

☞ bàogào   scholarly paper (N); report (V/N)

> (1) Shàng dàxué lǎo děi xiě **bàogào**.   In college, we always have to write papers.
>
> (2) Jīntiān shì shéi **bàogào**?   Who is presenting a report today?

9. kǎo   **give or take an examination, test or quiz (V)**

> (1) Lǎoshī tiāntiān **kǎo** wǒmen shēngzì.   The teacher tests us on vocabulary every day.
>
> (2) Nǐ jīntiān **kǎo** de zěnmeyàng?   How did you do on your test today?

☞ xiǎokǎo   quiz (N)

> (1) Xué Zhōngwén gēn Rìwén, tiāntiān dōu yǒu **xiǎokǎo**.   There are quizzes every day when you study Chinese and Japanese.
>
> (2) A: Lǎoshī, wǒmen **xiǎokǎo** kǎo shénme?   Teacher, what is the quiz going to be about?
>
> B: Kǎo dì-wǔ kè de shēngzì.   You will be tested on the new vocabulary of Lesson 5.

☞ dàkǎo   end-of-term examination, final examination (N)

> A: Lǎoshī, wǒmen de **dàkǎo** nán-bu-nán?   Teacher, is our final exam going to be hard?
>
> B: Bú tài nán.   It won't be too hard.

☞ qīzhōng-kǎo   midterm examination (N)

> A: Nǐ zhīdào wǒmen de **qīzhōngkǎo** zài jǐ yuè ma?   Do you know in which month our midterm will be?
>
> B: Zài shíyuè.   (It will be) in October.

10. shì   **try, test** (V)

☞ shìshi   try (V)

   A: Sīwén, wǒ hěn pà kǎoshì.   Siwen, I really dread taking the
                                         test.

   B: Bú yào pà, shìshi. Kǎo bù   Don't be afraid, give it a try. It's
      hǎo, bú yàojǐn.   no big deal if you don't do well.

☞ kǎoshì   examination (V / N)

   (1) Wǒmen yì xuéqī yǒu hěn   We have many exams and reports
       duō kǎoshì, yě yǒu hěn   to work on in a semester.
       duō bàogào.

   (2) A: Nǐ xǐhuan kǎoshì háishì   Do you like to take exams or to
          xǐhuan xiě bàogào?   write papers?

       B: Dōu bù xǐhuan.   (I) don't like either.

☞ kǒushì   oral examination, oral test (N)

   Wǒ xǐhuan kǎo kǒushì, bù   I'd like to take oral exams, (but)
   xǐhuan kǎo bǐshì.   I don't like to take written exams.

☞ bǐshì   written examination (N)

   A: Nǐ xiǎng shì kǒushì yàojǐn,   Which is more important? Oral
      háishì bǐshì yàojǐn?   exam or written exam?

   B: Lǎoshī shuō dōu yàojǐn.   The teacher says both are
                                        important.

🌸 Pattern Drills

The Chinese language employs several ways to express comparisons. This lesson
introduces patterns that assert a similarity or difference between two things or
persons, for example, X and Y.

6.1 Yíyàng AS A STATIVE VERB TO EXPRESS SIMILARITY OR DIFFERENCE

To assert a similarity or difference between X and Y, a coverbial expression consisting of the coverb gēn/hé and its object is placed between the subject of the sentence and the main stative verb yíyàng. When yíyàng is used as a stative verb, it means "be alike, be like, identical." The negative form is bù yíyàng.

6.1.1 X gēn/hé Y yíyàng

X	gēn/hé	Y	yíyàng/bù yíyàng
Nǐ de shū	gēn/hé	wǒ de shū	yíyàng.
Your book(s) and my book(s) is/are the same.			

1. A: Tā de biǎo gēn nǐ de biǎo yíyàng ma?

   Is his watch the same as yours?

   B: Tā de biǎo gēn wǒ de biǎo bù yíyàng.

   His watch and my watch are not the same.

2. A: Nǐ xuǎn de kè gēn wǒ xuǎn de kè yíyàng-bu-yíyàng?

   Are the courses you picked the same as mine?

   B: Yǒude yíyàng, yǒude bù yíyàng.

   Some are the same and some are not.

6.1.2 "XY" yíyàng

When two compared items do not require specific identification, the following pattern is used.

XY	yíyàng/bù yíyàng
Zhè liǎng běn shū	yíyàng/bù yíyàng?
Are these two books the same?	

1. A: Zhè liǎng ge cài yíyàng ma?

   Are these two dishes the same?

   B: Bú tài yíyàng.

   (They are) not quite the same.

2. A: Tāmen liǎng ge rén de xìng
    <mark>yíyàng</mark> ma?

    B: Tāmen liǎng gè rén de xìng
    <mark>bù yíyàng</mark>.

    Do they have the same family name?

    They don't have the same family name.

6.2 <u>Yíyàng</u> AS AN ADVERB TO EXPRESS SIMILARITY IN SPECIFIC RESPECTS

To limit similarity to a specific respect, an appropriate stative verb is placed after <u>yíyàng</u> as a predicate complement. When <u>yíyàng</u> is used adverbially before a stative verb, it means "equally" or "as." The negative <u>bù</u> may be placed before the coverb or before <u>yíyàng</u>.

X	(<u>bù</u>) <u>gēn</u>	Y	(<u>bù</u>) <u>yíyàng</u>	SV
Wǒ jiějie	gēn	wǒ mèimei	yíyàng	hǎokàn.

My elder sister and younger sister are both good-looking.

1. A: Zhè mén kè <mark>gēn</mark> nà mén kè <mark>yíyàng yǒuyìsi</mark> ma?

    B: Wǒ xiǎng zhè liǎng mén kè yíyàng yǒuyìsi.

    Is this course and that course equally interesting?

    I think these two courses are equally interesting.

2. A: Zhōngguófàn <mark>gēn</mark> Měiguófàn <mark>yíyàng hǎochī</mark> ma?

    B: Shìde. Zhōngguófàn <mark>gēn</mark> Měiguófàn yíyàng hǎochī.

    Are Chinese food and American food equally tasty?

    Yes. Both American food and Chinese food are equally delicious.

3. A: Nǐ chī de <mark>gēn</mark> tā <mark>yíyàng duō</mark> ma?

    B: Wǒ chī de bù <mark>gēn</mark> tā <mark>yíyàng duō</mark>.

    Did you eat as much as he did?

    I didn't eat as much as he did.

6.3 THE QUESTION WORD zěnme

<u>Zěnme</u> "why, how" is an adverb. It is used to ask about the reason for something or how to do something.

1. A: Nǐ **zěnme** hái bù chīfàn?   Why haven't you eaten yet?

   B: Wǒ xiànzài děi xiě bàogào.   I have to write a report.

2. A: Tā shuō jīntiān lái, **zěnme** hái méi lái?   He said he was coming today. Why hasn't he shown up yet?

   B: Yěxǔ tā hěn máng.   Maybe he is very busy.

3. A: Zhège zì **zěnme** xiě?   How does one write this character?

   B: Wǒ yě bù zhīdào **zěnme** xiě.   I don't know how to write it either.

The expression **zěnmeyàng** is usually used as a complement or predicate object to inquire about the condition or nature of something.

1. A: Nǐ jìnlái **zěnmeyàng**?   How have you been lately?

   B: Hěn hǎo.   Very well.

2. A: Nǐ xuǎn de nà mén kè **zěnmeyàng**?   How is that course you picked?

   B: Hěn yǒuyìsi.   (It's) very interesting.

3. A: Tā de Zhōngguóhuà **zěnmeyàng**?   How is her Chinese?

   B: Hěn hǎo.   Very good.

The expression **bù zěnme(yàng)** is used to indicate that something or some condition is not very good. It is usually used as a predicate object or complement in a sentence.

1. A: Nàge xuésheng de Yīngwén **zěnmeyàng**?   How is that student's English?

   B: **Bù zěnme(yàng)**.   Not very good.

2. A: Zhège cài hǎochī ma?   Is this dish tasty?

   B: **Bù zěnme(yàng)**.   Not really.

6.4 THE QUESTION WORD duōshǎo

Duōshǎo "how many, how much" can be used with numbers and amounts of any size. It may be used directly with a noun, making the use of a measure word optional.

S	V	<u>duōshǎo</u>	*(MW)*	N ?
Nǐ	yǒu	duōshǎo	(ge)	xuéshēng?
How many students do you have?				

1. A: Nǐ yǒu <u>duōshǎo</u> qián?   How much money do you have?

   B: Wǒ méiyǒu qián.   I don't have any money.

2. A: Nǐ yǒu <u>duōshǎo</u> tóngxué?   How many classmates do you have?

   B: Wǒ yǒu èrshí ge tóngxué.   I have twenty classmates.

6.5 THE PARTICLE <u>de</u> (得)

The character <u>de</u> introduced in pattern 6.5 is 得. It is different from the subordinating particle <u>de</u> (的) introduced in Lesson 2. De (得) has several pronunciations and many uses. When <u>de</u> follows a verb to describe the manner or degree of an action, it is pronounced in its neutral tone.

6.5.1 The V-<u>de</u> with stative verbs

When <u>de</u> is placed after a verb it depicts the manner or degree of an action or condition to form a noun clause, which then stands as the subject of a stative verb or other descriptive expression.

S	V-<u>de</u>	SV
Tā	chīde	hěn duō.
He eats a lot.		

1. A: Tā <u>zǒude</u> hěn kuài ma?   Does he walk very fast?

   B: Bù. Tā <u>zǒude</u> hěn màn. Nǐ ne?   No. He walks very slowly. What about you?

   A: Wǒ <u>pǎode</u> hěn kuài.   I run very fast.

2. A: Tā <u>shuōde</u> kuài-bu-kuài?   Does she speak fast?

   B: Tā <u>shuōde</u> hěn kuài.   She speaks very fast.

When the verb of an action has an object, several patterns can be used:

(A)	*S*	*V*	*O*	*V-<u>de</u>*	*SV*
	Tā	shuō	Zhōngguóhuà,	shuōde	hěn hǎo.

As for speaking Chinese, he speaks (it) very well.

(B)	*O*		*S*	*V-<u>de</u>*	*SV*
	Zhōngguóhuà,		tā	shuōde	hěn hǎo.

(As for) Chinese, he speaks (it) very well.

(C)	*S*	<u>de</u>	*O*	*V-<u>de</u>*	*SV*
	Tā	de	Zhōngguóhuà,	shuōde	hěn hǎo.

His Chinese, he speaks very well.
(His spoken Chinese is excellent.)

1. A: Nǐ de qīzhōngkǎo kǎode zěnmeyàng?

    How did you do on your midterm examination?

    B: Wǒ kǎode bú tài hǎo. Nǐ jiějie ne?

    I didn't do well on this test. How about your elder sister?

    A: Tā kǎode hěn hǎo.

    She did very well.

2. A: Tā zhè běn xiǎoshuō xiěde zěnmeyàng?

    (As for) this novel of his, was it well written?

    B: Zhè běn xiǎoshuō xiěde hěn hǎo.

    This one was very well written.

    A: Nà běn ne?

    How about that one?

    B: Nà běn xiěde bú tài hǎo.

    That one wasn't very well written.

6.6 A PAST EVENT USING <u>shì</u> … <u>de</u>

The <u>shì</u> … <u>de</u> pattern is used to emphasize various circumstances connected with the action of a verb, such as the time, place, purpose, etc., of a **past occurrence**, rather than the action itself. The <u>shì</u> is placed before the particular circumstance to be stressed, and the <u>de</u> follows the main verb. <u>Shì</u> is not obligatory unless the sentence contains the negative <u>bù</u>.

1. A: Zhè běn shū shì shéi xiě de?   Who wrote this book?

    B: Shì wǒ tóngxué xiě de.   (It) was written by my classmate.

    A: Nà běn yě shì tā xiě de ma?   Did he write that one too?

    B: Bú shì. Nà běn bú shì tā xiě de.   No. That one wasn't written by him.

2. A: Nǐ bàba lái le ma?   Has your father come?

    B: Tā lái le.   Yes, he has come.

    A: Tā shì jīnnián lái de ma?   Did he arrive this year?

    B: Bú shì. Tā shì qùnián lái de.   No. He arrived last year.

    A: Tā wèishénme lái zhèr?   Why did he come?

    B: Tā shì lái xué Yīngwén de.   He came here to learn English.

3. A: Zhège biǎo shì shéi de?   Whose watch is this?

    B: Shì wǒ de.   It's mine.

    A: Shì nǐ māma gěi nǐ de ma?   Did your mother give you this watch?

    B: Bú shì wǒ māma gěi wǒ de, shì   No. It wasn't my mother (who) gave
       wǒ nǚpéngyou gěi wǒ de.   it to me. It was my girlfriend (who)
                                  gave it to me.

6.7 THE DOUBLING VERBS

The doubling of a verb, with or without **yī** between the two verbs, gives a
touch of informality to the verb and suggests the idea "for a while, a little bit."
Yī is optional when it is used between two verbs and it is pronounced in its
neutral tone.

1. A: Lǎoshī, wǒ de Zhōngguóhuà   Teacher, my spoken Chinese is not
       shuōde bù hǎo.   good.

    B: Bú yàojīn. Nǐ shì(-yi-)shì.   It doesn't matter. Try!

2. A: Nǐ míngnián qù Zhōngguó ma?   Are you going to China next year?

    B: Wǒ hái bù zhīdào ne. Wǒ děi   I don't know yet. I have to think about
       xiǎng(-yi-)xiǎng.   it.

❁ Sentence Building

1.

Zěnme?

Zěnme xiě?

Zhège zì zěnme xiě?

Qǐngwèn, zhège zì zěnme xiě?

2.

Zhè yàng

Zhè yàng de rén.

Xiǎoxīn zhè yàng de rén.

Nǐ děi xiǎoxīn zhè yàng de rén.

3.

Zěnmeyàng?

Kǎode zěnmeyàng?

Xiǎokǎo kǎode zěnmeyàng?

Zhōngwén xiǎokǎo kǎode zěnmeyàng?

Nǐ de Zhōngwén xiǎokǎo kǎode
zěnmeyàng?

4.

Bù zěnmeyàng.

Xiěde bù zěnmeyàng.

Bàogào xiěde bù zěnmeyàng.

Zhège bàogào xiěde bù zěnmeyàng.

Wǒ zhège bàogào xiěde bù zěnmeyàng.

❁ Questions and Responses

1. Guóyīng, zěnmeyàng?
   Guoying, what's up?

   Hěn máng, kuài yào kǎoshì le.
   (I am) very busy. (I) am going to
   have an exam soon.

2. Nǐ yǒu-méiyǒu xiànjīn?

   Do you have any cash?

   Wǒ méiyǒu xiànjīn. Wǒ de qián dōu zài
   yínháng.
   I don't have any cash. All my money
   is in the bank.

3. Nǐ gēn nǐ gēge yíyàng xǐhuan dǎ
   qiú ma?
   Do you like to play ball games as
   much as your brother does?

   Tā xǐhuan dǎ qiú, wǒ bù xǐhuan dǎ qiú.

   He likes to play ball games. I don't like
   to play ball games.

4. Jīntiān rè-bu-rè?
   Is today hot?

   Bú rè, hěn lěng.
   It's not hot. It's very cold.

5. Tā shì nàme hǎo de rén, nǐ wèishénme
   bù xǐhuan tā?
   He is such a good person. Why don't
   you like him?

   Shéi shuō de? Nǐ zěnme zhīdào wǒ
   bù xǐhuan tā?
   Says who? How do you know I don't
   like him?

6. Wǒmen tiāntiān yǒu xiǎokǎo.
    Nǐmen ne?
    We have quizzes every day.
    How about you?

    Wǒmen yě gēn nǐmen yíyàng, tiāntiān yǒu xiǎokǎo.
    We are just like you. We also have quizzes every day.

7. Nǐ xǐhuan zhège yàngzi de shǒubiǎo ma?
    Do you like this watch's design?

    Bù zěnme xǐhuan. Wǒ xǐhuan nàge yàngzi de.
    (I) don't care too much for this design. I like that watch's design.

8. Nǐ de bàogào zěnme xiě de zhème kuài?
    Why did you write your report so quickly?

    Yīnwèi zhège bàogào bù nán xiě.

    Because it was not difficult to write this report.

9. Nǐ xiǎng dà duōshù de xuésheng dōu pà kǎoshì ma?
    Do you think the great majority of students are afraid of taking tests?

    Wǒ xiǎng yǒude xuésheng pà, yǒude xuésheng bú pà.
    I think some students dread taking tests and some don't.

10. Nǐ zěnme nàme máng?

    Why are you so busy?

    Yīnwèi mǎshàng kuài yào kǎoshì le. Nándào nǐ bù máng ma?
    Because we are going to have an exam in a short while. Do you mean you are not busy?

Pronunciation Review

Differentiating ou - uo

(a)	gōu	guō	(d)	dōu	duō	(g)	zhōu	zhuō
(b)	tóu	tuó	(e)	hòu	huò	(h)	zòu	zuò
(c)	chōu	chuō	(f)	ròu	ruò	(i)	còu	cuò

🌼 Supplementary Vocabulary

School Life

shàng kè	attend class; go to class; conduct a class
xià kè	get out of class; finish class
yì táng kè	one class
quē kè	miss a class
jiàoshì	classroom
bàngōngshì	office
túshūguǎn	library

Terms of Address

xiǎojie	miss; young lady
nǚshì	Ms. (a polite term for a woman, married or unmarried); lady; madam
tàitai	Mrs.; madam
jiàoshòu	professor
lǎoshī	teacher
xiānsheng	teacher; mister (Mr.); gentleman; sir

第六課
漢字本

內容

🐾 課 文

你選的課怎麼樣？

許小美：愛文，你選的課怎麼樣？

馬愛文：我現在還不太知道呢。你呢？

許小美：我也還不知道。我們還沒上課呢。

馬愛文：我們老師說我們這學期有很多功課，也有很多考
試。有小考，也有期中考。

許小美：沒有大考嗎？

馬愛文：沒有大考，不過，得寫一個長報告。

許小美：你喜歡寫報告嗎？

馬愛文：不喜歡。我很怕寫報告。你呢？

許小美：我不喜歡寫長報告。

🐾 生詞及例句

1. **怎**   **why, how** (QW)

☞ 怎麼   how, what, why (QW)

　　(1) A: 你今天早上怎麼沒來上課？

　　　　 B: 我太累了。

　　(2) A: 這個字怎麼寫？

　　　　 B: 老師說這麼寫。

　　(3) A: 你怎麼有這麼多錢？

　　　　 B: 不太多。

☞ 不怎麼   not very, not particularly (IE)

　　(1) A: 今天的考試難不難？

　　　　 B: 還好，不怎麼難。

　　(2) A: 他說的話有意思嗎？

　　　　 B: 不怎麼有意思。

2. **樣**   **appearance, shape, sample, type** (N)

☞ 樣子   appearance, shape, manner, sample, model (N)

　　A: 這個人的樣子很有意思。

　　B: 為甚麼？

　　A: 因為他跟我們很不一樣。

☞ 這樣   like this, this way (Adv)

　　(1) 這個字，王老師叫我這樣寫，金老師叫我那樣寫。現在我
　　　　不知道怎樣寫了。

　　(2) 我不喜歡這樣不小心的人。

☞ 那樣   of that kind, like that (Adv)

　　(1) 我不喜歡吃那樣的中國菜。

　　(2) 那樣難的課我不選。

☞ 一樣   the same, equally, alike (SV)

     (1) 他們姐妹兩個人不一樣，一個愛說話，一個不愛說話。

     (2) 我跟你一樣，不喜歡喝酒。

☞ 怎麼樣   how, what (QW)

     (1) A: 這個酒怎麼樣？

          B: 很好，是哪年的？

     (2) A: 你考得怎麼樣？

          B: 不太好。

☞ 不怎麼樣   not much, nothing much (IE)

     (1) A: 這個菜好吃嗎？

          B: 不怎麼樣。

     (2) A: 你想她很美嗎？

          B: 不怎麼樣。

3. 現   **present, current** (TW)

☞ 現在   now, at present (TW)

     (1) A: 你現在有錢嗎？

          B: 沒有。

     (2) A: 你現在知道他的名字了嗎？

          B: 知道了。

☞ 現錢/現金   cash (N)

     A: 我的錢都在銀行，現在沒有現錢，明天給你，好嗎？

     B: 好。

4. 上   **upper, up, upward; preceding; previous** (V)

☞ 上來   come up (V)

     A: 妹妹，媽媽叫你現在上來。

     B: 為甚麼？

     A: 我也不知道。

☞ 上去   go up (V)

          A: 媽媽問你上不上來？

          B: 我現在很忙，不要上去。

☞ 馬上   at once, immediately, right away (Adv)

          A: 快上來，媽媽要給你錢。

          B: 好，我馬上上去。

☞ 上課   attend class, go to class, conduct a class (VO)

          (1) 同學們，王老師今天不來上課。葉老師給你們上課。

          (2) 不早了，我得去上課了。

☞ 上班   go to work, start work (VO)

          A: 你哪天去上班？

          B: 明天。

          A: 那麼快！你在哪兒上班？

          B: 我在中國銀行上班。

☞ 早上   (early) morning (TW)

          A: 你今天早上有沒有課？

          B: 沒有。

☞ 晚上   (in the) evening, (at) night (TW)

          A: 我不喜歡晚上寫報告。

          B: 為甚麼？

          A: 因為晚上我太累了，寫不好。

5. 多   **many, much, excessive; odd (SV)**

          (1) 老師給我們的功課太多了。

          (2) A: 這一課有三十多個生字，太多了。

              B: 不多，不多。

☞ 多數　　majority, most (Adj)

(1) 多數學生不喜歡考試。

(2) 老師說，這個考試多數人考得很好。

☞ 大多數　great majority, vast majority (Adj)

(1) 大多數的學生都說，今天不要考試。

(2) 大多數的中國人愛喝茶。

6. 功　　**work, achievement** (N)

☞ 功課　　schoolwork, homework (N)

(1) A: 大學的功課多不多？

　　B: 還好。

(2) A: 他的功課怎麼樣？

　　B: 他的功課很好，他老考第一名。

7. 寫　　**write, compose** (V)

(1) A: 你在寫甚麼？

　　B: 我在寫今天的功課。

(2) A: 這本小說是誰寫的？

　　B: 是我一個同學寫的。

　　A: 寫得好不好？

　　B: 寫得很好。

☞ 寫字　　write characters (VO)

A: 我很喜歡寫字。

B: 寫甚麼字？

A: 寫中國字。

8. 告　　**tell, inform, notify** (V)

☞ 報告　　scholarly paper (N); report (V/N)

(1) 上大學老得寫報告。

(2) 今天是誰報告？

9. 考　　**give or take an examination, test or quiz** (V)

(1) 老師天天考我們生字。

(2) 你今天考得怎麼樣？

☞ 小考　　quiz (N)

(1) 學中文跟日文，天天都有小考。

(2) A: 老師，我們小考考甚麼？

　　B: 考第五課的生字。

☞ 大考　　end-of-term examination, final examination (N)

A: 老師，我們的大考難不難？

B: 不太難。

☞ 期中考　　midterm examination (N)

A: 你知道我們的期中考在幾月嗎？

B: 在十月。

10. 試　　**try, test** (V)

☞ 試試　　try (V)

A: 思文，我很怕考試。

B: 不要怕，試試。考不好，不要緊。

☞ 考試　　examination (V/N)

(1) 我們一學期有很多考試，也有很多報告。

(2) A: 你喜歡考試還是喜歡寫報告？

　　B: 都不喜歡。

☞ 口試　　　oral examination, oral test (N)

　　　　　　我喜歡考口試，不喜歡考筆試。

☞ 筆試　　　written examination (N)

　　　　　　A: 你想是口試要緊，還是筆試要緊？

　　　　　　B: 老師說都要緊。

🌸 句型練習

The Chinese language employs several ways to express comparisons. This lesson introduces patterns that assert a similarity or difference between two things or persons, for example, X and Y.

6.1 一樣 AS A STATIVE VERB TO EXPRESS SIMILARITY OR DIFFERENCE

To assert a similarity or difference between X and Y, a coverbial expression consisting of the converb 跟/和 and its object is placed between the subject of the sentence and the main stative verb 一樣. When 一樣 is used as a stative verb, it means "be alike, be like, identical." The negative form is 不一樣.

6.1.1 X 跟/和 Y 一樣

X	跟/和	Y	一樣/不一樣
你的書	跟/和	我的書	一樣。

Your book(s) and my book(s) is/are the same.

1. A: 他的錶跟你的錶一樣嗎？

　 B: 他的錶跟我的錶不一樣。

2. A: 你選的課跟我選的課一樣不一樣？

　 B: 有的一樣，有的不一樣。

6.1.2 "XY" 一樣

When two compared items do not require specific identification, the following pattern is used.

> XY   一樣/不一樣
> 這兩本書   一樣/不一樣？
> Are these two books the same?

1. A: 這兩個菜一樣嗎？

   B: 不太一樣。

2. A: 他們兩個人的姓一樣嗎？

   B: 他們兩個人的姓不一樣。

6.2 一樣 AS AN ADVERB TO EXPRESS SIMILARITY IN SPECIFIC RESPECTS

To limit similarity to a specific respect, an appropriate stative verb is placed after 一樣 as a predicate complement. When 一樣 is used adverbially before a stative verb, it means "equally" or "as." The negative 不 may be placed before the coverb or before 一樣.

> X   (不) 跟   Y   (不) 一樣   SV
> 我姐姐   跟   我妹妹   一樣   好看。
> My elder sister and younger sister are both good-looking.

1. A: 這門課跟那門課一樣有意思嗎？

   B: 我想這兩門課一樣有意思。

2. A: 中國飯跟美國飯一樣好吃嗎？

   B: 是的。中國飯跟美國飯一樣好吃。

3. A: 你吃的跟他一樣多嗎？

   B: 我吃的不跟他一樣多。

6.3 THE QUESTION WORD 怎麼

怎麼 "why, how" is an adverb. It is used to ask about the reason for something or how to do something.

1. A: 你怎麼還不吃飯？

    B: 我現在得寫報告。

2. A: 他説今天來，怎麼還沒來？

    B: 也許他很忙。

3. A: 這個字怎麼寫？

    B: 我也不知道怎麼寫。

The expression 怎麼樣 is usually used as a complement or predicate object to inquire about the condition or nature of something.

1. A: 你近來怎麼樣？

    B: 很好。

2. A: 你選的那門課怎麼樣？

    B: 很有意思。

3. A: 他的中國話怎麼樣？

    B: 很好。

The expression 不怎麼 (樣) is used to indicate that something or some condition is not very good. It is usually used as a predicate object or complement in a sentence.

1. A: 那個學生的英文怎麼樣？

    B: 不怎麼 (樣)。

2. A: 這個菜好吃嗎？

    B: 不怎麼 (樣)。

6.4 THE QUESTION WORD 多少

多少 "how many, how much" can be used with numbers and amounts of any size. It may be used directly with a noun, making the use of a measure word optional.

S	V	多少	(MW)	N ?
你	有	多少	(個)	學生？
How many students do you have?				

A: 你有多少錢？

B: 我沒有錢。

A: 你有多少同學？

B: 我有二十個同學。

6.5 THE PARTICLE 得 (de)

The character 得 introduced in pattern 6.5 is 得. It is different from the subordinating particle 的 (de) introduced in Lesson 2. 得 has several pronunciations and many uses. When 得 follows a verb to describe the manner or degree of an action, it is pronounced in its neutral tone.

6.5.1 The V-得 with stative verbs

When 得 is placed after a verb, it depicts the manner or degree of an action or condition to form a noun clause, which then stands as the subject of a stative verb or other descriptive expression.

S	V-得	Adj
他	吃得	很多。
He eats a lot.		

1. A: 他走得很快嗎？

   B: 不。他走得很慢。你呢？

   A: 我跑得很快。

2. A: 他說得快不快？

    B: 他說得很快。

When the verb of an action has an object, several patterns can be used:

(A)	*S*	*V*	*O*	*V-得*	*SV*
	他	說	中國話，	說得	很好。

As for speaking Chinese, he speaks (it) very well.

(B)	*O*	*S*	*V-得*	*SV*
	中國話，	他	說得	很好。

(As for) Chinese, he speaks (it) very well.

(C)	*S*	*的*	*O*	*V-得*	*SV*
	他	的	中國話，	說得	很好。

His Chinese, he speaks very well.
(His spoken Chinese is excellent.)

1. A: 你的期中考考得怎麼樣？

    B: 我考得不太好。你姐姐呢？

    A: 她考得很好。

2. A: 他這本小說寫得怎麼樣？

    B: 這本小說寫得很好。

    A: 那本呢？

    B: 那本寫得不太好。

6.6 A PAST EVENT USING 是……的

The 是……的 pattern is used to emphasize various circumstances connected with the action of a verb, such as the time, place, purpose, etc., of a **past occurrence**, rather than the action itself. The 是 is placed before the particular circumstance to be stressed, and the 的 follows the main verb. 是 is not obligatory unless the sentence contains the negative 不.

1. A: 這本書是誰寫的？

   B: 是我同學寫的。

   A: 那本也是他寫的嗎？

   B: 不是。那本不是他寫的。

2. A: 你爸爸來了嗎？

   B: 他來了。

   A: 他是今年來的嗎？

   B: 不是。他是去年來的。

   A: 他為甚麼來這兒？

   B: 他是來學英文的。

3. A: 這個錶是誰的？

   B: 是我的。

   A: 是你媽媽給你的嗎？

   B: 不是我媽媽給我的，是我女朋友給我的。

6.7 THE DOUBLING VERBS

The doubling of a verb, with or without 一 between the two verbs, gives a touch of informality to the verb and suggests the idea "for a while, a little bit." 一 is optional when it is used between two verbs and it is pronounced in its neutral tone.

1. A: 老師，我的中國話說得不好。

   B: 不要緊。你試 (一) 試。

2. A: 你明年去中國嗎？

   B: 我還不知道呢，我得想 (一) 想。

造句

1.

怎麼？

怎麼寫？

這個字怎麼寫？

請問，這個字怎麼寫？

2.

這樣

這樣的人。

小心這樣的人。

你得小心這樣的人。

3.

怎麼樣？

考得怎麼樣？

小考考得怎麼樣？

中文小考考得怎麼樣？

你的中文小考考得怎麼樣？

4.

不怎麼樣。

寫得不怎麼樣。

報告寫得不怎麼樣。

這個報告寫得不怎麼樣。

我這個報告寫得不怎麼樣。

問答

1. 國英，怎麼樣？　　　　　　　很忙，快要考試了。

2. 你有沒有現金？　　　　　　　我沒有現金。我的錢都在銀行。

3. 你跟你哥哥一樣喜歡打球嗎？　他喜歡打球，我不喜歡打球。

4. 今天熱不熱？　　　　　　　　不熱，很冷。

5. 他是那麼好的人，你為甚麼不　誰說的？你怎麼知道我不喜歡他？
   喜歡他？

6. 我們天天有小考，你們呢？　　我們也跟你們一樣，天天有小考。

7. 你喜歡這個樣子的手錶嗎？　　不怎麼喜歡。我喜歡那個樣子的。

8. 你的報告怎麼寫得這麼快？　　因為這個報告不難寫。

9. 你想大多數的學生都怕考試嗎？我想有的學生怕，有的學生不怕。

10. 你怎麼那麼忙？　　　　　　　因為馬上快要考試了。難道你不忙嗎？

❀ 閱讀練習

馬思文的日記

　　我這學期選的課很好。天天早上沒有課，下午有課。老師給我們很多功課。我很喜歡作功課。中文課跟日文課也天天有小考，不過小考不怎麼難。我現在還不太忙。過幾天，兩門課有期中考，兩門課得寫報告。我不喜歡考試，我喜歡寫報告，我的同學多數不喜歡寫報告，他們喜歡考試。大學的考試跟中學的不一樣。大學的考試得寫得很長。

　　現在我在考試，我得寫得很好、很快、很小心。這是我進大學第一個期中考。我很怕，我怕我考不好。媽媽說，考不好不要緊。

問 題

1. 馬思文的課是在上午還是在下午？
2. 馬思文的日文課跟中文課有沒有小考？
3. 為甚麼過幾天馬思文很忙？
4. 馬思文喜歡考試還是喜歡寫報告？他的同學呢？
5. 為甚麼馬思文現在很怕考試？他媽媽跟他說甚麼？
6. 你想學中文一定得有很多小考嗎？為甚麼？
7. 你有沒有寫過中文報告？你想寫中文報告難還是寫英文報告難？

第七課　晚會
Lesson 7　Evening party

Lesson 7
Pinyin Text

• •

🐾 Text

Wǎnhuì
Evening Party

(1) Qù wǎnhuì
(1) Going to an evening party

Xǔ Xiǎoměi:	Mǎ Àiwén, nǐ yào qù xīngqīliù de wǎnhuì ma?	Ma Aiwen, do you want to go to the evening party this Saturday?
Mǎ Àiwén:	Yào qù. Nǐ zhīdào zài nǎr ma?	I'd like to go. Do you know where it will be?
Xǔ Xiǎoměi:	Zài Xuésheng Zhōngxīn.	It will be at the Student Center.
Mǎ Àiwén:	Wǒmen shénme shíhou qù?	When shall we go?
Xǔ Xiǎoměi:	Xīngqīliù wǎnshang wǒ lái zhǎo nǐ.	I will come to meet you on Saturday evening.
Mǎ Àiwén:	Hǎo. Wǒ děng nǐ.	Okay. I will wait for you.

(2) Tán wǎnhuì
(2) Talking about the evening party

Lín Hǎiyīng:	Xīngqīliù de wǎnhuì zěnmeyàng?	How was the evening party last Saturday?
Xǔ Xiǎoměi:	Hěn yǒuyìsi. Yǒu hěn duō rén.	It was very interesting. There were a lot of people.
Lín Hǎiyīng:	Nǐmen dōu zuò shénme le?	What did you do at the party?
Xǔ Xiǎoměi:	Yǒude rén tánhuà, yǒude rén tiàowǔ, yǒude rén hē qìshuǐ.	Some people were talking, some people were dancing and some people were having soft drinks.
Lín Hǎiyīng:	Méiyǒu jiǔ ma?	No wine?

Xǔ Xiǎoměi: Méiyǒu. Wànhuì shàng bù kěyǐ hē jiǔ. Wǒmen jiù kěyǐ hē Kěkǒukělè, Qīxǐ, shuǐ, shénme de. Nǐ wèishénme méi qù?

No. We were not allowed to drink wine at the evening party. We could only drink Coca-Cola, Seven-up, water, etc. Why didn't you go?

Lín Hǎiyīng: Wǒ běnlái xiǎng qù, kěshì wǒ nà tiān wǎnshang děi xiě yí ge bàogào.

I was planning to go, but I had to write a paper that evening.

🐾 Vocabulary and Illustrative Sentences

1. huì   **will; know how to, be able to** (AV); **meeting(s), get-together, assembly, conference; association** (N)

    (1) A: Nǐ xiǎng míngtiān lǎoshī huì gěi wǒmen kǎoshì ma?

    Do you think the teacher will give us a quiz tomorrow?

    B: Wǒ xiǎng bú huì.

    I don't think (she) will.

    (2) A: Nǐ huì-bu-huì xiě nǐ de míngzi?

    Do you know how to write your name?

    B: Huì.

    (Yes, I) know.

☞ wǎnhuì   evening party, an evening of entertainment (N)

Nǐ lái wǒmen de wǎnhuì ma?

Are you coming to our evening party?

☞ cháhuì   tea party (N)

Míngtiān wǎnshang de cháhuì bù zhīdào huì yǒu jǐ ge rén lái.

(I) don't know how many people will attend tomorrow night's tea party.

☞ jiǔhuì   cocktail party (N)

A: Wǒ bú qù lǎoshī jiā de jiǔhuì, yīnwèi wǒ bú huì hē jiǔ, qù le yě méiyìsi.

I'm not going to the cocktail party at the teacher's house because I don't drink wine. It would be no fun going to the party.

B: Jiǔhuì bú shì jiù hē jiǔ, nǐ
kěyǐ gēn rén tánhuà.

A cocktail party is not only for
drinking. You can talk to people.

☞ huìhuà   conversation (N)

Jīntiān de huìhuà kè, wǒmen
shuō le hěn duō huà.

During today's conversation
class, we spoke a lot.

2. xīng   **star** (N)

☞ xīngxing   star (N)

Wǎnshang wǒ xǐhuan gēn jiārén
kàn tiānshàng de xīngxing.

I like to watch stars in the sky
with my family at night.

☞ míngxīng   a famous performer (N)

A: Tā jiùshì nǐ shuō de nàge
hěn yǒumíng de míngxīng
ma?

Is he the famous performer you
were talking about?

B: Shì. Tā xiànzài hěn hóng.

Yes. He is very popular right
now.

☞ xīngqī   week (TW)

(1) A: Jīntiān xīngqī jǐ?

What day of the week is it today?

B: Jīntiān xīngqīliù.

Today is Saturday.

(2) A: Yí ge xīngqī yǒu jǐ tiān?

How many days are there in a
week?

B: Qī tiān.

Seven days.

(3) Xīngqītiān yě jiào xīngqīrì.

Sunday (*xingqitian*) is also called
Sunday (*xingqiri*).

☞ zhè xīngqī   this week (TW)

Zhè xīngqī wǒmen méiyǒu
kǎoshì, zhēn hǎo.

We don't have a test this week.
How great!

☞ shàng
  xīngqī   last week (TW)

Shàng xīngqī wǒ bàba māma
qù Zhōngguó le.

My father and mother went to
China last week.

3. **shí**　　**time, hour** (N)

☞ xiǎoshí　　hour (N)

(1) A: Nǐ jǐ ge xiǎoshí kěyǐ xiě　　In how many hours can you
hǎo zhège bàogào?　　finish writing this paper?

B: Wǒ xiǎng sān ge duō　　I think I'll be able to finish
xiǎoshí jiù kěyǐ xiě hǎo le.　　writing it in about three hours.

(2) A: Yì tiān yǒu jǐ ge xiǎoshí?　　How many hours are there in a
day?

B: Yì tiān yǒu èrshísì ge　　There are twenty-four hours in a
xiǎoshí.　　day.

☞ shíqī　　period (N)

(1) Wǒ bú tài xǐhuan nàge　　I don't really like the literature of
shíqī de wénxué.　　that period.

(2) Nàge shíqī de wénxué　　Literature of that period is
gēn xiànzài de bù yíyàng.　　different from that of today.

4. **hòu**　　**time** (N); **wait** (V)

☞ shíhou　　(duration of) time, (point in) time, moment (N)

(1) A: Nǐ shì shénme shíhou lái　　When did you get here? Why
de? Wǒ zěnme bù zhīdào?　　didn't I know about it?

B: Wǒ qùnián jiù lái le.　　I came last year.

(2) A: Māma lái de shíhou, nǐ　　Do you know when mother
zhīdào-bu-zhīdào?　　came?

B: Wǒ bù zhīdào, yīnwèi　　I don't know because I was
wǒ zài shàng kè.　　attending class.

☞ yǒushíhou　sometimes (Adv)

(1) Wǒ yǒushíhou bù xǐhuan　　Sometimes I don't enjoy talking
gēn tā shuōhuà.　　to him.

(2) Wǒmen yǒushíhou hē chá,　　Sometimes we drink tea, some-
yǒushíhou hē Kěkǒukělè.　　times we drink Coca-Cola.

☞ xiǎoshíhou in one's childhood, when one was young (Adv)

> (1) Wǒ xiǎoshíhou bù xǐhuan shàng xué.
>
> I didn't like going to school when I was a child.

> (2) Māma shuō wǒ xiǎoshíhou hěn kě'ài. Dàjiā dōu xǐhuan wǒ.
>
> Mother says that I was cute when I was a child. Everyone loved me.

5. tán   **talk, chat, discuss** (V)

> A: Nǐ zhīdào tāmen zài tán shénme ma?
>
> Do you know what they are talking about?

> B: Wǒ zěnme zhīdào?
>
> How would I know?

☞ tánhuà conversation, talk, chat; statement (N/VO)

> Tāmen de tánhuà hěn yǒuyìsi.
>
> Their conversation was very interesting.

☞ tántiānr chat, make conversation (N/V)

> Dàjiā dōu hěn xǐhuan gēn tā tántiānr.
>
> Everyone likes to talk to him.

☞ tánxīn heart-to-heart talk (N/V)

> Zhǎo yí ge kěyǐ tánxīn de rén hěn nán.
>
> It's very hard to find someone with whom you can have a heart-to-heart talk.

☞ huìtán formal talks (N/V)

> Jìnlái Zhōngguó gēn Měiguó yǒu huìtán ma?
>
> Have China and the United States had some talks recently?

6. zuò   **do, make, compose** (V)

> A: Nǐ tiāntiān zài nǎr zuò gōngkè?
>
> Where do you do your homework every day?

> B: Zài túshūguǎn.
>
> At the library.

☞ zuòwén   student's essay or composition (N)

        A: Lǎoshī, wǒmen de zuòwén   Teacher, how long does our essay
            děi xiě duō cháng?   have to be?

        B: Nǐ xiǎng xiě duō cháng jiù   Write as much as you want.
            xiě duō cháng.

☞ xiězuò   writing (V/N)

        Zhè xuéqī wǒ xuǎn le yì mén   This semester, I am taking a
        xiězuò kè, wǒmen chángcháng   writing class. We often write
        xiě zuòwén.   essays.

☞ zuòjiā   writer (N)

        A: Bīngxīn shì Zhōngguó hěn   Bingxin is a famous Chinese
            yǒumíng de nǚ zuòjiā, nǐ   woman writer. Have you read
            kànguo tā xiě de xiǎoshuō   her novels?
            ma?

        B: Wǒ xiǎoshíhou kànguo.   I read them when I was little.

        A: Nǐ xǐhuan tā de xiǎoshuō ma? Do you like her novels?

        B: Wǒ hěn xǐhuan.   I like her novels very much.

7. wǔ   **dance (V/N)**

☞ tiàowǔ   to dance (V/VO)

        (1) Tā xiǎoshíhou hěn xǐhuan   She loved to dance when she was
            tiàowǔ, xiànzài bù xǐhuan   a child. Now she doesn't like it
            tiào le.   anymore.

        (2) Jīntiān wǎnshang, tā gēn   He danced three times with Ma
            Mǎ Hóng tiào le sān ge wǔ.   Hong tonight.

☞ wǔhuì   dance party, ball (N)

        Yàoshì nǐ bù xǐhuan tiàowǔ,   It would be no fun to go to a
        qù wǔhuì jiù méiyìsi le.   dance party if one didn't like to
                                         dance.

8. **kě**   can, may (Adv); but, yet (Conj)

☞ kěshì   but, yet, however (Conj)

A: Nǐ wèishénme bú tiàowǔ?   Why don't you dance? Don't you
Nǐ bù xǐhuan tiàowǔ ma?   like to dance?

B: Xǐhuan shì xǐhuan, kěshì   I like to dance all right, but I'm
wǒ jīntiān tài lèi le.   too tired today.

☞ kěpà   fearful, frightful, terrible, terrifying (SV)

A: Tiāntiān děi kǎoshì, kěpà.   We have exams every day. How
frightful!

B: Bú yào pà, nà dōu shì   Don't be scared! They're all
xiǎokǎo, bù nán.   quizzes. They won't be hard.

☞ kěkǒu   good to eat, tasty, delicious, palatable (SV)

A: Nǐ shìshi zhège cài kěkǒu-   Try this dish! Is it tasty?
bu-kěkǒu.

B: Hěn hǎochī.   (It's) delicious.

☞ Kěkǒukělè   Coca-Cola, Coke (N)

A: Nǐ xǐhuan hē shénme qìshuǐ?   What kind of soft drinks do you
like to have?

B: Wǒ xǐhuan hē Kěkǒukělè.   I like to drink Coca-Cola.

☞ xǔkě   permit, permission, allow (V/N)

(1) Māma bù xǔkě wǒ hē jiǔ,   Mother does not allow me to
yīnwèi wǒ hái xiǎo.   drink because I am still young.

(2) Méiyǒu lǎoshī de xǔkě, nǐ   Without the permission of the
kěyǐ bù kǎoshì ma?   teacher, can you not take the test?

☞ kě'ài   lovable, likable, lovely, adorable (SV)

(1) Nǐ de xiǎo mèimei hěn kě'ài.   Your younger sister is adorable.

(2) Tā shì yí ge hěn bù kě'ài   He is not a likable person.
de rén.

9. **yǐ**   **use, according to, because of** (CV)

☞ **kěyǐ**   can, may; not bad (AV)

(1) A: **Wǒ kěyǐ jìnlai ma?**   May I come in?

   B: **Kěyǐ. Qǐng jìn.**   (Yes, you) may. Please come in.

(2) A: **Zhège cài kěkǒu ma?**   Is this dish tasty?

   B: **Bù zěnme hǎo, hái kěyǐ.**   It's not so great. It's okay.

☞ **yǐhòu**   after, afterwards, later, hereafter, in the future (Conj/Adv)

(1) **Tā hē jiǔ yǐhòu, jiù hěn**   He talks a lot after he drinks.
    xǐhuan shuōhuà.

(2) **Nǐ yǐhòu xiǎng zuò shénme?**   What would you like to do in
                                          the future?

☞ **yǐwéi**   think, consider; thought (V)

(1) A: **Wǒ yǐwéi xuǎn wǔ mén**   I think taking five courses is too
       kè tài nán. Nǐ shuō ne?   difficult. What do you say?

   B: **Wǒ xiǎng hái kěyǐ.**   I think it will be okay.

(2) **Wǒ yǐwéi tā shì Zhōng-**   I thought he was Chinese, but he
    guórén, kěshì tā shì   is Japanese.
    Rìběnrén.

10. **jiù**   **already, as early as; just, only** (AV)

(1) A: **Lǎoshī, zhège zì wǒmen**   Teacher, we haven't learned
       méi xuéguo.   this character before.

   B: **Zhège zì wǒmen**   We learned this character last
      shàng xīngqī jiù xuéguo   week.
      le.

(2) **Lǎoshī yì lái, wǒmen jiù bù**   As soon as the teacher gets here,
    shuōhuà le.   we'll stop talking.

(3) **Wǒmen jīntiān bù xué hěn**   We will not be learning many
    duō shēngzì, jiù xué bā ge.   new words today. (We'll) just
                                          learn eight.

☞ jiùyào   be about to, be going to, be on the point of (AV)

Wǒmen mǎshàng jiùyào kǎo qīzhōngkǎo le.	We are just about to have our midterm exam.

☞ jiùshì   exactly, precisely; even if (EV / Adv)

(1) A: Shéi shì Lín Hǎiyīng?   Who is Lin Haiying?

     B: Wǒ jiùshì.   I am.

(2) A: Jiùshì tā hěn bèn, wǒ hái xǐhuan tā.   Even if he is very stupid, I still like him.

     B: Wèishénme?   Why?

     A: Yīnwèi tā shì yí ge hǎorén.   Because he is a nice person.

🐾 Pattern Drills

7.1 ASKING TIME

1. A: Nǐ māma shénme shíhou lái?   When is your mother coming?

     B: Míngtiān wǎnshang.   Tomorrow night.

2. A: Wǒmen shénme shíhou kǎoshì?   When is our test?

     B: Xīngqīwǔ.   Friday.

3. A: Nǐ shénme shíhou qù Zhōngguó?   When are you going to China?

     B: Míngnián liùyuè.   June of next year.

4. A: Míngtiān xīngqī jǐ?   What day of the week is tomorrow?

     B: Xīngqītiān/Xīngqīrì.   Sunday.

5. A: Nǐ zǎoshang lái háishì wǎnshang lái?   Are you coming in the morning or in the evening?

     B: Wǎnshang lái.   (I will) come in the evening.

The sequence of telling time in Chinese always begins with the largest unit followed by progressively smaller ones: year, month, week, day, part of day, hour, minute. For example, 3:15 p.m. on 15 March 1932 should be formulated as follows:

> yījiǔsānèr nián   sānyuè   shíwǔrì   xiàwǔ   sān diǎn   shíwǔ fēn
> 1932, March 15, afternoon, three o'clock, fifteen (minutes)

7.2 RELATIVE-TIME WORDS

The relative-time words <u>shíhou</u> "when, while," <u>yǐqián</u> "before," and <u>yǐhòu</u> "after" appear at the **end** of a clause, rather than the beginning, as in English:

Nǐ lái de <u>shíhou</u>	**When** you come
Nǐ lái <u>yǐqián</u>	**Before** you come
Nǐ lái (le) <u>yǐhòu</u>	**After** you come

1. A: Tā lái de shíhou nǐ zài nǎr?   Where were you when he came?

    B: Wǒ zài shàng kè.   I was in class.

2. A: Tā lái Měiguó yǐqián huì-bu-huì shuō Yīngwén?   Did he know how to speak English before he came to the States?

    B: Bú huì.   (He) didn't.

3. A: Wǒmen shénme shíhou kǎoshì?   When are we going to have the test?

    B: Lǎoshī lái (le) yǐhòu jiù kǎoshì.   (We) will have the test after the teacher arrives.

7.3 THE LINKING ADVERBS yǒu(de)shíhou ... yǒu(de)shíhou

The linking adverbs <u>yǒu(de)shíhou</u> ... <u>yǒu(de)shíhou</u> "sometimes ... sometimes" are inserted between two verbs, adjectives or phrases which are opposite or similar in meaning, to indicate that different actions or phenomena take place alternately within a given time.

1. Wǒ yǒu(de)shíhou xǐhuan hē chá, yǒu(de)shíhou xǐhuan hē qìshuǐ.   Sometimes I like to drink tea, sometimes I like to have soft drinks.

2. Wǒmen lǎoshī yǒu(de)shíhou gěi wǒmen kǎoshì, yǒu(de)shíhou bù gěi wǒmen kǎoshì.   Sometimes our teacher gives us tests, sometimes he doesn't.

3. Zhōngwén yǒu(de)shíhou hěn nán,
    yǒu(de)shíhou bù nán.

    Chinese is sometimes very difficult
    and sometimes not.

7.4 Huì AS AN AUXILIARY VERB

When huì functions as an auxiliary verb, it means "can, be able to" and has
three basic meanings.

7.4.1 A learned skill

To express a learned or acquired ability or skill, that is, "to know how" or "to
learn how to."

1. A: Nǐ huì-bu-huì shuō Yīngwén?

    Can you speak English?

    B: Wǒ bú huì shuō Yīngwén.

    I can't speak English.

2. A: Nǐ huì xiě Zhōngguózì ma?

    Do you know how to write Chinese
    characters?

    B: Wǒ huì.

    (Yes,) I do.

7.4.2 Possibility of an event

To express the possibility or the likelihood of the occurrence of an event, that
is, "will, could possibly."

1. A: Tā zěnme hái méi lái?

    Why isn't he here yet?

    B: Wǒ xiǎng tā bú huì lái le.

    I don't think he is coming.

2. A: Jīntiān lǎoshī huì-bu-huì gěi
    wǒmen kǎoshì?

    Do you think the teacher will give us
    a test today?

    B: Wǒ xiǎng huì.

    I think she will.

7.4.3 To describe someone

To describe someone who possesses a certain skill or talent, that is, "truly can,
to know how to." It is often preceded by the adverbs hěn "very," zhēn "really"
(see Lesson 9), or zuì "the most" (see Lesson 10).

1. Tā hěn huì zuò Zhōngguócài.

    She is very good at cooking Chinese food.

2. Tā hěn huì hē jiǔ.

    He can really drink.

3. Wáng tàitai zhēn huì shuōhuà.

    Mrs. Wang is very eloquent.

4. Mǎ Sīwén zuì huì tiàowǔ le.

    Ma Siwen is very good at dancing.

7.5 THE AUXILIARY VERB kěyǐ

Kěyǐ "may, can, be allowed" is used to express permissibility.

1. A: Māma, wǒ kěyǐ-bu-kěyǐ gēn tā tiàowǔ?

    Mom, may I dance with him?

    B: Bù kěyǐ.

    You may not.

2. A: Lǎoshī, wǒmen shàng kè de shíhou kěyǐ shuō Yīngwén ma?

    Teacher, may we speak English during class?

    B: Yǒushíhou kěyǐ, yǒushíhou bù kěyǐ.

    Sometimes you may, sometimes you may not.

3. A: Nǐ kěyǐ xiě zhège bàogào ma?

    Can you write this report?

    B: Wǒ xiǎng wǒ kěyǐ. Wǒ kěyǐ shìshi.

    I think I can. I can give it a try.

7.6 THE ADVERB jiù

The adverb jiù "only, soon" has many uses. Sometimes it shares an autonomous relationship with respect to time and expectation.

7.6.1 Jiù indicative of a future event

When jiù is followed by a verb in a sentence with or without an overt future time expression, it indicates that the event or action in question will happen soon.

1. Tā jiù lái.

    He will be here soon.

2. Wǒ jiù qù.

    I am going right away.

3. Wǒmen xiànzài jiù kǎoshì.   We are going to have the test now.

4. Wǒ míngtiān jiù qù zhǎo tā.   I am going to look for him tomorrow.

7.6.2 Jiù ... le with future time expressions

When jiù ... le is used in conjunction with future adverbs such as yào "will, soon," mǎshàng "at once," kuài yào "soon will," or a future time expression, it indicates something will happen or will complete **very soon**.

1. Zhè xuéqī jiù yào guòqu le.   The semester is almost over.

2. Wǒmen lǎoshī mǎshàng jiù lái le.   Our teacher will be here very soon.

3. Míngtiān jiù shì xīngqīliù le!   Tomorrow will be Saturday!

4. Wǒ de bàogào jiù kuài xiě hǎo le.   My paper will soon be finished.

7.6.3 Jiù ... le with past time expressions

When jiù ... le comes in conjunction with adverbs such as yǐjīng "already," zǎo "long ago," or a past time expression, it indicates that the action **has taken place** sooner than expected.

1. Tā shuō míngtiān lái, zěnme jīntiān jiù lái le?   She said she would come tomorrow. Why is she already here today?

2. Tā de qián zǎo jiù méiyǒu le.   He was out of money long ago.

3. Zhège zì wǒmen shàng xīngqī jiù xuéguo le.   We already learned this character last week.

7.6.4 Jiù with number-measure words

When jiù is used before a number-measure word, it means "only, merely." It indicates that the speaker considers the amount to be small.

1. Wǒ jiù yǒu yí ge nǚ'ér.   I only have one daughter.

2. Tā jiù xuéguo yì xuéqī de Zhōngwén.   She only studied Chinese for one semester.

7.6.5 The pattern yī ... jiù

The pattern <u>yī</u> ... <u>jiù</u> is made up of two linking nonmovable adverbs. <u>Yī</u> "as soon as" in the first clause and <u>jiù</u> "then" in the second clause indicate that the second action is going to happen as soon as the first action takes place.

1. Tā yì lái wǒmen jiù kǎoshì.

    We will start the test as soon as he gets here.

2. Wǒmen yì kāi wǔhuì tā jiù lái.

    She comes whenever we have a dance party.

3. Wǒ yì huì shuō Zhōngguóhuà jiù qù Zhōngguó.

    I will go to China as soon as I can speak Chinese.

7.6.6 The pattern yī ... jiù ... le

When <u>yī</u> ... <u>jiù</u> "as soon as, whenever" is followed by the particle <u>le</u>, it indicates the sequence of two actions, both of which have happened.

1. Tā yì lái wǒmen jiù kǎoshì le.

    We started the exam as soon as he came.

2. Nàge míngxīng yì lái wǒmen jiù tiàowǔ le.

    We started to dance as soon as the movie star arrived.

3. Tā yì shuōhuà, wǒ jiù zhīdào tā bú shì Zhōngguórén le.

    As soon as he spoke, I knew that he was not Chinese.

✿ Sentence Building

1.

Kěyǐ

Kěyǐ-bu-kěyǐ?

Kěyǐ-bu-kěyǐ hē jiǔ?

Xiànzài bù kěyǐ hē jiǔ.

Nǐmen xiànzài bù kěyǐ hē jiǔ.

2.

Yǒushíhou

Yǒushíhou tiàowǔ.

Yǒushíhou xǐhuan tiàowǔ.

Wǒ yǒushíhou xǐhuan tiàowǔ,
yǒushíhou bù xǐhuan tiàowǔ.

3.

Shénme?

Shénme shíhou?

Shénme shíhou lái?

Nǐmen shénme shíhou lái?

Wǒmen liǎng xiǎoshí yǐhòu lái.

4.

Yào

Jiù yào

Jiù yào qù shàng kè le.

Shéi jiù yào qù shàng kè le ?

Wǒmen jiù dōu yào qù shàng kè le.

✿ Questions and Responses

1. Qǐngwèn, Kěkǒukělè shì shénme?
   May I ask, what is Coca-Cola?

   Kěkǒukělè shì Měiguó de qìshuǐ.
   Coca-Cola is an American soft drink.

2. Nǐ xiǎoshíhou xǐhuan shàng xué ma?

   Did you like to go to school when
   you were a kid?

   Wǒ māma shuō wǒ xiǎoshíhou bú tài
   xǐhuan shàng xué.
   My mother says I didn't like to go to
   school very much when I was a kid.

3. Nǐ de Yīngwén zhēn hǎo, shì shénme
   shíhou xué de ?
   Your English is very good. When
   did you learn it?

   Wǒ lái Měiguó yǐhǒu jiù xué Yīngwén
   le.
   I learned English after I came to the
   United States.

4. Nǐ shàng Zhōngwén kè de shíhou
   xǐhuan shuōhuà ma?
   Do you like to speak in Chinese class?

   Wǒ yǒu shíhou xǐhuan shuōhuà, yǒu
   shíhou bù xǐhuan shuōhuà.
   Sometimes I like to speak, sometimes
   I don't.

5. Nǐ wèishénme yǒu shíhou bù xǐhuan
   shuōhuà?
   Why sometimes you don't like to
   speak?

   Yīnwèi wǒ bù huì shuō wǒ xiǎng shuō
   de huà.
   Because I don't know how to say what
   I want to say.

6. Zhōngguó zài nǎge shíqī bú tài hǎo?

    In which period were the circum-
    stances in China not very good?

    Zhōngguó zài yìjiǔliùliù nián dào
    yìjiǔqīliù nián de shíqī bú tài hǎo.
    The circumstances in China from 1966
    to 1976 were not too good.

7. Tā huì tiàowǔ ma?
    Does he know how to dance?

    Huì. Tā shénme wǔ dōu huì tiào.
    Yes, he can dance all types of dances.

8. Méiyǒu lǎoshī de xǔkě, xuésheng
    kěyǐ bú shàng kè ma?
    Can students skip class without
    permission from the teacher?

    Kěyǐ shì kěyǐ, kěshì bú tài hǎo.

    It's okay, but it's not very nice.

9. Nǐ zěnme le? Pà de zhège yàngzi!
    What's the matter? You look so
    terrified!

    Nǐ kàn! Nàge rén de yàngzi hǎo kěpà!
    Look! That person looks very
    frightening!

10. Wǒ yǐwéi tā huì lái. Tā zěnme
    hái méi lái?
    I thought he would come. Why
    isn't he here?

    Wǒ xiǎng tā mǎshàng jiù huì lái le.

    I think he will be here soon.

⚘ Pronunciation Review

Differentiating i - e after Retroflexes and Sibilants

(a)	zhī	zhē	(d)	zì	zè	(g)	rì	rè
(b)	chì	chè	(e)	cí	cé	(h)	shí	shé
(c)	shì	shè	(f)	sì	sè	(i)	cì	cè

⚘ Supplementary Vocabulary

gǔdiǎn yīnyuè	classical music		jiǔhuì	cocktail party
yīnyuèhuì	concert		wǔhuì	dance party; ball
qīng yīnyuè	light music		tīng yīnyuè	listen to music
yīnyuè	music		liúxínggē	popular songs
juéshì yīnyuè	jazz		chànggē	sing
cháhuì	tea party			

第七課
漢字本

....

內 容

❀❀ 課文

晚 會

(一)去晚會

許小美：馬愛文，你要去星期六的晚會嗎？

馬愛文：要去。你知道在哪兒嗎？

許小美：在學生中心。

馬愛文：我們甚麼時候去？

許小美：星期六晚上我來找你。

馬愛文：好。我等你。

(二)談晚會

林海英：星期六的晚會怎麼樣？

許小美：很有意思。有很多人。

林海英：你們都作甚麼了？

許小美：有的人談話、有的人跳舞、有的人喝汽水。

林海英：沒有酒嗎？

許小美：沒有。晚會上不可以喝酒。我們就可以喝可口可樂、七喜、水、甚麼的。你為甚麼沒去？

林海英：我本來想去，可是我那天晚上得寫一個報告。

🌸 生詞及例句

1. **會**　　**will; know how to, be able to** (AV); **meeting(s), get-together, assembly, conference; association** (N)

    (1) A: 你想明天老師會給我們考試嗎？

    　　B: 我想不會。

    (2) A: 你會不會寫你的名字？

    　　B: 會。

☞ 晚會　　evening party, an evening of entertainment (N)

　　你來我們的晚會嗎？

☞ 茶會　　tea party (N)

　　明天晚上的茶會不知道會有幾個人來。

☞ 酒會　　cocktail party (N)

　　A: 我不去老師家的酒會，因為我不會喝酒，去了也沒意思。

　　B: 酒會不是就喝酒，你可以跟人談話。

☞ 會話　　conversation (N)

　　今天的會話課，我們說了很多話。

2. **星**　　**star** (N)

☞ 星星　　star (N)

　　晚上我喜歡跟家人看天上的星星。

☞ 明星　　a famous performer (N)

　　A: 他就是你說的那個很有名的明星嗎？

　　B: 是。他現在很紅。

☞ 星期　　week (TW)

    (1) A: 今天星期幾？

    　　B: 今天星期六。

(2) A: 一個星期有幾天？

　　　B: 七天。

(3) 星期天也叫星期日。

☞ 這星期　　this week (TW)

　　　這星期我們沒有考試，真好。

☞ 上星期　　last week (TW)

　　　上星期我爸爸媽媽去中國了。

3. 時　　　**time, hour** (N)

☞ 小時　　hour (N)

　　　(1) A: 你幾個小時可以寫好這個報告？

　　　　　 B: 我想三個多小時就可以寫好了。

　　　(2) A: 一天有幾個小時？

　　　　　 B: 一天有二十四個小時。

☞ 時期　　period (N)

　　　(1) 我不太喜歡那個時期的文學。

　　　(2) 那個時期的文學跟現在的不一樣。

4. 候　　　**time** (N); **wait** (V)

☞ 時候　　(duration of) time, (point in) time, moment (N)

　　　(1) A: 你是甚麼時候來的？我怎麼不知道。

　　　　　 B: 我去年就來了。

　　　(2) A: 媽媽來的時候，你知道不知道？

　　　　　 B: 我不知道，因為我在上課。

☞ 有時候　　sometimes (Adv)

　　　(1) 我有時候不喜歡跟他說話。

　　　(2) 我們有時候喝茶，有時候喝可口可樂。

☞ 小時候   in one's childhood, when one was young (Adv)

(1) 我小時候不喜歡上學。

(2) 媽媽說我小時候很可愛。大家都喜歡我。

5. **談**   **talk, chat, discuss** (V)

A: 你知道他們在談甚麼嗎？

B: 我怎麼知道？

☞ 談話   conversation, talk, chat; statement (N/VO)

他們的談話很有意思。

☞ 談天兒   chat, make conversation (N/V)

大家都很喜歡跟他談天兒。

☞ 談心   heart-to-heart talk (N/V)

找一個可以談心的人很難。

☞ 會談   formal talks (N/V)

近來中國跟美國有會談嗎？

6. **作**   **do, make, compose** (V)

A: 你天天在哪兒作功課？

B: 在圖書館。

☞ 作文   student's essay or composition (N)

A: 老師，我們的作文得寫多長？

B: 你想寫多長就寫多長。

☞ 寫作   writing (V/N)

這學期我選了一門寫作課，我們常常寫作文。

☞ 作家   writer (N)

A: 冰心是中國很有名的女作家，你看過她寫的小說嗎？

B: 我小時候看過。

A:　　你喜歡她的小說嗎？

B:　　我很喜歡。

7. **舞**　　**dance** (V/N)

☞ 跳舞　　to dance (V/VO)

(1) 她小時候很喜歡跳舞，現在不喜歡跳了。

(2) 今天晚上，他跟馬紅跳了三個舞。

☞ 舞會　　dance party, ball (N)

要是你不喜歡跳舞，去舞會就沒意思了。

8. **可**　　**can, may** (Adv); **but, yet** (Conj)

☞ 可是　　but, yet, however (Conj)

A: 你為甚麼不跳舞？你不喜歡跳舞嗎？

B: 喜歡是喜歡，可是我今天太累了。

☞ 可怕　　fearful, frightful, terrible, terrifying (SV)

A: 天天得考試，可怕。

B: 不要怕，那都是小考，不難。

☞ 可口　　good to eat, tasty, delicious, palatable (SV)

A: 你試試這個菜可口不可口。

B: 很好吃。

☞ 可口可樂 Coca-Cola, Coke (N)

A: 你喜歡喝甚麼汽水？

B: 我喜歡喝可口可樂。

☞ 許可　　permit, permission, allow (V/N)

(1) 媽媽不許可我喝酒，因為我還小。

(2) 沒有老師的許可，你可以不考試嗎？

☞ 可愛   lovable, likable, lovely, adorable (SV)

(1) 你的小妹妹很可愛。

(2) 他是一個很不可愛的人。

9. 以   **use, according to, because of** (CV)

☞ 可以   can, may; not bad (AV)

(1) A: 我可以進來嗎？

　　 B: 可以。請進。

(2) A: 這個菜可口嗎？

　　 B: 不怎麼好，還可以。

☞ 以後   after, afterwards, later, hereafter; in the future (Conj/Adv)

(1) 他喝酒以後，就很喜歡說話。

(2) 你以後想作甚麼？

☞ 以為   think, consider; thought (V)

(1) A: 我以為選五門課太難，你說呢？

　　 B: 我想還可以。

(2) 我以為他是中國人，可是他是日本人。

10. 就   **already, as early as; just, only** (AV)

(1) A: 老師，這個字我們沒學過。

　　 B: 這個字我們上星期就學過了。

(2) 老師一來，我們就不說話了。

(3) 我們今天不學很多生字，就學八個。

☞ 就要   be about to, be going to, be on the point of (AV)

我們馬上就要考期中考了。

☞ 就是   exactly, precisely; even if (EV/Adv)

    (1) A: 誰是<u>林海英</u>？

        B: 我就是。

    (2) A: 就是他很笨，我還喜歡他。

        B: 為甚麼？

        A: 因為他是一個好人。

🐾 句型練習

7.1 ASKING TIME

1. A: 你媽媽甚麼時候來？
   B: 明天晚上。

2. A: 我們甚麼時候考試？
   B: 星期五。

3. A: 你甚麼時候去<u>中國</u>？
   B: 明年六月。

4. A: 明天星期幾？
   B: 星期天/星期日。

5. A: 你早上來還是晚上來？
   B: 晚上來。

The sequence of telling time in Chinese always begins with the largest unit followed by progressively smaller ones: year, month, week, day, part of day, hour, minute. For example, 3:15 p.m. on 15 March 1932 should be formulated as follows:

一九三二年三月十五日下午三點十五分
1932, March 15, afternoon, three o'clock, fifteen (minutes)

7.2 RELATIVE-TIME WORDS

The relative-time words 時候 "when, while," 以前 "before," and 以後 "after" appear at the **end** of a clause, rather than the beginning, as in English:

你來的時候	**When** you come
你來以前	**Before** you come
你來(了)以後	**After** you come

1. A: 他來的時候你在哪兒？

    B: 我在上課。

2. A: 他來美國以前會不會說英文？

    B: 不會。

3. A: 我們甚麼時候考試？

    B: 老師來(了)以後就考試。

7.3 THE LINKING ADVERBS 有(的)時候……有(的)時候

The linking adverbs 有(的)時候……有(的)時候 "sometimes ... sometimes" are inserted between two verbs, adjectives or phrases which are opposite or similar in meaning, to indicate that different actions or phenomena take place alternately within a given time.

1. 我有(的)時候喜歡喝茶，有(的)時候喜歡喝汽水。

2. 我們老師有(的)時候給我們考試，有(的)時候不給我們考試。

3. 中文有(的)時候很難，有(的)時候不難。

7.4 會 AS AN AUXILIARY VERB

When 會 functions as an auxiliary verb, it means "can, be able to" and has three basic meanings.

7.4.1 A learned skill

To express a learned or acquired ability or skill, that is, "to know how" or "to learn how to."

1. A: 你會不會説英文？

    B: 我不會説英文。

2. A: 你會寫中國字嗎？

    B: 我會。

7.4.2 Possibility of an event

To express the possibility or the likelihood of the occurrence of an event, that is, "will, could possibly."

1. A: 他怎麼還沒來？

    B: 我想他不會來了。

2. A: 今天老師會不會給我們考試？

    B: 我想會。

7.4.3 To describe someone

To describe someone who possesses a certain skill or talent, that is, "truly can, to know how to." It is often preceded by the adverbs 很 "very," 真 "really" (see Lesson 9), or 最 "the most" (see Lesson 10).

1. 他很會作中國菜。

2. 他很會喝酒。

3. 王太太真會説話。

4. 馬思文最會跳舞了。

7.5 THE AUXILIARY VERB 可以

可以 "may, can, be allowed" is used to express permissibility.

1. A: 媽媽，我可以不可以跟他跳舞？

    B: 不可以。

2. A: 老師，我們上課的時候可以説英文嗎？

    B: 有時候可以，有時候不可以。

3. A: 你可以寫這個報告嗎？

    B: 我想我可以。我可以試試。

7.6 THE ADVERB 就

The adverb 就 "only, soon" has many uses. Sometimes it shares an autonomous relationship with respect to time and expectation.

7.6.1 就 indicative of a future event

When 就 is followed by a verb in a sentence with or without an overt future time expression, it indicates that the event or action in question will happen soon.

1. 他就來。

2. 我就去。

3. 我們現在就考試。

4. 我明天就去找他。

7.6.2 就……了 with future time expressions

When 就……了 is used in conjunction with future adverbs such as 要 "will, soon," 馬上 "at once," 快要 "soon will," or a future time expression, it indicates something will happen or will complete **very soon**.

1. 這學期就要過去了。

2. 我們老師馬上就來了。

3. 明天就是星期六了。

4. 我的報告就快寫好了。

7.6.3 就……了 with past time expressions

When 就……了 comes in conjunction with adverbs such as 已經 "already," 早 "long ago," or a past time expression, it indicates that the action **has taken place** sooner than expected.

1. 她說明天來，怎麼今天就來了？

2. 他的錢早就沒有了。

3. 這個字我們上星期就學過了。

7.6.4 就 with number-measure words

When 就 is used before a number-measure word, it means "only, merely." It indicates that the speaker considers the amount to be small.

1. 我就有一個女兒。

2. 他就學過一學期的中文。

7.6.5 The pattern 一……就

The pattern 一……就 is made up of two linking nonmovable adverbs. 一 "as soon as" in the first clause and 就 "then" in the second clause indicate that the second action is going to happen as soon as the first action takes place.

1. 他一來我們就考試。

2. 我們一開舞會她就來。

3. 我一會說中國話就去中國。

7.6.6 The pattern 一……就……了

When 一……就 "as soon as, whenever" is followed by the particle 了, it indicates the sequence of two actions, both of which have happened.

1. 他一來我們就考試了。

2. 那個明星一來我們就跳舞了。

3. 他一說話，我就知道他不是中國人了。

🐾 造 句

1.

可以

可以不可以？

可以不可以喝酒？

現在不可以喝酒。

你們現在不可以喝酒。

2.

有時候

有時候跳舞。

有時候喜歡跳舞。

我有時候喜歡跳舞，有時候
不喜歡跳舞。

3.

甚麼

甚麼時候？

甚麼時候來？

你們甚麼時候來？

我們兩小時以後來。

4.

要

就要

就要去上課了。

誰就要去上課了？

我們就都要去上課了。

🐾 問 答

1. 請問，可口可樂是甚麼？　　　　可口可樂是美國的汽水。

2. 你小時候喜歡上學嗎？　　　　　我媽媽說我小時候不太喜歡上學。

3. 你的英文真好，是甚麼時候學的？　我來美國以後就學英文了。

4. 你上中文課的時候喜歡說話嗎？　我有時候喜歡說話，有時候不喜歡
　　　　　　　　　　　　　　　　說話。

5. 你為甚麼有時候不喜歡說話？　　因為我不會說我想說的話。

6. 中國在哪個時期不太好？　　　　中國在一九六六年到一九七六年的
　　　　　　　　　　　　　　　　時期不太好。

7. 他會跳舞嗎？　　　　　　　　　會。他甚麼舞都會跳。

8. 沒有老師的許可，學生可以不　　可以是可以，可是不太好。
　　上課嗎？

9. 你怎麼了？怕得這個樣子！　　　你看！那個人的樣子好可怕！

10. 我以為他會來。他怎麼還沒來？　我想他馬上就會來了。

閱讀練習

金建的日記

上個星期六晚上，我們學校在學生中心有一個晚會。我本來不想去，因為我有很多功課得作。可是海英說，你不可以老作功課。天天作功課多沒意思。我想想也是，就跟她去了。那天的晚會有很多人。有的人談話、有的人跳舞、有的人喝可口可樂。有幾個人想喝酒，可是那兒沒有酒，因為學校的晚會不可以喝酒。我不會跳舞，所以我有時候坐在那兒看別人跳舞，有時候跟別人談話。我跟一個同學談我們喜歡的作家的時候，一個很可愛的女生過來請我跳舞。我說我不會跳舞。她以為我不喜歡跟她跳舞，就很不好意思地找人談話了。我很難過，可是我怎麼跟她說呢？我想我以後得好好學跳舞。

問 題

1. 金建為甚麼不想去學校的晚會？
2. 海英跟金建說甚麼？
3. 那天的晚會上金建作甚麼？
4. 為甚麼那天的晚會沒有酒？
5. 金建很會跳舞嗎？那天晚上他有沒有跳舞？
6. 金建為甚麼要學跳舞了？
7. 你在晚會上喜歡作甚麼？你很會跳舞嗎？
8. 你們學校有很多晚會嗎？

第八課　給爸爸媽媽的信
Lesson 8　A letter to father and mother

Lesson 8
Pinyin Text

· ·

CONTENTS

Text

Gěi bàba māma de xìn

A letter to father and mother

Bàba, māma:

    Nǐmen hǎo ma? Gēge, jiějie, dìdi dōu hǎo ma? Wǒmen hěn xiǎng nǐmen. Wǒmen yǐjīng kāixué liǎng ge duō xīngqī le. Wǒmen zài zhèr hěn hǎo, hěn kuàilè. Wǒmen de lǎoshī hěn yǒu jīngyàn. Wǒmen de tóngxué yǒude shì Zhōngguórén, yǒude shì Rìběnrén, yǒude shì Měiguórén. Tāmen dōu hěn héqi. Wǒmen zhè xuéqī dōu xuǎn le sì mén kè. Wǒmen yǐjīng huì shuō Zhōngguóhuà le. Xiànzài gōngkè hái bú tài duō, wǒmen yě bú tài máng. Wǒmen xiǎng zhège xīngqīliù (jiǔyuè èrshírì) huí jiā kàn nǐmen. Qǐng huí xìn gàosu wǒmen, nǐmen zài-bu-zài jiā. Wǒmen děi qù kànshū le.

Sīwén
Àiwén
Jiǔyuè shísìrì

Dear Dad and Mom,

    How are you? How are my elder brother, elder sister and younger brother? We miss you all very much. School has been in session for over two weeks now. We are doing well here and we are very happy. Our teachers are very experienced. Some of our classmates are Chinese, some are Japanese, and some are Americans. They are all very nice. We are taking four classes this semester. We already know how to speak Chinese. As of now, we don't have much homework, so we are not too busy. We are thinking about coming home this Saturday (20 September) to visit you all. Please write to tell us whether you will be home. We have to go to study (read books) now.

Siwen
Aiwen
14 September

🌸 Vocabulary and Illustrative Sentences

1. **xìn**   **believe** (V); **letter** (N)

   (1) A: Wǒ shuō de huà, nǐ   Do you believe what I have said?
          xìn-bu-xìn?

       B: Wǒ bú xìn.   I don't believe (it).

   (2) A: Zhè shì shéi gěi nǐ de xìn?   Who is this letter from?

       B: Wǒ māma.   (It is from) my mother.

☞ **xiě xìn**   write letters (VO)

   A: Wǒ māma hěn shēngqì,   My mother was very upset and
      wèn wǒ wèishénme bù gěi   asked me why I had not written
      tā xiě xìn.   to her.

   B: Nǐ jǐ ge xīngqī méi gěi tā   For how many weeks haven't
      xiě xìn le?   you written her?

   A: Hǎo jǐ ge xīngqī le.   (It has been) quite a few weeks
                                         now.

   B: Wèishénme?   Why?

   A: Yīnwèi wǒ de gōngkè tài   Because I have too much
      duō.   homework.

☞ **lái xìn**   mail (VO)

   (1) Wǒ gēge jìnlái méiyǒu gěi   My elder brother hasn't written
       wǒ lái xìn.   to me recently.

   (2) Wǒ zhōngxué de tóngxué   My high school classmate wrote
       lái xìn shuō tā jìnlái hěn   me to say that he has been quite
       máng.   busy lately.

☞ **jièshàoxìn**   recommendation letter, reference (N)

   A: Lǎoshī, wǒ xiǎng qù   Teacher, I'd like to go to China
      Zhōngguó xué Zhōngwén,   to study Chinese. Can you write
      nǐ kěyǐ gěi wǒ xiě jièshàoxìn   me a recommendation letter?
      ma?

   B: Wǒ hěn gāoxìng gěi nǐ xiě   I will be very happy to write a
      jièshàoxìn.   recommendation letter for you.

☞ xìnzhǐ   letter sheets (N)

    A: Wǒ děi xiě xìn. Wǒ de xìnzhǐ   I have to write a letter. But I don't
       méiyǒu le. Nǐ yǒu-méiyǒu   have any writing paper. Have
       xìnzhǐ?   you got any?

    B: Yǒu. Nǐ yào duōshǎo?   Yes, I have. How many do you
                            want?

☞ xìnxīn   confidence (N)

   (1) A: Wǒ bù zhīdào wǒ xué   I don't know if I can do well in
        Zhōngwén xuédehǎo   my study of Chinese.
        xuébuhǎo?

     B: Nǐ xuédehǎo. Nǐ yào   You can do well. You must have
       yǒu xìnxīn.   confidence.

   (2) A: Zhège kǎoshì kǎodehǎo   I don't have any confidence that
        kǎobuhǎo, wǒ méiyǒu   I can do well on this exam.
        xìnxīn.

     B: Wǒ zhīdào nǐ huì kǎode   I know you will do well.
       hěn hǎo.

2. **yǐ**   **already** (Adv)

☞ zǎoyǐ   long ago, for a long time (Adv)

    A: Lǎoshī, zhège zì wǒmen   Teacher, we haven't learned this
       méiyǒu xuéguo.   word before.

    B: Nǐmen zǎoyǐ xuéguo le.   You have already learned it. It
       Zài dì-sì kè.   was in Lesson 4.

☞ bùdéyǐ   act against one's will; have no alternative but to; have to (IE)

    A: Nǐ hěn xǐhuan shùxué,   You like math so much. Why
       wèishénme bù xuǎn   don't you take math?
       shùxué kè ne?

    B: Wǒ bù xuǎn shùxué kè shì   I have no choice but not to take
       bùdéyǐ, yīnwèi wǒ tài máng math, because I am too busy.
       le.

3. **jīng**　　**through** (V)

☞ yǐjīng　　already (Adv)

　　(1) A: Lái, wǒ gěi nǐmen　　　Come, I will introduce you.
　　　　　jièshào jièshào.

　　　　B: Nǐ yǐjīng gěi wǒmen　　You have already introduced us.
　　　　　jièshàoguo le.

　　(2) A: Nǐ mèimei shénme　　　When is your little sister coming?
　　　　　shíhou lái?

　　　　B: Tā yǐjīng lái le liǎng　　She has already been here for two
　　　　　tiān le.　　　　　　　　days.

☞ jīngguò　　pass, go through, undergo; happening (V/N)

　　A: Nǐ qùnián qù Zhōngguó,　　Did you stop in Japan when you
　　　yǒu-méiyǒu jīngguò Rìběn?　went to china last year?

　　B: Méi jīngguò Rìběn.　　　No, (I) didn't stop in Japan.

4. **yàn**　　**examine, check, test** (V)

☞ jīngyàn　　experience (N)

　　(1) A: Nǐ yǒu shénme jīngyàn?　What kind of experience do you
　　　　　　　　　　　　　　　　have?

　　　　B: Wǒ méiyǒu tài duō　　　I don't have much experience.
　　　　　jīngyàn. Wǒ háishì　　　I'm still a student.
　　　　　xuésheng.

　　(2) A: Qǐng nǐ bàogào nǐ　　　Please tell us about your
　　　　　zài Zhōngguó xué　　　experience of learning Chinese
　　　　　Zhōngwén de jīngyàn.　in China.

　　　　B: Hǎo. Dì-yī, zài Zhōng-　Okay. First, learning Chinese
　　　　　guó xué Zhōngwén hěn　in China was very interesting.
　　　　　yǒuyìsi. Dì-èr, Zhōng-　Second, people in China speak
　　　　　guórén shuōhuà hěn kuài.　very fast. Third, my Chinese
　　　　　Dì-sān, wǒ de Zhōngwén　teachers were very friendly.
　　　　　lǎoshī dōu hěn héqi.　　Some of them had experience,
　　　　　Tāmen yǒude yǒu　　　some of them did not (have
　　　　　jīngyàn, yǒude méiyǒu.　experience).

5. kāi   **open, make an opening; start; operate** (V)

☞ kāixué   school opens, term begins (V)

     A: Nǐmen shénme shíhou kāixué?   When does your school start?

     B: Wǒmen yǐjīng kāixué hǎo   Our school started a few days
         jǐ tiān le.   ago.

     A: Nàme zǎo!   So early!

☞ kāimén   open the door (VO)

     A: Yǒu rén jiàomén, kuài qù   Somebody's at the door. Hurry
         kāimén!   up and open the door.

     B: Shì Wáng lǎoshī! Nǐ hǎo!   It's Professor Wang! How are
         Qǐng jìn.   you? Please come in.

☞ kāikǒu   open one's mouth; start to talk (VO)

     (1) Tā yì kāikǒu, wǒ jiù zhīdào   Once he started to talk, I knew
         tā bú shì Měiguórén.   he wasn't American.

     (2) A: Kāihuì de shíhou, dàjiā   During the meeting, nobody
            dōu bù kāikǒu shuōhuà.   would talk.

        B: Nà kāihuì hái yǒu shénme   Then, what's the point of having
            yìsi?   a meeting?

☞ kāishuǐ   boiled water (N)

     A: Shénme shì "lěng kāishuǐ"?   What is "cold boiled water"?

     B: Kāishuǐ lěng le jiùshì "lěng   After boiled water gets cold, it is
         kāishuǐ."   "cold boiled water."

     A: Xiànzài wǒ zhīdao le.   Now I know.

☞ kāixīn   feel happy, rejoice (SV)

     (1) A: Nǐ jīntiān zěnme zhème   Why are you so happy today?
            kāixīn?

        B: Yīnwèi wǒ de Zhōngwén   Because I did well on my Chinese
            kǎode hěn hǎo.   exam.

     (2) A: Wǒ jiějie kāixīn de shíhou   When my elder sister is feeling
            wǒ yě hěn kāixīn.   happy, I feel happy too.

| | B: Wèishénme? | Why? |
| | A: Yīnwèi tā yì kāixīn jiù gěi wǒ qián. | Because whenever she feels happy, she gives me money. |

☞ **kāihuì**   hold or attend a meeting (VO)

| | A: Wǒmen shénme shíhou kāihuì? | When is our meeting? |
| | B: Xiànzài jiù kāi. | (We are) going to have the meeting right now. |

☞ **kāimíng**   enlightened, open-minded (SV)

| | (1) Xiànzài de lǎoshī dōu hěn kāimíng. | Teachers now are all very open-minded. |
| | (2) Wǒ māma hěn kāimíng, kěshì wǒ bàba bú tài kāimíng. | My mother is very open-minded, but my father is not. |

☞ **xìnkǒu-kāihé**   talk irresponsibly; talk nonsense (IE)

| | (1) Zhège rén lǎoshì xǐhuan xìnkǒukāihé, shénme dōu shuō. | This person always talks irresponsibly. He'll say anything. |
| | (2) Nǐ zhīdào tā shì yí ge xìnkǒu-kāihé de rén, bú yào xìn tā shuō de huà. | You know that he is one who talks nonsense. Don't believe what he says. |

6. **qì**   **gas, air, breath; smell, odor; energy of life** (N)

☞ **tiānqì**   weather (N)

| | A: Jīntiān de tiānqì zěnmeyàng? | How's the weather today? |
| | B: Hěn rè. | It's very hot. |

☞ **qìhòu**   climate (N)

| | A: Nǐmen lǎojiā de qìhòu zěnmeyàng? | How is the climate in your hometown? |
| | B: Hěn hǎo, bù lěng yě bú rè. | Very nice, neither too cold nor too hot. |

☞ shēngqì　　take offence, get angry (V/SV)

(1) Bú yào shēngqì, tā shì xìnkǒukāihé.

Don't be mad. He's just joking.

(2) Māma xiànzài shēng
wǒ de qì, yīnwèi wǒ jìnlái
huā hěn duō qián.

Mother is mad at me right now
because I have been spending a
lot of money recently.

☞ xiǎoqì　　stingy; narrow-minded (SV)

(1) Nàge rén hěn xiǎoqì, shénme
qián dōu bù huā.

That person is very stingy. He
doesn't spend any money.

(2) Tā bú shì nàme xiǎoqì de
rén, tā bú huì shēngqì de.

He is not a narrow-minded
person. He wouldn't get angry.

7. sù　　**tell, inform** (V)

☞ gàosu　　tell, let know (V)

(1) A: Shéi gàosu nǐ wǒ huì
tiàowǔ?

Who told you that I know how
to dance?

B: Nǐ tóngxué gàosu wǒ de.

Your classmate told me.

(2) A: Qǐng nǐ gàosu lǎoshī, wǒ
míngtiān bù lái shàng kè.

Please tell the teacher that I am
not coming to class tomorrow.

B: Hǎo.

Okay.

8. huí　　**return, go back, turn around** (V)

☞ huí xìn　　write in reply, write back (VO)

A: Wǒ māma zěnme hái méi gěi
wǒ huí xìn?

Why hasn't my mother written
back to me yet?

B: Yěxǔ tā hěn máng.

Maybe she is very busy.

☞ huílai　　come back (V)

A: Nǐ shénme shíhou huílai?

When are you coming back?

B: Hòutiān wǎnshang.

The evening after tomorrow.

☞ huíqu　　go back (V)

A: Nǐ shénme shíhou húi jiā?

When are you going home?

B: Wǒ zhè xuéqī bù húiqu.

I am not going back this semester.

☞ huí guó   go back to one's country (VO)

A: Nǐ yǐjīng zài Měiguó nàme duō nián le, nǐ bù xiǎng huí guó kànkan ma?

You have been in the States for so many years. Don't you want to go back and visit your country?

B: Xiǎng shì xiǎng, kěshì méi qián huíbuqù.

I want to, but without money I can't go back.

9. **kàn**   **see, look at; read; think, consider** (V)

(1) A: Wǒ hòutiān qù kàn nǐ, kěyǐ ma?

I will visit you the day after tomorrow. Is that okay?

B: Kěyǐ.

That's fine.

(2) A: Nǐ zài kàn shénme?

What are you reading?

B: Wǒ zài kàn jīntiān de bào.

I am reading today's paper.

(3) A: Nǐ kàn wǒmen yào-bu-yào gàosu tā?

Do you think we should tell her?

B: Wǒ xiǎng bú yào gàosu tā hǎo.

I think it's best not to tell her.

☞ kàn bào   read a newspaper (VO)

(1) A: Nǐ jīntiān kàn bào le méiyǒu?

Have you read today's paper(s)?

B: Hái méi kàn ne.

Not yet.

(2) A: Nǐ kàn Zhōngwén bào háishì kàn Yīngwén bào?

Do you read the Chinese or the English paper?

B: Wǒ kàn Yīngwén bào, yīnwèi wǒ hái bú huì kàn Zhōngwén bào.

I read the English paper, because I can't read the Chinese paper yet.

☞ hǎokàn   good-looking; interesting (SV)

(1) Nàge rén hěn hǎokàn.

That person is very good-looking.

(2) A: Nǐ kàn de nà běn xiǎoshuō, hǎokàn-bu-hǎokàn?

Is the novel that you are reading interesting?

B: Bú tài hǎokàn.

It's not that great.

☞ xiǎokàn   look down upon; belittle (V)

(1) Nǐ bù kěyǐ xiǎokàn tā.

You shouldn't belittle him.

(2) Nǐ bú yào xiǎokàn tā, tā yǒu hěn duō jīngyàn.

Don't look down upon him. He has a lot of experience.

10. shū   **book** (N)

Wǒ nǚ'ér cóng xiǎo jiù hěn xǐhuan kàn shū.

My daughter has loved to read books since she was a little girl.

☞ shūbào   books and newspapers (N)

Wǒ hěn xǐhuan qù tā jiā, yīnwèi tā jiā yǒu hěn duō shūbào.

I like to go to his house because his family has a lot of books and newspapers.

☞ shūmíng   title of a book (N)

A: Nǐ māma sòng nǐ de nà běn shū de shūmíng shì shénme?

What is the title of the book that your mother gave you?

B: Shì Zěnyàng Xiě Zhōngguó-zì.

The title is *How to Write Chinese Characters*.

☞ Sìshū   The Four books, namely, *Daxue* (The Great Learning), *Zhongyong* (The Doctrine of the Mean), *Lunyu* (The Analects of Confucius), and *Mengzi* (The Mencius) (N)

A: Lǎoshī, wǒmen shénme shíhou huì kàn Sìshū?

Teacher, when will we be able to read the Four Books?

B: Sìshū hěn nán. Yěxǔ liǎng nián yǐhòu, búguò nǐmen xiànzài kěyǐ kàn Yīngwén de.

The Four Books are very difficult. Maybe after two years, but meanwhile you can read the English version.

❧ Pattern Drills

8.1 THE PATTERN yǐjīng ... le

The adverb yǐjīng "already" is often used with le to indicate that an action has already happened.

S	yǐjīng	V	le
Xuésheng	yǐjīng	lái	le.
The students have already come.			

1. A: Zhège zì nǐmen xuéguo méiyǒu?

    Have you learned this character before?

    B: Zhège zì wǒmen yǐjīng xuéguo le.

    We have already learned this character.

2. A: Nǐmen kāixué le ma?

    Has your school started?

    B: Wǒmen yǐjīng kāixué yì xīngqī le.

    Our school has already started for a week.

3. A: Wǒ gěi nǐmen jièshào jièshào.

    I will introduce you to each other.

    B: Hǎiyīng yǐjīng gěi wǒmen jièshào-guo le.

    Haiying has already introduced us.

8.2 THE WORD gěi

The word gěi can function as a verb as well as a coverb.

8.2.1 Gěi as a verb

When gěi is used as a verb, it means "to give."

S	gěi	DO	IO
Tā	gěi	wǒ	yì běn shū.
She gave me a book.			

1. A: Nǐ gěi nǐ mèimei shénme?

    What are you going to give your younger sister?

    B: Wǒ gěi tā yì běn xiǎoshuō.

    I am going to give her a novel.

2. A: Shéi gěi nǐ qián qù Zhōngguó?

    Who gave you the money to go to China?

    B: Wǒ bàba māma.

    My dad and mom.

8.2.2 Gěi as a coverb

When gěi comes before another verb in a sentence, it functions as a coverb, meaning "for."

S	gěi	DO	V	IO
Lǎoshī	gěi	wǒ	xiě	jièshàoxìn le.

The teacher wrote a recommendation letter for me.

1. A: Nǐ zuìjìn yǒu-méiyǒu gěi nǐ nǚpéngyou xiě xìn?

    Have you written to your girlfriend recently?

    B: Méiyǒu.

    (No,) I haven't.

2. A: Nǐ wèishénme gěi dìdi zuò gōngkè?

    Why do you do homework for your younger brother?

    B: Yīnwèi tā bú huì zuò.

    Because he doesn't know how to do it.

3. A: Nǐ kěyǐ gěi wǒmen jièshào jièshào Zhōngguó ma?

    Can you give us an introduction to China?

    B: Hǎo. Wǒ xiànzài gěi nǐmen jièshào wǒ de guójiā.

    Okay, I'll give you an introduction to my country now.

8.3 THE PATTERN bù ... bù ...

The pattern bù … bù … is used before two stative verbs opposite in meaning to indicate an intermediate state.

S	bù	SV	bù	SV
Jīntiān	bù	lěng	bù	rè.

Today is neither too cold nor too hot.

1. A: Nǐmen lǎoshī shuō Zhōngguóhuà shuō de hěn kuài ma?

   Does your teacher speak Chinese very quickly?

   B: Ta shuō de bú kuài yě bú màn.

   She speaks neither too quickly nor too slowly.

2. A: Jīntiān māma zuò de cài duō-bu-duō?

   Did Mom cook too much food today?

   B: Bù duō yě bù shǎo.

   (No,) neither too much nor too little.

3. A: Jīntiān de gōngkè zěnmeyàng?

   How is today's homework?

   B: Hěn hǎo. Bù duō yě bù shǎo.

   Very good, neither too much nor too little.

8.4 SV/V <u>shì</u> SV/V, <u>kěshì</u> ...

The pattern SV/V <u>shì</u> SV/V, <u>kěshì</u> ... is a two-clause sentence in which the first clause states the fact, while the second clause states a countering fact or situation. The <u>shì</u> in the first clause can be understood in English as "all right" at the end of the first clause.

S	SV/V	<u>shì</u>	SV/V,	<u>kěshì</u> ...
Zhōngwén	nán	shì	nán,	kěshì wǒ hái yào xué.

Chinese is difficult all right, but I still want to learn it.

1. A: Nǐ xiǎng qù Zhōngguó ma?

   Would you like to go to China?

   B: Xiǎng shì xiǎng qù, kěshì wǒ méiyǒu qián.

   (I'd) like to go all right, but I don't have the money to go.

2. A: Zhège zì, nǐmen méi xuéguo ma?

   Haven't you learned this character before?

   B: Xué shì xuéguo le, kěshì wǒmen xiànzài bú huì le.

   (We) have learned it all right, but we don't know it anymore.

3. A: Nǐ bù xǐhuan tiàowǔ ma?

    B: Xǐhuan shì xǐhuan, kěshì xiànzài
    wǒ tài lèi le.

Don't you like to dance?

I like (to dance) all right, but I am too
tired now.

8.5 THE PATTERN shénme ... jiù ... shénme

The question word shénme can function as an indefinite pronoun. The shénme
... jiù ... shénme pattern denotes the notion "whatever, whichever."

1. A: Nǐ xià xuéqī yào xuǎn shénme kè?

    B: Shénme kè yǒuyìsi, wǒ jiù xuǎn
    shénme kè.

What courses are you going to take
next semester?

I will take whatever courses are
interesting.

2. A: Wǒ kěyǐ chī shénme?

    B: Nǐ xiǎng chī shénme jiù chī shénme.

What can I eat?

You can eat whatever you want.

3. A: Nǐ xiǎng hē shénme?

    B: Nǐ yǒu shénme, wǒ jiù hē shénme.

What would you like to drink?

I will drink whatever you have.

Sentence Building

1.
Yǐjīng
Yǐjīng kāixué le.
Yǐjīng kāixué liǎng ge xīngqī le.
Wǒmen yǐjīng kāixué liǎng ge xīngqī le.

2.
Zǎoyǐ
Zǎoyǐ huì xiě zì le.
Zǎoyǐ huì xiě Zhōngguózì le.
Tā zǎoyǐ huì xiě Zhōngguózì le.

3.
Jīngyàn
Shénme jīngyàn?
Nǐ yǒu shénme jīngyàn?
Gàosu wǒ nǐ yǒu shénme jīngyàn.

4.
Héqi
Héqi de rén
Xǐhuan héqi de rén.
Rénrén dōu xǐhuan héqi de rén.

🌼 Questions and Responses

1. Nǐ xuéguo Zhōngwén ma?
   Have you studied Chinese before?

   Xuéguo.
   (Yes, I) have studied Chinese before.

2. Nǐ zài nǎr xué de Zhōngwén?
   Where did you learn Chinese?

   Wǒ zài jiā xué de Zhōngwén.
   I learned Chinese at home.

3. Nǐ huì xiě Zhōngguózì ma?

   Do you know how to write Chinese characters?

   Huì, búguò wǒ jiù huì xiě shí ge Zhōngguózì.
   Yes, but I only know how to write ten Chinese characters.

4. Nǐ wèishénme nàme kāixīn?
   Why are you so happy?

   Yīnwèi wǒ mā lái xìn le.
   Because I got my mother's letter.

5. Nǐ shénme shíhou huí guó?

   When are you going back to your country?

   Wǒ xiànzài hái bù zhīdào ne. Bàba māma lái xìn jiào wǒ shénme shíhou huí qù, wǒ jiù shénme shíhou huí qù.
   I don't know yet. I will go back whenever my father and mother want me back.

6. Zhège kǎoshì nǐ yǒu-méiyǒu xìnxīn?
   Are you confident about this test?

   Wǒ yìdiǎnr xìnxīn dōu méiyǒu.
   I don't have any confidence at all.

7. Wāng Sān shuō de huà nǐ xìn-bu-xìn?

   Do you believe what Wang San says?

   Wǒ bú xìn. Yīnwèi wǒ zhīdào tā shì yí ge xǐhuan xìnkǒukāihé de rén.
   No, I don't, because I know he is a person who likes to talk nonsense.

8. Wèishénme Mǎ Àiwén jīntiān nàme shēngqì?
   Why is Ma Aiwen so angry today?

   Wǒ xiǎng shì yīnwèi tā lǎoshī shuō tā de bàogào xiě de bú tài hǎo.
   I think it is because her teacher said her paper was not very good.

9. Míngtiān kāihuì, qǐng nǐ gàosu Sīwén.
   Tomorrow we are going to have a meeting. Please inform Siwen.

   Tā zǎoyǐ zhīdào le.
   He has known about it for a long time.

10. Nǐ xīngqī jǐ yǒu kè?
    What days of the week do you have class?

    Wǒ yī, sān, wǔ yǒu kè.
    I have class on Monday, Wednesday and Friday.

🐾 Pronunciation Review

Differentiating <u>en</u> - <u>eng</u>

(a)	chén	chéng	(d)	zěn	zěng	(g)	fèn	fèng
(b)	shěn	shěng	(e)	cén	céng	(h)	hěn	hěng
(c)	zhēn	zhēng	(f)	sēn	sēng	(i)	mén	méng

🐾 Fun Activity

Try Another Tongue Twister

Sìshísì Zhī Shīzi
Forty-four Lions

Mén wài yǒu sìshísì zhī shīzi,	There are forty-four lions outside the door,
bù zhīdào shì sìshísì zhī shí shīzi,	(we) don't know if they are forty-four stone-lions,
háishì sìshísì zhī sǐ shīzi.	or forty-four dead-lions.

(The purpose of this tongue twister is to practice the retroflexes <u>zhi</u> and <u>shi</u>, and the sibilants <u>zi</u> and <u>si</u>.)

🐾 Supplementary Vocabulary

Days of the Week

For spoken Chinese only:

lǐbàiyī	Monday
lǐbài'èr	Tuesday
lǐbàisān	Wednesday
lǐbàisì	Thursday
lǐbàiwǔ	Friday
lǐbàilìu	Saturday
lǐbàirì / lǐbàitiān	Sunday

For both spoken and written Chinese:

xīngqīyī	Monday
xīngqī'èr	Tuesday
xīngqīsān	Wednesday
xīngqīsì	Thursday
xīngqīwǔ	Friday
xīngqīliù	Saturday
xīngqīrì / xīngqītiān	Sunday
zhōumò	weekend

第八課
漢字本

課 文

給爸爸媽媽的信

爸爸，媽媽：

你們好嗎？哥哥、姐姐、弟弟，都好嗎？我們很想你們。我們已經開學兩個多星期了。我們在這兒很好，很快樂。我們的老師很有經驗。我們的同學有的是中國人、有的是日本人、有的是美國人。他們都很和氣。我們這學期都選了四門課。我們已經會說中國話了。現在功課還不太多，我們也不太忙。我們想這個星期六(九月二十日)回家看你們。請回信告訴我們，你們在不在家。我們得去看書了。

思文

愛文

九月十四日

🌸 生詞及例句

1. **信**　**believe** (V); **letter** (N)

　　(1) A: 我說的話，你信不信？

　　　　B: 我不信。

　　(2) A: 這是誰給你的信？

　　　　B: 我媽媽。

☞ 寫信　write letters (VO)

　　A: 我媽媽很生氣，問我為甚麼不給她寫信。

　　B: 你幾個星期沒給她寫信了？

　　A: 好幾個星期了。

　　B: 為甚麼？

　　A: 因為我的功課太多。

☞ 來信　mail (VO)

　　(1) 我哥哥近來沒有給我來信。

　　(2) 我中學的同學來信說他近來很忙。

☞ 介紹信　recommendation letter, reference (N)

　　A: 老師，我想去中國學中文，你可以給我寫介紹信嗎？

　　B: 我很高興給你寫介紹信。

☞ 信紙　letter sheets (N)

　　A: 我得寫信。我的信紙沒有了。你有沒有信紙？

　　B: 有。你要多少？

☞ 信心　confidence (N)

　　(1) A: 我不知道我學中文學得好學不好？

　　　　B: 你學得好。你要有信心。

　　(2) A: 這個考試考得好考不好，我沒有信心。

　　　　B: 我知道你會考得很好。

2. **已**　　　　**already** (Adv)

☞ 早已　　　long ago, for a long time (Adv)

A: 老師，這個字我們沒有學過。

B: 你們早已學過了。在第四課。

☞ 不得已　　act against one's will; have no alternative but to; have to (IE)

A: 你很喜歡數學，為甚麼不選數學課呢？

B: 我不選數學課是不得已，因為我太忙了。

3. **經**　　　　**through** (V)

☞ 已經　　　already (Adv)

(1) A: 來，我給你們介紹介紹。

　　B: 你已經給我們介紹過了。

(2) A: 你妹妹甚麼時候來？

　　B: 他已經來了兩天了。

☞ 經過　　　pass, go through, undergo; happening (V/N)

A: 你去年去中國，有沒有經過日本？

B: 沒經過日本。

4. **驗**　　　　**examine, check, test** (V)

☞ 經驗　　　experience (N)

(1) A: 你有甚麼經驗？

　　B: 我沒有太多經驗。我還是學生。

(2) A: 請你報告你在中國學中文的經驗。

　　B: 好。第一，在中國學中文很有意思。第二，中國人說話
　　　很快。第三，我的中文老師都很和氣。他們有的有經
　　　驗，有的沒有。

5. 開   **open, make an opening; start; operate** (V)

☞ 開學   school opens, term begins (V)

A: 你們甚麼時候開學？

B: 我們已經開學好幾天了。

A: 那麼早！

☞ 開門   open the door (VO)

A: 有人叫門，快去開門！

B: 是王老師！你好！請進。

☞ 開口   open one's mouth; start to talk (VO)

(1) 他一開口，我就知道他不是美國人。

(2) A: 開會的時候，大家都不開口說話。

B: 那開會還有甚麼意思？

☞ 開水   boiled water (N)

A: 甚麼是"冷開水"？

B: 開水冷了就是"冷開水。"

A: 現在我知道了。

☞ 開心   feel happy, rejoice (SV)

(1) A: 你今天怎麼這麼開心？

B: 因為我的中文考得很好。

(2) A: 我姐姐開心的時候我也很開心。

B: 為甚麼？

A: 因為她一開心就給我錢。

☞ 開會   hold or attend a meeting (VO)

A: 我們甚麼時候開會？

B: 現在就開。

☞ 開明　　　enlightened, open-minded (SV)

(1) 現在的老師都很開明。

(2) 我媽媽很開明，可是我爸爸不太開明。

☞ 信口開河　talk irresponsibly; talk nonsense (IE)

(1) 這個人老是喜歡信口開河，甚麼都說。

(2) 你知道他是一個信口開河的人，不要信他說的話。

6. 氣　　gas, air, breath; smell, odor; energy of life (N)

☞ 天氣　　　weather (N)

A: 今天的天氣怎麼樣？

B: 很熱。

☞ 氣候　　　climate (N)

A: 你們老家的氣候怎麼樣？

B: 很好，不冷也不熱。

☞ 生氣　　　take offence, get angry (V/SV)

(1) 不要生氣，他是信口開河。

(2) 媽媽現在生我的氣，因為我近來花很多錢。

☞ 小氣　　　stingy; narrow-minded (SV)

(1) 那個人很小氣，甚麼錢都不花。

(2) 他不是那麼小氣的人，他不會生氣的。

7. 訴　　tell, inform (V)

☞ 告訴　　　tell, let know (V)

(1) A: 誰告訴你我會跳舞？

B: 你同學告訴我的。

(2) A: 請你告訴老師，我明天不來上課。

B: 好。

8. **回**   **return, go back, turn around** (V)

☞ 回信   write in reply, write back (VO)

A: 我媽媽怎麼還沒給我回信？

B: 也許她很忙。

☞ 回來   come back (V)

A: 你甚麼時候回來？

B: 後天晚上。

☞ 回去   go back (V)

A: 你甚麼時候回家？

B: 我這學期不回去。

☞ 回國   go back to one's country (VO)

A: 你已經在美國那麼多年了，你不想回國看看嗎？

B: 想是想，可是沒錢回不去。

9. **看**   **see, look at; read; think, consider** (V)

(1) A: 我後天去看你，可以嗎？

B: 可以。

(2) A: 你在看甚麼？

B: 我在看今天的報。

(3) A: 你看我們要不要告訴她？

B: 我想不要告訴她好。

☞ 看報   read a newspaper (VO)

(1) A: 你今天看報了沒有？

B: 還沒看呢。

(2) A: 你看中文報還是看英文報？

B: 我看英文報，因為我還不會看中文報。

☞ 好看　good-looking; interesting (SV)

(1) 那個人很好看。

(2) A: 你看的那本小説，好看不好看？

　　 B: 不太好看。

☞ 小看　look down upon; belittle (V)

(1) 你不可以小看他。

(2) 你不要小看他，他有很多經驗。

10. 書　**book** (N)

我女兒從小就很喜歡看書。

☞ 書報　books and newspapers (N)

我很喜歡去他家，因為他家有很多書報。

☞ 書名　title of a book (N)

A: 你媽媽送你的那本書的書名是甚麼？

B: 是《怎樣寫中國字》。

☞ 四書　The Four Books, namely, *Daxue* (The Great Learning), *Zhongyong* (The Doctrine of the Mean) , *Lunyu* (The Analects of Confucius), and *Mengzi* (The Mencius) (N)

A: 老師，我們甚麼時候會看四書？

B: 四書很難。也許兩年以後，不過你們現在可以看英文的。

☘ 句型練習

8.1 THE PATTERN 已經……了

The adverb 已經 "already" is often used with 了 to indicate that an action has already happened.

```
S          已經      V        了
學生        已經      來        了。
The students have already come.
```

1. A: 這個字你們學過沒有？
    B: 這個字我們已經學過了。

2. A: 你們開學了嗎？
    B: 我們已經開學一星期了。

3. A: 我給你們介紹介紹。
    B: 海英已經給我們介紹過了。

8.2 THE WORD 給

The word 給 can function as a verb as well as a coverb.

8.2.1 給 as a verb

When 給 is used as a verb, it means "to give."

```
S          給        DO       IO
她          給        我        一本書。
She gave me a book.
```

1. A: 你給你妹妹甚麼？
    B: 我給她一本小說。

2. A: 誰給你錢去中國？
    B: 我爸爸媽媽。

8.2.2 給 as a coverb

When 給 comes before another verb in a sentence, it functions as a coverb, meaning "for."

S	給	DO	V	IO
老師	給	我	寫	介紹信了。

The teacher wrote a recommendation letter for me.

1. A: 你最近有沒有給你女朋友寫信？
   B: 沒有。

2. A: 你為甚麼給弟弟作功課？
   B: 因為他不會作。

3. A: 你可以給我們介紹介紹中國嗎？
   B: 好。我現在給你們介紹我的國家。

8.3 THE PATTERN 不⋯⋯不⋯⋯

The pattern 不⋯⋯不⋯⋯ is used before two stative verbs opposite in meaning to indicate an intermediate state.

S	不	SV	不	SV
今天	不	冷	不	熱。

Today is neither too cold nor too hot.

1. A: 你們老師說中國話說得很快嗎？
   B: 她說得不快也不慢。

2. A: 今天媽媽作的菜多不多？
   B: 不多也不少。

3. A: 今天的功課怎麼樣？
   B: 很好。不多也不少。

8.4 SV/V 是 SV/V, 可是……

The pattern SV/V 是 SV/V, 可是…… is a two-clause sentence in which the first clause states the fact, while the second clause states a countering fact or situation. The 是 in the first clause can be understood in English as "all right" at the end of the first clause.

S	*SV/V*	*是*	*SV/V,*	*可是*……
中文	難	是	難，	可是我還要學。

Chinese is difficult all right, but I still want to learn it.

1. A: 你想去中國嗎？

    B: 想是想去，可是我沒有錢。

2. A: 這個字，你們沒學過嗎？

    B: 學是學過了，可是我們現在不會了。

3. A: 你不喜歡跳舞嗎？

    B: 喜歡是喜歡，可是現在我太累了。

8.5 THE PATTERN 甚麼……就……甚麼

The question word 甚麼 can function as an indefinite pronoun. The 甚麼……就……甚麼…… pattern denotes the notion "whatever, whichever."

1. A: 你下學期要選甚麼課？

    B: 甚麼課有意思，我就選甚麼課。

2. A: 我可以吃甚麼？

    B: 你想吃甚麼就吃甚麼。

3. A: 你想喝甚麼？

    B: 你有甚麼，我就喝甚麼。

🏵 造句

1.

已經

已經開學了。

已經開學兩個星期了。

我們已經開學兩個星期了。

2.

早已

早已會寫字了。

早已會寫中國字了。

他早已會寫中國字了。

3.

經驗

甚麼經驗？

你有甚麼經驗？

告訴我你有甚麼經驗。

4.

和氣

和氣的人

喜歡和氣的人。

人人都喜歡和氣的人。

🏵 問答

1. 你學過中文嗎？　　　　　學過。

2. 你在哪兒學的中文？　　　我在家學的中文。

3. 你會寫中國字嗎？　　　　會，不過我就會寫十個中國字。

4. 你為甚麼那麼開心？　　　因為我媽來信了。

5. 你甚麼時候回國？　　　　我現在還不知道呢。爸爸媽媽來信叫我甚麼時候回去，我就甚麼時候回去。

6. 這個考試你有沒有信心？　我一點兒信心都沒有。

7. 王三說的話你信不信？　　我不信。因為我知道他是一個喜歡信口開河的人。

8. 為甚麼馬愛文今天那麼生氣？我想是因為她老師說她的報告寫得不太好。

9. 明天開會，請你告訴思文。他早已知道了。

10. 你星期幾有課？　　　　　我一、三、五有課。

🍀 閱讀練習

馬思文的日記

時間過得太快了，開學已經有幾個星期了。我也有兩個多星期沒給爸爸媽媽寫信了。我很想爸爸、媽媽、姐姐跟弟弟。我想他們也會想我。我今天要給他們寫信，告訴他們我在學校很好，很快樂。老師都很有經驗，同學們都很和氣。大學的課沒有中學多，可是功課很多。我天天不是看書，就是寫報告。星期六、星期日，我有時候跟同學談天兒，有時候去跳舞，有時候去開會。開會的時候，大家都有不同的意見，很有意思。下星期要是天氣好，我很想回家去看看，跟他們談談、吃媽媽作的菜。我得問他們在家不在家。我想，要是我可以回家，他們會很開心。

問題

1. 馬思文最近有沒有給他家人寫信？
2. 思文今天給他爸爸媽媽寫信要告訴他們學校怎麼樣？
3. 星期六、星期天思文作甚麼？
4. 開會的時候，大家的意見都一樣嗎？
5. 思文為甚麼下星期要回家？
6. 你喜歡你的學校嗎？為甚麼？

第九課　爸爸媽媽的回信
Lesson 9　Father and mother's reply

Lesson 9
Pinyin Text

🐾 Text

Bàba māma de huíxìn
Father and mother's reply

Sīwén, Àiwén:

Jīntiān zǎoshang jiēdào nǐmen de láixìn, zhīdào nǐmen hěn kuàilè, tóngxué hěn héqi, lǎoshī hěn yǒu jīngyàn. Wǒmen zhēn gāoxìng. Wǒmen yě dōu hěn xiǎng nǐmen. Nǐmen gēge, jiějie kànjian nǐmen xiě de xìn dōu shuō, xiǎngbudào xiànzài nǐmen de Zhōngwén nàme hǎo le, jìnbù de nàme kuài. Nǐ dìdi shuō, tā yě xiǎng nǐmen, kěshì nǐmen bú zài jiā tā yě hěn gāoxìng. Yīnwèi tā kěyǐ qǐng hěn duō péngyou lái jiā. Tā míngtiān yěxǔ huì gěi nǐmen xiě xìn. Nǐmen shuō nǐmen xīngqīliù (jiǔyuè èrshírì) yào huíjiā, wǒmen tài kāixīn le. Wǒmen yídìng zài jiā děng nǐmen. Nǐmen de qián gòu ma? Yàoshì bú gòu, gàosu wǒmen, wǒmen huì mǎshàng gěi nǐmen.

Zhù
kuàilè!

Māma
Jiǔyuè shíqīrì

Dear Siwen and Aiwen,

We received your letter this morning and we know that you are happy, having nice classmates, and experienced teachers. We are so happy for you. We also miss you very much. After reading your letter, both your elder brother and sister said that they were surprised that your Chinese is now so good and that you have improved so quickly. Your younger brother said he misses you too, but he is also happy that you are not home, because he can invite a lot of friends home. He might write to you tomorrow. We are overjoyed to hear that you want to come home this Saturday (20 September). We will definitely be home waiting for you. Do you have enough money? If not, tell us, (and) we'll send you some money immediately.

Wishing you happiness,
Mom
17 September

🐾 Vocabulary and Illustrative Sentences

1. gāo   **tall, high** (SV); **a surname** (N)

   Nàge rén zhēn gāo.   That person is really tall.

☞ gāodà   tall and big, tall (SV)

   A: Nàge gāodà de rén shì shéi?   Who is that big, tall person?

   B: Shì wǒ gēge.   That's my elder brother.

☞ gāozhōng   high school (N)

   (1) Tā shì wǒ gāozhōng de   He is my classmate from high
       tóngxué.   school.

   (2) Wǒ de gāozhōng hěn dà.   My high school is very big.

☞ gāomíng   brilliant, wise (SV)

   A: Nǐ zhège yìjiàn zhēn gāomíng.   This idea of yours is brilliant.

   B: Méishénme.   It's nothing.

2. xìng   **interest, excitement** (SV)

☞ gāoxìng   glad, happy, cheerful; be willing to (SV)

   (1) Wǒ dìdi kǎoshàng le hǎo   My younger brother got into a
       dàxué, wǒ jiārén dōu hěn   good college. My family is very
       gāoxìng.   happy.

   (2) Nǐ kǎode zhème hǎo, wǒ   You did so well in your exam.
       zhēn wèi nǐ gāoxìng.   I'm so happy for you.

3. jiē   **receive; come in contact with; catch; meet; pick up** (V)

   A: Nǐ xīngqīliù huílái, yào-bu-   You're coming back on Saturday.
      yào wǒmen qù jiē nǐ?   Do you want us to pick you up?

   B: Nǐ děi lái jiē wǒ.   You'll have to pick me up.

4. **dào**   **arrive, reach (V); up until (CV)**

    (1) A: Nǐ shénme shíhou kěyǐ dào wǒ jiā lái? — When can you come to my house?

       B: Yěxǔ xīngqīwǔ wǎnshang. — Maybe Friday night.

    (2) A: Wǒ de shēngrì kuài dào le. — My birthday is coming up soon.

       B: Nǎ tiān? — Which day?

       A: Hòutiān. — The day after tomorrow.

☞ **jiēdào**   receive (V)

    (1) Wǒ yì jiēdào xìn jiù hěn kāixīn. — I'm happy whenever (I) receive a letter.

    (2) A: Nǐ jiēdào nǐ bàba gěi nǐ de xìn le ma? — Did you receive the letter your father sent you?

       B: Hái méi jiēdào ne. — I haven't received it yet.

☞ **dédào**   get, obtain, gain, receive (V)

    (1) Wǒ jīnnián de shùxué dàkǎo dédào le yí ge "A." — I got an "A" on my final exam in math this year.

    (2) Yàoshì wǒ kěyǐ dédào tā de "xīn," wǒ jiù kāixīn le. — If I can win her "heart," I will be happy.

☞ **děngdào**   by the time, wait until (V)

    (1) A: Nǐ shénme shíhou gàosu wǒ nǐ qù Zhōngguó de jīngyàn? — When are you going to tell me about your experiences in China?

       B: Děngdào nǐ yào qù Zhōngguó de shíhou wǒ jiù gàosu nǐ. — I'll tell you when you are going to China.

    (2) A: Wǒ děngdào xiànzài tā hái méi lái. Nǐ shuō wǒ hái yào-bu-yào děng tā? — I have been waiting till now. He still hasn't shown up. Tell me, should I wait for him any longer?

       B: Wǒ xiǎng nǐ bú yào děng le. Yěxǔ tā bú huì lái le. — I don't think you should wait for him anymore. He might not come.

☞ xiǎngdào   think of; call to mind (V)

    (1) Yì xiǎngdào kǎoshì, wǒ   Once I think of the exam, I get
        jiù jǐnzhāng.   really nervous.

    (2) Nǐmen zěnme huì xiǎngdào   How did you ever think of such
        zhème gāomíng de yìjiàn?   a brilliant idea?

☞ yìtiān-   from morning till night, from dawn to dusk, all day long (IE)
  dàowǎn

    (1) Yǒude xuéshēng yìtiān-   Some students study Chinese
        dàowǎn zài xué Zhōngwén. from dawn to dusk.

    (2) Wǒ dìdi yìtiāndàowǎn bú   My younger brother isn't home
        zài jiā.   all day.

    (3) Wǒ māma wèi wǒmen yìtiān My mother is busy all day long
        máng dàowǎn.   just for our sake.

5. zhēn   **true, real, genuine; really, truly, indeed (Adv)**

    (1) Tā zhēn shì yí ge hǎo   He is really a good student.
        xuéshēng.

    (2) A: Nǐ zhēn bú ài tā le ma?   You really don't love her anymore?

        B: Zhēn de.   Really.

☞ zhēnxīn   wholehearted, heartfelt, sincere (Adv)

    Wǒ gàosu tā wǒ shì zhēnxīn   I told her that I love her whole-
    ài tā, kěshì tā bú xìn. Wǒ hěn   heartedly, but she didn't believe
    shēngqì.   me. I was very angry.

☞ tiānzhēn   innocent; simple and unaffected; naive (SV)

    (1) Wǒ mèimei zhēn shì tiānzhēn My little sister is really innocent
        kě'ài.   and lovable.

    (2) Nǐ xiǎng rénrén dōu shì   You think everybody is good-
        hǎorén, zhēn tài tiānzhēn le. hearted. You're really too naive.

6. jiàn   **see, catch sight of (V)**

    (1) A: Nǐ de lǎoshī shénme   When can your teacher see you?
        shíhou kěyǐ jiàn nǐ?

        B: Xīngqī'èr.   Tuesday.

(2) Wǒ bù gāoxìng de shíhou, bù xǐhuan jiàn rén.

When I'm not happy, I don't like to see people.

☞ kànjian   caught sight of; saw (V)

A: Nǐ jīntiān shàng kè de shíhou, yǒu-méiyǒu kànjian Mǎ Sīwén?

When you went to class today, did you see Ma Siwen?

B: Kànjian le.

(Yes, I) saw (him).

☞ bújiàn le   disappear, be missing (IE)

A: Wǒ de biǎo bújiàn le, nǐ kànjian le ma?

My watch is missing. Have you seen it?

B: Méiyǒu.

(No, I) haven't (seen it).

☞ yìjiàn   idea, view, opinion, suggestion; objection (N)

A: Lǎoshī, wǒmen yǒu jǐ ge yìjiàn.

Teacher, we have a few suggestions.

B: Qǐng shuō.

Please speak out.

A: Wǒmen kěyǐ-bu-kěyǐ míngtiān bù kǎoshì?

Can we not have the test tomorrow?

B: Wèishénme?

Why?

A: Yīnwèi wǒmen de gōngkè tài duō le.

Because we have too much homework.

C: Wǒmen kěyǐ-bu-kěyǐ jiù kǎo bǐshì, bù kǎo kǒushì?

Can we just take the written exam but not the oral exam?

D: Wǒmen kěyǐ jiù xiě bàogào, bù kǎoshì ma?

Can we write a paper but not take the exam?

B: Nǐmen de yìjiàn hěn duō. Wǒ děi kàn dà duōshù xuésheng de yìjiàn shì shénme.

You all have so many suggestions. I need to see what the majority of the students think about them.

☞ yuǎnjiàn   foresight, vision (N)

Wǒ hěn xǐhuan tā, yīnwèi tā shì yí ge hěn yǒu yuǎnjiàn de rén.

I like him very much, because he is a person with vision.

7. gòu   **enough, sufficient, adequate** (SV)

(1) A: Bù zhīdào wèishénme,   (I) don't know why I never seem
       wǒ de qián lǎo bú gòu.   to have enough money.

   B: Nǐ huāde tài duō le.   You spend too much.

(2) Wǒ zhège bàogào xiěde   I didn't write my paper very
    bú gòu hǎo.   well.

☞ zúgòu   enough; ample (V)

Zhège yuè wǒ de qián zúgòu le.   I have an ample amount of money
                                    this month.

☞ gòuyìsi   really something; generous, really kind (IE)

(1) Wǒ yì huílái Xiǎoměi mǎshàng   Once I got back, Xiaomei came
    jiù lái kàn wǒ, zhēn gòuyìsi.   to see me right away. That's really
                                    something.

(2) Wǒ yào shénme, tā jiù gěi   He will give me whatever I want.
    wǒ shénme, zhēn gòuyìsi.   He is really generous.

8. dìng   **set, decide; certainly, definitely** (V)

(1) Wǒmen dìng hǎo le hòutiān   We decided to meet the morning
    zǎoshang jiàn.   after tomorrow.

(2) Shuōbudìng tā jīntiān bù   Maybe he's not coming to the
    lái kāihuì.   meeting today.

☞ yídìng   definitely, certainly, surely (Adv)

(1) A: Hǎiyīng, qǐng nǐ lái wǒ   Haiying, please come to my
       de shēngrì cháhuì.   birthday party.

   B: Hǎo, wǒ yídìng qù.   Okay, I will definitely be there.

(2) A: Jīntiān de kǎoshì, yídìng   Today's exam will definitely be
       hěn nán.   difficult.

   B: Nǐ zěnme zhīdào?   How do you know?

   A: Lín Hǎiyīng gàosu wǒ de.   Lin Haiying told me.

(3) Wǒmen jīntiān qù. Míngtiān   The weather may not be that
    de tiānqì bù yídìng hǎo.   good tomorrow.

9. **bù**   **step, pace, go on foot** (N)

Wǒmen děi yíbùyíbùde xué Zhōngwén.

We must learn Chinese step by step.

☞ **jìnbù**   advance, progress, improve; (politically) progressive (V/N)

Lǎoshī shuō, wǒmen de Zhōngwén jìnbùde hěn kuài.

The teacher says our Chinese is improving rapidly.

☞ **pǎobù**   run (V)

Wǒ tiāntiān zǎoshang pǎobù.

I go running every morning.

10. **zhù**   **express good wishes, wish** (V)

Zhù nǐ kuàilè!

I wish you happiness!

✿ Pattern Drills

9.1 THE PATTERN dào

The word dào has many functions. It can function as a main verb "reach, arrive," as a coverb "to," or as an unstressed postverb.

9.1.1 Dào "arrive" as a verb

1. A: Nǐ tóngxué shénme shíhou dào?   When will your classmates arrive?

   B: Tāmen mǎshàng jiù dào le.   They will be here very soon.

2. A: Wǒmen shénme shíhou chīfàn?   When are we going to eat?

   B: Tāmen yí dào wǒmen jiù chīfàn.   We will eat as soon as they arrive.

3. A: Tā shénme shíhou dào Měiguó?   When will he arrive in America?

   B: Tā yǐjīng dào le.   He has already arrived.

9.1.2 Dào "to" as a coverb

Dào is used to express movement toward a place with the verb lái "come" or qù "go."

S	dào	PW	lái/qù
Tā	dào	Zhōngguó	qù.

He is going to China.

1. A: Nǐ jīntiān yào dào nǎr qù?
   Where are you going today?

   B: Wǒ dào Lín Hǎiyīng jiā qù.
   I am going to Lin Haiying's house.

   A: Nǐ dào tā jiā qù zuò shénme?
   Why are you going to her house?

   B: Wǒ qù tiàowǔ.
   I am going (to her house) to dance.

2. A: Nǐ míngtiān kěyǐ dào wǒ jiā lái chī wǎnfàn ma?
   Can you come to my house for dinner tomorrow?

   B: Kěyǐ.
   (I) can.

3. A: Wǒ gēn nǚpéngyou hěn xǐhuan dào zhèr lái hē chá. Nǐmen ne?
   My girlfriend and I like to come here to drink tea very much. How about you?

   B: Wǒmen yě hěn xǐhuan dào zhèr lái.
   We also like to come here very much.

9.1.3 The pattern cóng ... dào ...

Movement from one place to another is expressed by the coverbs cóng "from" and dào "to."

S	cóng	PW1	dào	PW2
Sīwén	cóng	tā jiā	dào	wǒ jiā lái.

Siwen is coming from his house to my house.

1. A: Qǐngwèn, cóng zhèr dào Hǎiyīng jiā zěnme zǒu?
   May I ask, how do I go to Haiying's house from here?

   B: Wǒ bù zhīdào.
   I don't know.

2. A: Cóng nǐ jiā dào Sīwén jiā yuǎn-bu-yuǎn?

Is it far to go to Siwen's house from your house?

B: Hěn yuǎn.

Very far.

3. A: Cóng Měiguó dào Zhōngguó jìn, háishì cóng Rìběn dào Zhōngguó jìn?

Which is closer? From America to China or from Japan to China?

B: Cóng Rìběn jìn duō le.

It's much closer (to go to China) from Japan.

9.1.4 Dào as a postverb to form a compound verb

When dào is suffixed to other verbs to form a compound verb, it adds a sense of completion, attainment, or success.

S	V-dào	O
Tā	mǎidào le	nà běn xiǎoshuō.
He bought that novel.		

1. Wǒ jīntiān zài wǔhuì shàng kàndào le yí ge lǎopéngyou.

I ran into an old friend at the dance today.

2. Wǒ méi xiǎngdào nǐ jīntiān lái le.

I have never expected you to come today.

3. Māma zhǎodào le wǒ de biǎo.

My mom found my watch.

9.2 THE COVERB wèi

The coverb wèi "for, for the sake of " comes in the pattern "wèi O V/SV," meaning "to V/SV for the sake of the object," where the object is a noun or pronoun.

S	wèi	O	V/SV
Māma	wèi	wǒmen	zuò fàn.
Mom cooks for us.			

1. Tā hěn xǐhuan wèi tā nǚpéngyou zuò gōngkè.

   He likes to do homework for his girlfriend.

2. A: Wǒ de Yīngwén kǎode hěn hǎo.

   I did very well in my English exam.

   B: Zhēn de ma! Wǒ zhēn wèi nǐ gāoxìng.

   Really! I am very happy for you.

3. A: Lǎoshī děi wèi xuésheng xiǎngxiang, bú yào tiāntiān kǎoshì.

   Teachers need to think about the students and should not give them tests every day.

   B: Tiāntiān kǎoshì shì wèi nǐmen hǎo.

   Having a test every day is for your own good.

9.3 THE DIFFERENCE BETWEEN kàn, jiàn AND kàndào/kànjian

The verbs kàn, jiàn and kàndào/kànjian all have the meaning "to meet, to see."

Wǒ jīntiān kàn / jiàn / kàndào / kànjian le yí ge yǒuyìsi de rén.

I met a very interesting person today.

9.3.1 The use of kàn

Besides the meaning "to see, to meet," kàn can also mean "to look, to watch, to read, to consider, to visit, etc." In the following situations, only kàn — not jiàn or kàndào/kànjian — can be used.

1. Kàn! Nà shì shénme?

   Look! What is that?

2. Wǒ hěn xǐhuan kàn diànyǐng.

   I like to watch movies very much.

3. Qǐng nǐmen xiànzài kàn shū.

   Please read your book now.

4. Wǒ kàn zhège kǎoshì hěn nán.

   I think this test is very difficult.

5. Wǒ shénme shíhou kěyǐ qù kàn nǐmen?

   When may I visit you?

9.3.2 The use of <u>jiàn</u>

In the following situations, only <u>jiàn</u> — not <u>kàn</u> or <u>kàndào</u>/<u>kànjian</u> — can be used.

1. A: Wǒmen shénme shíhou jiàn?

    When shall we meet?

    B: Míngtiān wǎnshang.

    Tomorrow evening.

    A: Hǎo, míngtiān jiàn.

    Okay, I'll see you tomorrow.

2. Tā bùhǎoyìsi jiàn nǐ.

    He feels embarrassed to see you.

3. Bàba, wǒ de nǚpéngyou xiǎng jiànjian nǐ.

    Dad, my girlfriend would like to meet you.

9.3.3 The use of <u>kàndào</u>/<u>kànjian</u>

In the following situations, only <u>kàndào</u>/<u>kànjian</u> — not <u>jiàn</u> or <u>kàn</u> — can be used.

1. A: Nǐ shàng kè de shíhou, yǒu-méiyǒu kàndào/kànjian tā?

    Did you see him in class?

    B: Méi kàndào/kànjian tā.

    I didn't see him.

2. Jīntiān de wǎnhuì shàng, wǒ kàndào le/kànjian le yí ge hěn yǒumíng de rén.

    I saw a very famous person at the party tonight.

3. Nǐ kàndào/kànjian wǒ de biǎo le ma?

    Did you see my watch?

9.4 THE PARTICLE -<u>de</u>

When -<u>de</u> is used as a particle, it is pronounced in its neutral tone. It is often attached to duplicated stative verbs or other expressions to turn them into adverbs. When the duplicated stative verb is monosyllabic, the second syllable is changed to its first tone, with the addition of an -<u>r</u> ending.

1. Xué Zhōngwén děi yíbùyíbùde xué.

    One has to learn Chinese step by step.

2. Qǐng nǐ hǎohāorde shuōhuà.

    Please speak nicely.

3. Bú yào máng. Mànmānrde zǒu.

    There is no hurry. Walk slowly.

🐾 Sentence Building

1.

Jiēdào

Jiēdào xìn.

Jiēdào nǐ de xìn.

Jīntiān jiēdào le nǐ de xìn.

Wǒmen jīntiān jiēdào le nǐ de xìn.

2.

Jìnbù

Guójiā jìnbù le.

Zhège guójiā jìnbù le.

Zhège guójiā jìnlái jìnbù le hěn duō.

Nǐmen zhège guójiā jìnlái jìnbù le hěn duō.

3.

Yìjiàn

Shénme yìjiàn?

Nǐ yǒu shénme yìjiàn?

Gàosu wǒ nǐ yǒu shénme yìjiàn.

4.

Gòu

Gòu-bu-gòu?

Qián gòu-bu-gòu?

Nǐ de qián gòu-bu-gòu?

🐾 Questions and Responses

1. Nǐ dìdi jīntiān wèishénme zhème gāoxìng?
   Why is your little brother so happy today?

   Yīnwèi tā jiēdào bàba māma de xìn le.
   Because he received a letter from Dad and Mom.

2. Zhège yìjiàn zhēn gāomíng, shéi xiǎngdào de?
   Who came up with this brilliant idea?

   Shì wǒmen dàjiā xiǎngdào de.
   We all thought it up.

3. Yàoshì nǐ kànjian Qián Guóyīng de shíhou, wèn tā hǎo.
   When you see Qian Guoying, please send her my best regards.

   Hǎo, yídìng.
   Okay, I will.

4. Nǐ zhège yuè de qián gòu-bu-gòu huā de?
   Do you have enough money to spend this month?

   Gòule gòule.
   (I have) enough.

5. Zhège xīngqīliù, nǐ zài-bu-zài jiā?
   Will you be home this Saturday?

   Hái bù yídìng. Yěxǔ bú zài.
   (I) am not sure yet. Maybe (I) will not be home.

6. Nǐ dìdi yìtiāndàowǎn zài máng
   shénme?

   What is your younger brother so
   busy about all day long?

   Tā zài máng gěi tā nǚtóngxué xiě xìn.

   He is busy writing letters to his
   female classmates.

7. Nǐ zài zhǎo shénme?

   What are you looking for?

   Wǒ de Zhōngwén kèběn bújiàn le.
   Nǐ yǒu-méiyǒu kànjian?
   My Chinese textbook is missing.
   Have you seen it?

8. Nǐ shuō wǒ de Yīngwén yǒu-
   méiyǒu jìnbù?

   Would you say my English has
   improved?

   Yǒu. Nǐ de Yīngwén zhè jǐ ge yuè
   jìnbù le hěn duō.
   Yes, your English has improved a lot
   in these few months.

9. Wèishénme rénrén dōu xǐhuan tā?
   Why does everyone like her?

   Yīnwèi tā hěn tiānzhēn kě'ài.
   Because she is very innocent and
   lovable.

10. Wǒmen shì zǎoshang qù pǎobù háishì
    wǎnshang qù pǎobù?
    Shall we go running in the morning
    or in the evening?

    Shénme shíhou dōu kěyǐ. Wǒ méi yìjiàn.

    Anytime will be fine for me. I have
    no objections.

🌺 Supplementary Vocabulary

Months of the Year

yīyuè	January	qīyuè	July
èryuè	February	bāyuè	August
sānyuè	March	jiǔyuè	September
sìyuè	April	shíyuè	October
wǔyuè	May	shíyīyuè	November
liùyuè	June	shí'èryuè	December

🐾 Cultural Notes

Shíèr Shēngxiào

Chinese Zodiac

The Chinese Zodiac consists of a twelve-year cycle of animals, each year of which is named after a different animal that imparts distinct characteristics to its year. Many Chinese people believe that the year of a person's birth is the primary factor in determining that person's personality traits, physical and mental attributes, and the degree of success and happiness attained throughout his/her lifetime. To find out your Chinese zodiac sign, read the year of your birth among the twelve signs. If you were born before 1936, add twelve to the year you were born to find your sign.

Sign	Years
Shǔ (Rat)	1936, 1948, 1960, 1972, 1984, 1996 ...
Niú (Ox)	1937, 1949, 1961, 1973, 1985, 1997 ...
Hǔ (Tiger)	1938, 1950, 1962, 1974, 1986, 1998 ...
Tù (Rabbit)	1939, 1951, 1963, 1975, 1987, 1999 ...
Lóng (Dragon)	1940, 1952, 1964, 1976, 1988, 2000 ...
Shé (Snake)	1941, 1953, 1965, 1977, 1989, 2001 ...
Mǎ (Horse)	1942, 1954, 1966, 1978, 1990, 2002 ...
Yáng (Goat)	1943, 1955, 1967, 1979, 1991, 2003 ...
Hóu (Monkey)	1944, 1956, 1968, 1980, 1992, 2004 ...
Jī (Rooster)	1945, 1957, 1969, 1981, 1993, 2005 ...
Gǒu (Dog)	1946, 1958, 1970, 1982, 1994, 2006 ...
Zhū (Pig)	1947, 1959, 1971, 1983, 1995, 2007 ...

第九課
漢字本

課 文

爸爸媽媽的回信

思文，愛文：

今天早上接到你們的來信，知道你們很快樂，同學很和氣，老師很有經驗。我們真高興。我們也都很想你們。你們哥哥姐姐看見你們寫的信都說，想不到現在你們的中文那麼好了，進步得那麼快。你弟弟說，他也想你們，可是你們不在家他也很高興。因為他可以請很多朋友來家。他明天也許會給你們寫信。你們說你們星期六（九月二十日）要回家，我們太開心了。我們一定在家等你們。你們的錢夠嗎？要是不夠，告訴我們，我們會馬上給你們。

祝

快樂！

媽媽

九月十七日

❀ 生詞及例句

1. 高   **tall, high** (SV); **a surname** (N)

那個人真高。

☞ 高大   tall and big, tall (SV)

A: 那個高大的人是誰？

B: 是我哥哥。

☞ 高中   high school (N)

(1) 他是我高中的同學。

(2) 我的高中很大。

☞ 高明   brilliant, wise (SV)

A: 你這個意見真高明。

B: 沒甚麼。

2. 興   **interest, excitement** (SV)

☞ 高興   glad, happy, cheerful; be willing to (SV)

(1) 我弟弟考上了好大學，我家人都很高興。

(2) 你考得這麼好，我真為你高興。

3. 接   **receive; come in contact with; catch; meet; pick up** (V)

A: 你星期六回來，要不要我們去接你？

B: 你得來接我。

4. 到   **arrive, reach** (V); **up until** (CV)

(1) A: 你甚麼時候可以到我家來？

    B: 也許星期五晚上。

(2) A: 我的生日快到了。

    B: 哪天？

    A: 後天。

☞ 接到   receive (V)

(1) 我一接到信就很開心。

(2) A: 你接到你爸爸給你的信了嗎？

    B: 還沒接到呢。

☞ 得到   get, obtain, gain, receive (V)

(1) 我今年的數學大考得到了一個"A"。

(2) 要是我可以得到她的"心"，我就開心了。

☞ 等到   by the time, wait until (V)

(1) A: 你甚麼時候告訴我你去中國的經驗？

    B: 等到你要去中國的時候我就告訴你。

(2) A: 我等到現在他還沒來。你說我還要不要等他？

    B: 我想你不要等了，也許他不會來了。

☞ 想到   think of; call to mind (V)

(1) 一想到考試，我就緊張。

(2) 你怎麼會想到這麼高明的意見？

☞ 一天到晚 from morning till night, from dawn to dusk, all day long (IE)

(1) 有的學生一天到晚在學中文。

(2) 我弟弟一天到晚不在家。

(3) 我媽媽為我們一天忙到晚。

5. 真   **true, real, genuine; really, truly, indeed** (Adv)

(1) 他真是一個好學生。

(2) A: 你真不愛她了嗎？

    B: 真的。

☞ 真心　　wholehearted, heartfelt, sincere (Adv)

我告訴她我是真心愛她，可是她不信。我很生氣。

☞ 天真　　innocent; simple and unaffected; naive (SV)

(1) 我妹妹真是天真可愛。

(2) 你想人人都是好人，真太天真了。

6. 見　　**see, catch sight of** (V)

(1) A: 你的老師甚麼時候可以見你？

　　 B: 星期二。

(2) 我不高興的時候，不喜歡見人。

☞ 看見　　caught sight of; saw (V)

A: 你今天上課的時候，有沒有看見馬思文？

B: 看見了。

☞ 不見了　　disappear, be missing (IE)

A: 我的錶不見了，你看見了嗎？

B: 沒有。

☞ 意見　　idea, view, opinion, suggestion; objection (N)

A: 老師，我們有幾個意見。

B: 請說。

A: 我們可以不可以明天不考試？

B: 為甚麼？

A: 因為我們的功課太多了。

C: 我們可以不可以就考筆試，不考口試？

D: 我們可以就寫報告，不考試嗎？

B: 你們的意見很多。我得看大多數學生的意見是甚麼。

☞ 遠見　　foresight, vision (N)

我很喜歡他，因為他是一個很有遠見的人。

7. **夠**   **enough, sufficient, adequate** (SV)

(1) A: 不知道為甚麼，我的錢老不夠。

     B: 你花得太多了。

(2) 我這個報告寫得不夠好。

☞ 足夠   enough; ample (V)

這個月我的錢足夠了。

☞ 夠意思   really something; generous, really kind (IE)

(1) 我一回來小美馬上就來看我，真夠意思。

(2) 我要甚麼，他就給我甚麼，真夠意思。

8. **定**   **set, decide; certainly, definitely** (V)

(1) 我們定好了後天早上見。

(2) 說不定他今天不來開會。

☞ 一定   definitely, certainly, surely (Adv)

(1) A: 海英，請你來我的生日茶會。

     B: 好，我一定去。

(2) A: 今天的考試，一定很難。

     B: 你怎麼知道？

     A: 林海英告訴我的。

(3) 我們今天去。明天的天氣不一定好。

9. **步**   **step, pace, go on foot** (N)

我們得一步一步地學中文。

☞ 進步   advance, progress, improve; (politically) progressive (V/N)

老師說，我們的中文進步得很快。

☞ 跑步   run (V)

我天天早上跑步。

10. 祝   **express good wishes, wish** (V)

祝你快樂！

🌸 句型練習

9.1 THE PATTERN 到

The word 到 has many functions. It can function as a main verb "reach,
arrive," a coverb "to," or as an unstressed postverb.

9.1.1 到 "arrive" as a verb

1. A: 你同學甚麼時候到？
    B: 他們馬上就到了。

2. A: 我們甚麼時候吃飯？
    B: 他們一到我們就吃飯。

3. A: 他甚麼時候到美國？
    B: 他已經到了。

9.1.2 到 "to" as a coverb

到 is used to express movement toward a place with the verb 來 "come" or 去
"go."

S	到	PW	來／去
他	到	中國	去。
He is going to China.			

1. A: 你今天要到哪兒去？
    B: 我到林海英家去。

A: 你到她家去作甚麼？

B: 我去跳舞。

2. A: 你明天可以到我家來吃晚飯嗎？

B: 可以。

3. A: 我跟女朋友很喜歡到這兒來喝茶。你們呢？

B: 我們也很喜歡到這兒來。

9.1.3 The pattern 從……到……

Movement from one place to another is expressed by the coverbs 從 "from" and 到 "to."

S	從	PW1	到	PW2	
思文	從	他家	到	我家	來。

Siwen is coming from his house to my house.

1. A: 請問，從這兒到海英家怎麼走？

B: 我不知道。

2. A: 從你家到思文家遠不遠？

B: 很遠。

3. A: 從美國到中國近，還是從日本到中國近？

B: 從日本近多了。

9.1.4 到 as a postverb to form a compound verb

When 到 is suffixed to other verbs to form a compound verb, it adds a sense of completion, attainment, or success.

S	V-到	O
他	買到了	那本小說。

He bought that novel.

1. 我今天在舞會上看到了一個老朋友。

2. 我沒想到你今天來了。

3. 媽媽找到了我的錶。

9.2 THE COVERB 為

The coverb 為 "for, for the sake of" comes in the pattern "為 O V/SV," meaning "to V/SV for the sake of the object," where the object is a noun or pronoun.

S	為	O	V/SV
媽媽	為	我們	作飯。
Mom cooks for us.			

1. 他很喜歡為他女朋友作功課。

2. A: 我的英文考得很好。

   B: 真的嗎！我真為你高興。

3. A: 老師得為學生想想，不要天天考試。

   B: 天天考試是為你們好。

9.3 THE DIFFERENCE BETWEEN 看, 見 AND 看到/看見

The verbs 看, 見 and 看到/看見 all have the meaning "to meet, to see."

我今天看/見/看到/看見了一個有意思的人。

9.3.1 The use of 看

Besides the meaning "to see, to meet," 看 can also mean "to look, to watch, to read, to consider, to visit, etc." In the following situations, only 看 — not 見 or 看到/看見 — can be used.

1. 看！那是甚麼？

2. 我很喜歡看電影。

3. 請你們現在看書。

4. 我看這個考試很難。

5. 我甚麼時候可以去看你們？

9.3.2 The use of 見

In the following situations, only 見 — not 看 or 看到/看見 — can be used.

1. A: 我們甚麼時候見？

   B: 明天晚上。

   A: 好，明天見。

2. 他不好意思見你。

3. 爸爸，我的女朋友想見見你。

9.3.3 The use of 看到/看見

In the following situations, only 看到/看見 — not 見 or 看 — can be used.

1. A: 你上課的時候，有沒有看到/看見他？

   B: 沒看到/看見他。

2. 今天的晚會上，我看到/看見了一個很有名的人。

3. 你看到/看見我的錶了嗎？

9.4 THE PARTICLE -地

When -地 is used as a particle, it is pronounced in its neutral tone. It is often attached to duplicated stative verbs or other expressions to turn them into adverbs. When the duplicated stative verb is monosyllabic, the second syllable is changed to its first tone, with the addition of an -兒 ending.

1. 學中文得一步一步地學。

2. 請你好好 (兒) 地說話。

3. 不要忙。慢慢 (兒) 地走。

🌼 造 句

1.

接到

接到信。

接到你的信。

今天接到了你的信。

我們今天接到了你的信。

2.

進步

國家進步了。

這個國家進步了。

這個國家近來進步了很多。

你們這個國家近來進步了很多。

3.

意見

甚麼意見？

你有甚麼意見？

告訴我你有甚麼意見。

4.

夠

夠不夠？

錢夠不夠？

你的錢夠不夠？

🌼 問 答

1. 你弟弟今天為甚麼這麼高興？　　因為他接到爸爸媽媽的信了。

2. 這個意見真高明，誰想到的？　　是我們大家想到的。

3. 要是你看見錢國英的時候，問她好。　好，一定。

4. 你這個月的錢夠不夠花的？　　夠了夠了。

5. 這個星期六你在不在家？　　還不一定，也許不在。

6. 你弟弟一天到晚在忙甚麼？　　他在忙給他女同學寫信。

7. 你在找甚麼？　　我的中文課本不見了。你有沒有看見？

8. 你說我的英文有沒有進步？　　有。你的英文這幾個月進步了很多。

9. 為甚麼人人都喜歡她？　　因為她很天真可愛。

10. 我們是早上去跑步還是晚上去跑步？　甚麼時候都可以。我沒意見。

閱讀練習

馬思文的日記

　　我今天早上去慢跑回來的時候，接到了爸爸媽媽的回信。他們說接到我的信以後很開心。他們問我錢夠不夠。說我的中文進步了很多。說姐姐弟弟也很高興可以看見我。他們一定在家等我回去。

　　我得想想送給他們甚麼。我不可以太小氣，可是我也沒有太多錢。爸爸愛看書，我送他一本四書，媽媽愛花，我就送她花。姐姐愛看小說，我也許送她一本有名的英國小說。弟弟呢，他愛打球，我就送他一個大球。他一定很高興。不過我得去銀行看看我還有多少錢。我得問問星期六銀行開門不開門。

問 題

1. 思文甚麼時候接到了爸爸媽媽的回信？
2. 爸爸媽媽的信上說甚麼？
3. 思文為甚麼要去銀行？
4. 思文想送他姐姐弟弟甚麼？
5. 你想思文是一個小氣的人嗎？為甚麼？
6. 銀行星期六開不開門？
7. 你回家的時候給爸爸媽媽買甚麼？

第十課　給朋友打電話
Lesson 10　A phone call to a friend

Lesson 10
Pinyin Text

• •

CONTENTS

✿ Text

Gěi péngyou dǎ diànhuà
A phonecall to a friend

Jīn Jiàn:	Wéi, Hǎiyīng, wǒ shì Jīn Jiàn. Nǐ hǎo ma?	Hello, Haiying, it's Jin Jian. How are you?
Hǎiyīng:	Jīn Jiàn, wǒ hěn hǎo. Nǐ ne?	Jin Jian, I'm fine. (And) you?
Jīn Jiàn:	Wǒ yě hěn hǎo. Wǒ zuìjìn rènshi le yí ge nǚpéngyou. Wǒ xiǎng qǐng nǐ gēn wǒmen qù fànguǎn chīfàn.	I'm fine too. I've got a girlfriend recently. I was thinking of asking you out to dine with us.
Hǎiyīng:	Hǎo. Shénme shíhou? Wǒ hěn xiǎng rènshi tā.	Okay. When? I would really like to meet her.
Jīn Jiàn:	Zhège xīngqīliù wǎnshang, wǒmen zài wǒ jiā děng nǐ.	This Saturday night. We'll wait for you at my place.
Hǎiyīng:	Wǒmen shì qù Zhōngguó fànguǎn háishì qù Měiguó fànguǎn?	Should we go to a Chinese restaurant or an American restaurant?
Jīn Jiàn:	Nǐ xǐhuan chī Zhōngguófàn háishì chī Měiguófàn?	Do you like eating Chinese food or American food?
Hǎiyīng:	Nǐ zhīdào wǒ zuì xǐhuan chī Zhōngguófàn. Nǐ nǚpéngyou ne?	You know that I like Chinese food. What about your girlfriend?
Jīn Jiàn:	Tā yě xǐhuan chī Zhōngguófàn.	She likes Chinese food too.
Hǎiyīng:	Nà wǒmen jiù qù Zhōngguó fànguǎn ba.	Let's go to a Chinese restaurant then.
Jīn Jiàn:	Wǒmen chī le fàn qù kàn diànyǐng, hǎo ma?	Let's go to a movie after dinner, okay?
Hǎiyīng:	Hǎo. Nǐ qǐng chīfàn, wǒ qǐng nǐmen kàn diànyǐng, hǎo ma?	You treat us to dinner, (and) I will treat you two to the movie, okay?

Jīn Jiàn:　　Hǎo ba. Xīngqīliù jiàn.　　　　Okay. See you on Saturday.

Hǎiyīng:　　Xīngqīliù jiàn.　　　　　　　See you on Saturday.

✿ Vocabulary and Illustrative Sentences

1. **diàn**　　**electricity** (N)

☞ diànhuà　　telephone; phone call (N)

    (1) Wǒ bù gěi wǒ māma dǎ　　　I don't call my mother. I write to
    diànhuà. Wǒ gěi tā xiě xìn.　　her.

    (2) A: Xiǎoměi, diànhuà!　　　Xiaomei, the phone!

    B: Hǎo, wǒ jiù lái.　　　　Okay, I'll be right there.

☞ diànbào　　wire (N)

    Wǒ bàba lái diànbào jiào wǒ　　My father sent me a wire and
    mǎshàng huí guó.　　　　　asked me to return to my
    　　　　　　　　　　　　homeland immediately.

2. **zuì**　　**-est** (Adj)

☞ zuìduō　　at most; maximum (Adj)

    (1) A: Nǐmen jǐ ge rén, shéi de　　Among you all, who has the most
    Zhōngwénshū zuìduō?　　Chinese books?

    B: Tāde. Tā yǒu shí jǐ běn　　He has. He has more than ten
    Zhōngwénshū.　　　　　Chinese books.

    (2) Wǒmen yì tiān zuìduō kěyǐ　　We can learn ten new words a
    xué shí ge shēngzì.　　　　day at most.

☞ zuìhǎo　　best, first-rate; it would be best (Adv)

    (1) Tā de Zhōngguóhuà, shuō　　He speaks Chinese best.
    de zuìhǎo.

    (2) Zhège diànyǐng shì jīnnián　　This movie is the best of the year.
    zuìhǎo de. Wǒmen děi qù　　We have to see it.
    kàn.

(3) Nǐ yào xiǎng kǎode hǎo, **zuìhǎo** tiāntiān lái shàng kè. — If you want to do well in tests, it would be best for you to attend class every day.

☞ **zuìgāo** highest, supreme, tallest (Adj)

Tā shì wǒmen tóngxué zhōng **zuìgāo** de. — He is the tallest in our class.

☞ **zuìhòu** final, last, ultimate (Adv)

(1) Jīntiān tā shì **zuìhòu** yí ge rén bàogào. — Today, he is the last one to give a report.

(2) Wǒ běnlái bù xiǎng gěi tā qián, **zuìhòu** hái shì gěi tā le. — Originally I wasn't going to give him any money, but in the end I gave him the money.

☞ **zuìjìn** recently, lately; in the near future, soon (Adv)

(1) **Zuìjìn** wǒ hěn máng, méiyǒu qù kàn nǐ. — I've been very busy lately, (so) I haven't been to see you.

(2) Nǐ **zuìjìn** hái yào qù Rìběn ma? — Are you still going to Japan soon?

3. **rèn** **recognize, identify; admit** (V)

☞ **rènde** know, recognize (V)

A: Lín Hǎiyīng, nǐ **rènde** nàge rén ma? — Lin Haiying, do you recognize that person?

B: **Rènde**. Tā shì wǒ tóngxué de nǚpéngyou. — I know her. She is my classmate's girlfriend.

☞ **rèn zì** know or learn how to read (VO)

(1) Wǒ hěn xiǎo de shíhou, māma jiù jiào wǒ **rèn zì**. — When I was very little, my mother started to teach me to read.

(2) A: **Rèn zì** nán háishì xiě zì nán? — Is it harder to read or write?

B: Wǒ xiǎng xiě zì nán, nǐ shuō ne? — I think writing is harder. What do you think?

A: Wǒ tóngyì. — I agree.

☞ **rènwéi** think, consider (V)

A: Wǒ **rènwéi** wǒmen zuìhǎo bú qù kāi nàge huì, nǐ shuō ne? | I think it is best if we don't attend that meeting. What do you say?

B: Wǒ tóngyì. | I agree.

☞ **rènzhēn** conscientious, earnest, serious, take seriously (SV)

(1) Nàge lǎoshī hěn **rènzhēn**. Xuésheng yě hěn **rènzhēn** ma? | That teacher takes things very seriously. Are the students serious too?

(2) A: Nǐ wèishénme nàme **rènzhēn**? | Why are you so serious?

B: Yīnwèi wǒ cóng xiǎo jiù hěn **rènzhēn**. | Because I've been serious ever since I was little.

(3) A: Nǐ gēn zhège nǚpéngyou shì **rènzhēn** de ma? | Are you serious about this girlfriend?

B: Shì. Wǒmen yǐjīng rènshi hǎo jǐ nián le. | Yes. We have known each other for many years already.

4. **shí**   **know (V); knowledge (N)**

☞ **shí zì** learn to read, become literate (VO)

A: Xiànzài Zhōngguó **shí zì** de rén duō-bu-duō? | Are there many literate people in China now?

B: Wǒ xiǎng xiànzài hěn duō rén dōu **shí zì** le. | I think that many people are literate these days.

☞ **rènshi** know, recognize (V)

(1) A: Nǐ **rènshi** nàge diànyǐng míngxīng ma? | Do you know that movie star?

B: Wǒ bú **rènshi** tā, kěshì wǒ kànguo hěn duō tā de diànyǐng. | I don't know him, but I have seen many of his movies.

(2) A: Nǐ **rènshi** jǐ ge Zhōng-guózì? | How many Chinese characters do you recognize?

B: Bùhǎoyìsi. Wǒ jiù rènshi "yī," "èr," "sān," sān ge Zhōngguózì.

It's embarrassing. I only know "one," "two," "three," these three Chinese characters.

(3) A: Lǎoshī, dì-sān ge zì, wǒ bú rènshi.

Teacher, I don't recognize the third character.

B: Shéi rènshi?

Who knows it?

A: Wǒ rènshi. Nàge zì shì "diàn" zì.

I know it. That character is "electricity."

☞ zhīshi   knowledge; pertaining to learning or culture (N)

(1) "Zhīshi" shì yìtiān yìtiān xuélái de.

Knowledge is obtained day by day.

(2) Bú yào gēn tā shēngqì, tā shì yí ge méiyǒu zhīshi de rén.

Don't be mad at him! He is an uneducated person.

☞ xuéshi   learning, knowledge, scholarly attainments (N)

(1) A: Wèishénme dàjiā dōu xǐhuan nàge rén?

Why does everyone like that person?

B: Yīnwèi tā xuéshi hǎo, hěn héqi, yě hěn rèxīn.

Because he is learned, friendly, and enthusiastic.

(2) A: Xuéshi hǎo de rén dōu shì hǎorén ma?

Are all well-educated people good people?

B: Nà kě bù yídìng.

That's not necessarily true.

☞ jiànshi   knowledge; experience (N)

(1) Wǒ de nǚpéngyou qùguo hěn duō guójiā, tā de jiànshi hěn duō.

My girlfriend has visited many countries. She knows a lot of things.

(2) Bàba shuō wǒ shì dàrén le, zuìhǎo qù Yīngguó, Měiguó jiànshi jiànshi.

Father says I am a grown-up now. It's best if I go to England and the States to widen my horizons.

5. péng   **friend** (N)

6. yǒu　　　**friend** (N); **friendly** (SV)

☞ péngyou　friend (N)

(1) Wǒ de **péngyou** hěn duō, kěshì hǎo**péngyou** bù duō.

I have a lot of friends, but I don't have many good friends.

(2) A: Wǒmen shì jǐ shí nián de lǎo**péngyou** le.

We have been good friends for many years.

B: Zhēn nándé.

That's really difficult to achieve.

☞ nǚpéng-you　girlfriend (N)

Tā shì wǒ de nǚ de péngyou, hái bú shì **nǚpéngyou** ne.

She is my female friend. She is not my girlfriend yet.

☞ xiǎo-péngyou　children (a form of address by adult to child), little boy or girl (N)

A: **Xiǎopéngyou**, wǒmen lái kàn yí ge Zhōngguó diànyǐng, hǎo ma?

Children, let's watch a Chinese movie, okay?

B: Hǎo, lǎoshī.

Okay, teacher.

☞ yǒuhǎo　friendly, amicable (SV)

(1) A: Zhōng-Měi liǎng guó shì **yǒuhǎo** de guójiā ma?

Are the two countries, China and America, on friendly terms?

B: Yǒude shíhou shì, yǒude shíhou bú shì.

Sometimes they are, sometimes they aren't.

(2) Bù zhīdào wèishénme, tā zuìjìn gēn wǒ hěn bù **yǒuhǎo**.

(I) don't know why he's been very unfriendly toward me lately.

7. fàn　　　**cooked rice or other cereals; meal** (N)

☞ chīfàn　eat; eat cooked rice; have a meal; main dish (VO)

(1) Nǐ zěnme jiù **chīfàn**, bù chīcài?

Why do you eat rice only, (but) not the main dishes?

(2) A: Nǐ xǐhuan **chī** nǎ guó **fàn**?　Which cuisine do you prefer?

B: Nǎ guó fàn wǒ dōu xǐhuan.

I like any cuisine.

(3) A: Wǒmen shénme shíhou
chīfàn? — When are we going to eat?

B: Kàn diànyǐng yǐhòu jiù
chīfàn. — After the movie, we'll eat.

☞ **zǎofàn** — breakfast (N)

Māma shuō wǒ děi tiāntiān
chī zǎofàn. — Mother says I have to eat breakfast every day.

☞ **zhōngfàn** — lunch, midday meal (N)

Wǒmen lǎoshì zài chī zhōngfàn
de shíhou kāihuì. — We always have lunch meetings.

☞ **wǎnfàn** — supper, dinner (N)

Tā lái de shíhou, wǒmen zài
chī wǎnfàn. — When he came, we were having our dinner.

☞ **fàncài** — meal, cuisine (N)

Jīntiān wǎnfàn de fàncài
dōu shì wǒ zuì xǐhuan chī de. — The dishes of today's dinner are all my favorites.

☞ **yàofànde** — beggar (N)

Wǒ zài lùshàng kànjian hěn
duō yàofànde. Tāmen bú yào
fàn, tāmen jiù yào qián. — I saw many beggars on the street. They didn't want food, they only wanted money.

8. **guǎn** — **accommodations for guests; a shop; a place for cultural activities (N)**

☞ **fànguǎn** — restaurant (PW)

(1) A: Rénrén dōu xǐhuan qù
fànguǎn chīfàn. — Everyone loves to eat out.

B: Nà kě bù yídìng. Wǒ
bàba jiù bù xǐhuan qù
fànguǎn chīfàn. — That's not true. My father doesn't like to eat out.

A: Zhēn de! Wèishénme? — Really! Why?

B: Dì-yī, tā pà huā qián,
dì-èr, tā pà děng.

Firstly, he doesn't feel like spending money, and secondly, he doesn't like to wait.

(2) A: Nǐ kěyǐ gěi wǒ jièshào jǐ ge hǎo fànguǎn ma?

Can you recommend a couple of good restaurants to me?

B: Wǒ cónglái bú qù fànguǎn chīfàn. Zěnme gěi nǐ jièshào?

I never eat at restaurants. How can I recommend them to you?

☞ cháguǎn　　teahouse (PW)

(1) Gēn péngyou zài cháguǎn hē chá hěn yǒuyìsi.

It's very enjoyable to have tea with friends at teahouses.

(2) Zuìjìn, zhèr kāi le jǐ ge cháguǎn.

Recently, several teahouses have been opened around here.

9. yǐng　　　**shadow** (N)

☞ diànyǐng　　movie, film (N)

Kàn Zhōngguó diànyǐng yě kěyǐ xué Zhōngguóhuà.

One can also learn Chinese by watching Chinese movies.

10. ba　　　(sentence final particle for suggestion or agreement)

(1) Tā jīntiān tài máng, nǐ zuìhǎo míngtiān lái ba!

He is too busy today. It is best if you come back tomorrow!

(2) A: Nǐ shì Měiguórén ba?

You are American, right?

B: Shì. Nǐ zěnme zhīdào?

Yes. How did you know?

🐾 Pattern Drills

10.1 THE PARTICLE le

10.1.1 V le O jiù ...

When the particle le is attached to the verb in a dependent clause and is not present in the main clause, it indicates that the action in the main clause will take place only after the action in the dependent clause is completed. Jiù is an adverb linking the two clauses in the sentence.

S	V	le	O	jiù ...
Wǒ	chī	le	fàn	jiù huí jiā.
I will go home after I finish my meal.				

1. A: Nǐ shénme shíhou qù kàn Jīn Jiàn?   When are you going to see Jin Jian?

   B: Wǒ xià le kè jiù qù.   I'll go (see him) right after class.

2. A: Wǒmen shénme shíhou qù kàn diànyǐng?   When are we going to watch the movie?

   B: Wǒ dǎ le diànhuà jiù qù.   We'll go after I make the phone call.

3. A: Nǐmen shénme shíhou kāihuì?   When are you going to have the meeting?

   B: Děng dàjiā dōu lái le jiù kāihuì.   We will hold the meeting when everyone is here.

10.1.2 V le O jiù V (O) le

When le appears in both a dependent clause and the main clause in a sentence, it indicates that the actions in both clauses have been completed.

S	V	le	O,	jiu	V	O	le
Wǒ	chī	le	fàn,	jiù	huí	jiā	le.
I went home after I finished my meal.							

1. A: Tāmen shénme shíhou zǒu de?

    B: Tāmen chī le fàn jiù zǒu le.

    When did they leave?

    They left right after (they) finished their meal.

2. A: Nǐ gěi Hǎiyīng dǎ diànhuà le ma?

    B: Dǎ le. Wǒ xià le kè jiù gěi tā dǎ le.

    Have you called Haiying?

    Yes, I have. I called her right after I got out of class.

3. A: Nǐmen chīfàn le ma?

    B: Chī le. Jīn Jiàn lái le wǒmen jiù chīfàn le.

    Have you eaten yet?

    (Yes,) we have eaten. We ate right after Jin Jian came.

4. A: Wèishénme tā lái le nǐ mǎshàng jiù zǒu le?

    B: Yīnwèi wǒ bù xǐhuan gēn tā shuōhuà.

    Why did you leave as soon as he arrived?

    Because I don't like to talk to him.

10.2 THE PARTICLE ba

Ba is a final particle for a sentence. The semantic functions of ba are determined by the sentence structure: ba can appear in an imperative, a declarative or a request sentence. The meaning of ba is determined by the structure and the context of the sentence.

10.2.1 Ba in imperative sentences

Ba is used at the end of an imperative sentence to indicate a suggestion. It has the effect of softening the imperative force in the second person command, as in the first three examples. Ba can be used in first person plural commands to convey the idea of "let's ...," as in the last two examples.

1. Wáng lǎoshī jīntiān bú zài jiā. Nǐ míngtiān lái ba!

    Professor Wang is not at home today. (Please) come tomorrow!

2. Nǐ bù xǐhuan tā, jiù bú yào jiàn tā ba!

    Since you don't like him, you don't have to see him.

3. Nǐ māma hěn xiǎng nǐ, huílái ba!

    Your mother misses you very much. (Please) come back!

4. Wǒmen qù chī Zhōngguófàn ba!   Let's go to have some Chinese food!

5. Bù zǎo le, wǒmen zǒu ba!   It's getting late. Let's go!

10.2.2 Ba in interrogative sentences

Ba can turn a declarative sentence into an interrogative sentence, indicating that the speaker is uncertain about his/her conjecture. Ba has the effect of soliciting the agreement or approval of the listener with respect to the statement to which ba is attached. In this pattern, ba can be described as similar to the "Isn't it true?" or "Don't you agree?" type of question that is tagged on to a statement in English.

1. A: Tā shì Měiguórén ba?   He is American, isn't he?

    B: Bú shì. Tā shì Yīngguórén.   (No,) he is not. He is English.

2. A: Zhè běn shū shì nǐ gěi tā de ba?   This is the book you gave her, right?

    B: Shì de.   Yes.

3. A: Zhōngguórén dōu xǐhuan hē chá ba?   All Chinese like to drink tea. Am I right?

    B: Bù yídìng. Yǒude rén xǐhuan,   Not necessarily. Some people like (to
       yǒude rén bù xǐhuan.   drink tea) and some do not.

4. A: Jīntiān de kǎoshì bù nán ba?   Today's test wasn't too difficult, right?

    B: Shéi shuō de? Wǒ xiǎng hěn nán.   Who said so? I think it was very difficult.

10.2.3 Ba in response to questions

When ba is used in response to a question, it expresses agreement or approval.

1. A: Nǐ míngtiān yídìng lái, hǎo ma?   Please make sure you are coming tomorrow, okay?

    B: Hǎo ba.   (Well,) okay.

2. A: Jīntiān wǒ zuòfàn, míngtiān nǐ   I will cook today, and you will cook
       zuò, hǎo ma?   tomorrow. Okay?

    B: Hǎo ba.   (Well,) okay.

3. A: Nǐ qǐng wǒ chīfàn, wǒ qǐng nǐ
       kàn diànyǐng, hǎo ma?

    B: Hǎo ba, jiù zhèyàng ba.

How about you treat me to dinner and
I treat you to a movie?

All right, (we'll) do it this way.

10.2.4 More than one ba in a sentence

When ba appears more than once in a sentence, it conveys a hypothetical
tone. It is often used after two opposite cases to show a dilemma.

1. A: Nǐ yào qǐng tā tiàowǔ ma?

    B: Bù zhīdào. Qǐng tā ba, tā yídìng
       bù gēn wǒ tiào, bù qǐng tā ba,
       tā huì hěn shēngqì.

Do you want to ask her to dance?

I don't know. (If) I ask her, she
definitely won't dance with me.
(But if) I don't ask her, she will be
very angry.

2. A: Nǐ qù-bu-qù Jīn Jiàn de wǔhuì?

    B: Hái bù yídìng.

    A: Wèishénme?

    B: Yīnwèi tā qǐng wǒ le, wǒ bú qù ba,
       bú tài hǎo, qù ba, wǒ zhīdào yídìng
       hěn méiyìsi.

Are you going to Jin Jian's party?

I am not sure yet.

Why?

Because he has invited me, it will not
be very nice (if) I don't go. (But if) I
go, I know I will not find the party
interesting.

3. A: Nǐ gàosu tā nǐ bú ài tā le ma?

    B: Hái méi ne. Wǒ bù zhīdào
       yào-bu-yào gàosu tā.

    A: Wèishénme?

    B: Yīnwèi wǒ gàosu tā ba, pà tā
       nánguò, bú gàosu tā ba, yě bú
       tài hǎo.

Have you told him that you no longer
love him?

Not yet. I don't know whether I should
tell him.

Why?

Because (if) I tell him, I am afraid he
will be very sad. (But) it is also not
right (if) I don't tell him.

10.3 THE DIFFERENCE BETWEEN rènshi/rènde AND zhīdào

Rènshi/rènde and zhīdào are verbs and can be rendered as "to know, to know of" in English. These two verbs are sometimes interchangeable; sometimes, however, they have distinct uses. Rènshi/rènde, in addition to meaning "to know, to know of," in common with zhīdào, can also mean "to recognize, to identify someone, some place or something previously known." Note the differences illustrated in the following examples.

1. A: Nǐ rènshi/rènde nàge rén ma?   Do you know that person?

        Nǐ zhīdào tā shì shéi ma?   Do you know who he is?

    B: Wǒ zhīdào tā shì shéi, kěshì wǒ bú rènshi/rènde tā.   I know who he is, but I don't know him.

2. A: Nǐ rènshi/rènde tā ma? Nǐ zhīdào tā jiào shénme míngzi ma?   Do you know her? Do you know her first name?

    B: Wǒ bú rènshi/rènde tā, yě bù zhīdào tā de míngzi.   I don't know her. Neither do I know her name.

3. A: Nǐ zhīdào Xuésheng Zhōngxīn zài nǎr ma?   Do you know where the Student Center is?

    B: Wǒ zhīdào.   I do.

    A: Nǐ rènshi/rènde qù nàr de lù ma?   Do you know how to get there?

    B: Rènshi/rènde.   (Yes,) I do.

4. A: Nǐ zěnme bú rènshi/rènde wǒ le? Wǒ shì nǐ xiǎoxué de tóngxué.   How come you don't recognize me any more? I was your elementary school classmate.

    B: Zhēn de? Nǐ bú gàosu wǒ, wǒ zhēn bú rènshi/rènde nǐ le.   Really! If you didn't tell me, I really couldn't have recognized you.

5. A: Nǐ zhīdào nǐ yínháng yǒu duōshǎo qián ma?   Do you know how much money you have in your bank?

    B: Wǒ zěnme huì bù zhīdào.   How can I not know? (Of course I know.)

6. A: Nǐ rènshi/rènde zhège zì ma?   Do you know this character?

    B: Wǒ rènshi/rènde, kěshì wǒ bú huì xiě.   I do, but I don't know how to write it.

7. A: Míngtiān zǎoshang kāihuì, nǐ
    zhīdào ma?

    Do you know there will be a meeting
    tomorrow morning?

    B: Wǒ zhīdào, kěshì lái kāihuì de rén
    wǒ dōu bú rènshi/rènde.

    I do. But I don't know anyone who will
    be at the meeting.

8. A: Nǐ zhīdào zhè shì shéi de bǐ ma?

    Do you know whose pen this is?

    B: Wǒ zhīdào, shì Sīwén de. Wǒ
    rènshi/rènde tā de bǐ.

    I know, (it) is Siwen's. I recognize his
    pen.

Sentence Building

1.
Rènshi
Rènshi zhège.
Rènshi zhège Zhōngguózì.
Shéi rènshi zhège Zhōngguózì?
Shéi dōu bú rènshi zhège Zhōngguózì.

2.
Zuìjìn
Zuìjìn hěn máng.
Zuìjìn bù hěn máng.
Shéi zuìjìn bù hěn máng?
Wǒmen zuìjìn dōu bù hěn máng.

3.
Xuéshi
Yǒu xuéshi.
Yǒu-méiyǒu xuéshi?
Nàge rén yǒu-méiyǒu xuéshi?
Nàge rén hěn yǒu xuéshi.

4.
Chīfàn.
Qù chīfàn.
Shì qù kàn diànyǐng háishì qù chīfàn?
Nǐ shì qù kàn diànyǐng háishì qù chīfàn?
Wǒ bú qù kàn diànyǐng yě bú qù chīfàn.

Questions and Responses

1. Nǐ zuì xǐhuan chī nǎ guó fàn?

    Which cuisine do you like most?

    Wǒ zuì xǐhuan chī Zhōngguófàn,
    yīnwèi wǒ shì Zhōngguórén.
    I like Chinese food best, because I
    am Chinese.

2. Shàng xīngqīliù, nǐ gēn shéi qù kàn
    diànyǐng le?
    With whom did you go to the movie
    last Saturday?

    Shàng xīngqīliù wǒ méi qù kàn diànyǐng.

    I didn't go to the movie last Saturday.

3. Nǐmen bú rènshi ba?
   You don't know each other, right?

   Wǒmen zǎo jiù rènshi le.
   We have known each other for a long time.

4. Nǐmen shéi de qián zuìduō?

   Who has the most money among you?

   Nàge diànyǐng míngxīng de qián zuìduō.
   That movie star has the most money.

5. Wǒmen shì zài zhège fànguǎn chīfàn háishì zài nàge fànguǎn chīfàn?
   Shall we eat at this restaurant or that restaurant?

   Wǒmen zài zhège fànguǎn chīfàn ba, zhège fànguǎn hěn yǒumíng.
   Let's eat at this restaurant. This restaurant is well-known.

6. Nǐ de nǚpéngyou shì Měiguórén ba?
   Your girlfriend is American, right?

   Bú shì. Tā shì Yīngguórén.
   She is not American, she is English.

7. Nǐ de xuésheng shàng kè de shíhou dōu hěn rènzhēn ma?
   Are all your students very conscientious in class?

   Yǒude rènzhēn, yǒude bú rènzhēn.

   Some (students) are very conscientious and some are not.

8. Nǐ zuìjìn rènshi de nàge péngyou zěnmeyàng?
   How is the friend with whom you just became acquainted?

   Tā hěn hǎo. Tā hěn yǒu xuéshi, gēn tā shuōhuà hěn yǒuyìsi.
   He is very nice. He is very knowledgeable and it is very interesting to talk to him.

9. Míngtiān wǒ qǐng nǐ chī zhōngfàn. Hǎo ma?
   I'd like to invite you to lunch tomorrow. Can you come?

   Zhōngfàn de shíhou wǒ děi kāihuì, wǎnfàn zěnmeyàng?
   We will have a meeting during lunchtime. How about dinner?

10. Wèishénme Zhōngguó yǒu nàme duō bù shí zì de rén?
    Why are there so many illiterates in China?

    Wǒ xiǎng shì yīnwèi Zhōngguózì tài nán xué ba.
    I think that is because Chinese characters are very difficult to learn.

🌸 Pronunciation Review

Differentiating Pairs

(a)	dàzhì	dàzì	(e)	chūbù	cùbù
(b)	jìnshì	jìnsì	(f)	yìjiàn	yùjiàn
(c)	zhǔfù	zǔfù	(g)	bùyǎn	bùyuǎn
(d)	zhījǐ	zìjǐ	(h)	búqù	búqì

🌸 Supplementary Vocabulary

Dìfang (Places)

jiǔbā	bar
kāfēiguǎnr	coffee shop
fàntīng	dining hall, dining room
shítáng	dining room, mess hall, canteen
cāntīng	dining room, restaurant
wǎngbā	internet bar
cānguǎnr	restaurant
cháguǎnr	teahouse

Càidān (Menu)

Tāng	Soups
suānlàtāng	hot and sour soup
dànhuātāng	egg drop soup
fānqiédànhuātāng	tomato egg drop soup

Zhǔshí	Staple foods
mǐfàn	rice
mántou	steamed bun
chǎofàn	fried rice

Càilèi	**Dishes**
Zuǒgōngjī	General Zuo's chicken
Mápó dòufu	Mapo bean curd
tángcù páigǔ	sweet and sour spare ribs
gānbiǎn sìjìdòu	stir-fried string beans
hóngshāo yú	fish braised in brown sauce
shīzitóu	big meat balls
chǎo dòumiáo	stir-fried pea shoots

Fēngwèi xiǎochī	**Local snacks**
xiǎolóng bāozi	steamed stuffed bun
dàndàn miàn	Sichuan noodles with spicy sauce
jiǎozi	boiled dumplings
guōtiē	lightly fried dumplings
húntún	wonton

第十課
漢字本

∙∙

內 容

🐾 課 文

給朋友打電話

金建：　喂，海英，我是金建。你好嗎？

海英：　金建，我很好。你呢？

金建：　我也很好。我最近認識了一個女朋友。我想請你
　　　　跟我們去飯館吃飯。

海英：　好。甚麼時候？我很想認識她。

金建：　這個星期六晚上，我們在我家等你。

海英：　我們是去中國飯館還是去美國飯館？

金建：　你喜歡吃中國飯還是吃美國飯？

海英：　你知道我最喜歡吃中國飯。你女朋友呢？

金建：　她也喜歡吃中國飯。

海英：　那我們就去中國飯館吧。

金建：　我們吃了飯去看電影，好嗎？

海英：　好。你請吃飯，我請你們看電影，好嗎？

金建：　好吧。星期六見。

海英：　星期六見。

🌸 生詞及例句

1. 電　**electricity** (N)

☞ 電話　telephone; phone call (N)

(1) 我不給我媽媽打電話，我給她寫信。

(2) A: 小美，電話！

　　B: 好，我就來。

☞ 電報　wire (N)

我爸爸來電報叫我馬上回國。

2. 最　**-est** (Adj)

☞ 最多　at most; maximum (Adj)

(1) A: 你們幾個人，誰的中文書最多？

　　B: 他的。他有十幾本中文書。

(2) 我們一天最多可以學十個生字。

☞ 最好　best, first-rate; it would be best (Adv)

(1) 他的中國話，說得最好。

(2) 這個電影是今年最好的。我們得去看。

(3) 你要想考得好，最好天天來上課。

☞ 最高　highest, supreme, tallest (Adj)

他是我們同學中最高的。

☞ 最後　final, last, ultimate (Adv)

(1) 今天他是最後一個人報告。

(2) 我本來不想給他錢，最後還是給他了。

☞ 最近　recently, lately; in the near future, soon (Adv)

(1) 最近我很忙，沒有去看你。

(2) 你最近還要去日本嗎？

3. 認　　**recognize, identify; admit** (V)

☞ 認得　　know, recognize (V)

　　A: 林海英，你認得那個人嗎？

　　B: 認得。她是我同學的女朋友。

☞ 認字　　know or learn how to read (VO)

　　(1) 我很小的時候，媽媽就教我認字。

　　(2) A: 認字難還是寫字難？

　　　　B: 我想寫字難，你説呢？

　　　　A: 我同意。

☞ 認為　　think, consider (V)

　　A: 我認為我們最好不去開那個會，你説呢？

　　B: 我同意。

☞ 認真　　conscientious, earnest, serious, take seriously (SV)

　　(1) 那個老師很認真，學生也很認真嗎？

　　(2) A: 你為甚麼那麼認真？

　　　　B: 因為我從小就很認真。

　　(3) A: 你跟這個女朋友是認真的嗎？

　　　　B: 是。我們已經認識好幾年了。

4. 識　　**know** (V); **knowledge** (N)

☞ 識字　　learn to read, become literate (VO)

　　A: 現在中國識字的人多不多？

　　B: 我想現在很多人都識字了。

☞ 認識　　know, recognize (V)

　　(1) A: 你認識那個電影明星嗎？

　　　　B: 我不認識他，可是我看過很多他的電影。

(2) A: 你認識幾個中國字？

B: 不好意思。我就認識"一、二、三"三個中國字。

(3) A: 老師，第三個字，我不認識。

B: 誰認識？

A: 我認識。那個字是"電"字。

☞ 知識　　knowledge; pertaining to learning or culture (N)

(1) 知識是一天一天學來的。

(2) 不要跟他生氣，他是一個沒有知識的人。

☞ 學識　　learning , knowledge, scholarly attainments (N)

(1) A: 為甚麼大家都喜歡那個人？

B: 因為他學識好、很和氣、也很熱心。

(2) A: 學識好的人都是好人嗎？

B: 那可不一定。

☞ 見識　　knowledge; experience (N)

(1) 我的女朋友去過很多國家，她的見識很多。

(2) 爸爸說我是大人了，最好去英國、美國見識見識。

5. **朋**　　**friend** (N)

6. **友**　　**friend** (N); **friendly** (SV)

☞ 朋友　　friend (N)

(1) 我的朋友很多，可是好朋友不多。

(2) A: 我們是幾十年的老朋友了。

B: 真難得。

☞ 女朋友　　girlfriend (N)

她是我的女的朋友，還不是女朋友呢。

☞ 小朋友　　　children (a form of address by adult to child), little boy or girl (N)

A: 小朋友，我們來看一個中國電影，好嗎？

B: 好，老師。

☞ 友好　　　friendly, amicable (SV)

(1) A: 中美兩國是友好的國家嗎？

B: 有的時候是，有的時候不是。

(2) 不知道為甚麼，他最近跟我很不友好。

7. 飯　　　cooked rice or other cereals; meal (N)

☞ 吃飯　　　eat; eat cooked rice; have a meal, main dish (VO)

(1) 你怎麼就吃飯，不吃菜？

(2) A: 你喜歡吃哪國飯？

B: 哪國飯我都喜歡。

(3) A: 我們甚麼時候吃飯？

B: 看電影以後就吃飯。

☞ 早飯　　　breakfast (N)

媽媽說我得天天吃早飯。

☞ 中飯　　　lunch, midday meal (N)

我們老是在吃中飯的時候開會。

☞ 晚飯　　　supper, dinner (N)

他來的時候，我們在吃晚飯。

☞ 飯菜　　　meal, cuisine (N)

今天晚飯的飯菜都是我最喜歡吃的。

☞ 要飯的　　　beggar (N)

我在路上看見很多要飯的。他們不要飯，他們就要錢。

8. **館**　　accommodations for guests; a shop; a place for cultural activities (N)

☞ 飯館　restaurant (PW)

(1) A: 人人都喜歡去飯館吃飯。

B: 那可不一定。我爸爸就不喜歡去飯館吃飯。

A: 真的！為甚麼？

B: 第一，他怕花錢。第二，他怕等。

(2) A: 你可以給我介紹幾個好飯館嗎？

B: 我從來不去飯館吃飯。怎麼給你介紹？

☞ 茶館　teahouse (PW)

(1) 跟朋友在茶館喝茶很有意思。

(2) 最近，這兒開了幾個茶館。

9. **影**　　**shadow** (N)

☞ 電影　movie, film (N)

看中國電影也可以學中國話。

10. **吧**　　(sentence final particle for suggestion or agreement)

(1) 他今天太忙，你最好明天來吧！

(2) A: 你是美國人吧？

B: 是。你怎麼知道？

句型練習

10.1 THE PARTICLE 了

10.1.1 V 了 O 就……

When the particle 了 is attached to the verb in a dependent clause and is not present in the main clause, it indicates that the action in the main clause will take place only after the action in the dependent clause is completed. 就 is an adverb linking the two clauses in the sentence.

S	*V*	了	*O*	就……	
我	吃	了	飯	就	回家。

I will go home after I finish my meal.

1. A: 你甚麼時候去看金建？
   B: 我下了課就去。

2. A: 我們甚麼時候去看電影？
   B: 我打了電話就去。

3. A: 你們甚麼時候開會？
   B: 等大家都來了就開會。

10.1.2 V 了 O 就 V (O) 了

When 了 appears in both a dependent clause and the main clause in a sentence, it indicates that the actions in both clauses have been completed.

S	*V*	了	*O,*	就	*V*	*O*	了
我	吃	了	飯，	就	回	家	了。

I went home after I finished my meal.

1. A: 他們甚麼時候走的？
   B: 他們吃了飯就走了。

2.　A:　你給<u>海英</u>打電話了嗎？

　　　B:　打了。我下了課就給她打了。

3.　A:　你們吃飯了嗎？

　　　B:　吃了。<u>金建</u>來了我們就吃飯了。

4.　A:　為甚麼他來了你馬上就走了？

　　　B:　因為我不喜歡跟他說話。

10.2 THE PARTICLE 吧

吧 is a final particle for a sentence. The semantic functions of 吧 are determined by the sentence structure: 吧 can appear in an imperative, a declarative , or a request sentence. The meaning of 吧 is determined by the sentence structure and the context of the sentence.

10.2.1 吧 in imperative sentences

吧 is used at the end of an imperative sentence to indicate a suggestion. It has the effect of softening the imperative force in the second person command, as in the first three examples. 吧 can be used in first person plural commands to convey the idea of "let's ...," as in the last two examples.

1.　<u>王</u>老師今天不在家，你明天來吧！

2.　你不喜歡他，就不要見他吧！

3.　你媽媽很想你，回來吧！

4.　我們去吃<u>中國</u>飯吧！

5.　不早了，我們走吧！

10.2.2 吧 in interrogative sentences

吧 can turn a declarative sentence into an interrogative sentence, indicating that the speaker is uncertain about his/her conjecture. 吧 has the effect of soliciting the agreement or approval of the listener with respect to the statement to which 吧 is attached. In this pattern, 吧 can be described as similar to the "Isn't it true?" or "Don't you agree?" type of question that is tagged on to a statement in English.

1. A: 他是美國人吧？

   B: 不是。他是英國人。

2. A: 這本書是你給她的吧？

   B: 是的。

3. A: 中國人都喜歡喝茶吧？

   B: 不一定。有的人喜歡，有的人不喜歡。

4. A: 今天的考試不難吧？

   B: 誰說的？我想很難。

10.2.3 吧 in response to questions

When 吧 is used in response to a question, it expresses agreement or approval.

1. A: 你明天一定來，好嗎？

   B: 好吧。

2. A: 今天我作飯，明天你作，好嗎？

   B: 好吧。

3. A: 你請我吃飯，我請你看電影，好嗎？

   B: 好吧，就這樣吧。

10.2.4 More than one 吧 in a sentence

When 吧 appears more than once in a sentence, it conveys a hypothetical tone. It is often used after two opposite cases to show a dilemma.

1. A: 你要請她跳舞嗎？

   B: 不知道。請她吧，她一定不跟我跳，不請她吧，她會很生氣。

2. A: 你去不去金建的舞會？

   B: 還不一定。

   A: 為甚麼？

   B: 因為他請我了，我不去吧，不太好，去吧，我知道一定很沒意思。

3. A: 你告訴他你不愛他了嗎？

   B: 還沒呢。我不知道要不要告訴他。

   A: 為甚麼？

   B: 因為我告訴他吧，怕他難過，不告訴他吧，也不太好。

10.3 THE DIFFERENCE BETWEEN 認識/認得 AND 知道

認識/認得 and 知道 are verbs and can be rendered as "to know, to know of" in English. These two verbs are sometimes interchangeable; sometimes, however, they have distinct uses. 認識/認得, in addition to meaning "to know, to know of" in common with 知道, can also mean "to recognize, to identify someone, some place or something previously known." Note the differences illustrated in the following examples.

1. A: 你認識/認得那個人嗎？你知道他是誰嗎？

   B: 我知道他是誰，可是我不認識/認得他。

2. A: 你認識/認得他嗎？你知道他叫甚麼名字嗎？

   B: 我不認識/認得他，也不知道他的名字。

3. A: 你知道學生中心在哪兒嗎？

   B: 我知道。

   A: 你認識/認得去那兒的路嗎？

   B: 認識/認得。

4. A: 你怎麼不認識/認得我了？我是你小學的同學。

   B: 真的？你不告訴我，我真不認識/認得你了。

5. A: 你知道你銀行有多少錢嗎？

　　B: 我怎麼會不知道。

6. A: 你認識/認得這個字嗎？

　　B: 我認識/認得，可是我不會寫。

7. A: 明天早上開會，你知道嗎？

　　B: 我知道，可是來開會的人我都不認識/認得。

8. A: 你知道這是誰的筆嗎？

　　B: 我知道，是思文的。我認識/認得他的筆。

🌸 造句

1.

認識

認識這個。

認識這個中國字。

誰認識這個中國字？

誰都不認識這個中國字。

2.

最近

最近很忙。

最近不很忙。

誰最近不很忙？

我們最近都不很忙。

3.

學識

有學識。

有沒有學識？

那個人有沒有學識？

那個人很有學識。

4.

吃飯

去吃飯。

是去看電影還是去吃飯？

你是去看電影還是去吃飯？

我不去看電影也不去吃飯。

🎴 問答

1. 你最喜歡吃哪國飯？　　　　　我最喜歡吃<u>中國</u>飯，因為我是<u>中國</u>人。

2. 上星期六，你跟誰去看電影了？　上星期六我沒有去看電影。
3. 你們不認識吧？　　　　　　　我們早就認識了。
4. 你們誰的錢最多？　　　　　　那個電影明星的錢最多。
5. 我們是在這個飯館吃飯還是　　我們在這個飯館吃飯吧，
   在那個飯館吃飯？　　　　　　這個飯館很有名。
6. 你的女朋友是<u>美國</u>人吧？　　不是，她是<u>英國</u>人。
7. 你的學生上課的時候都很認　　有的認真，有的不認真。
   真嗎？
8. 你最近認識的那個朋友怎麼樣？　他很好。他很有學識，跟他說話很有意思。
9. 明天我請你吃中飯，好嗎？　　中飯的時候我得開會，晚飯怎麼樣？
10. 為甚麼<u>中國</u>有那麼多不識字　我想是因為<u>中國</u>字太難學吧。
    的人？

🎴 閱讀練習

<u>金建</u>的日記

　　最近同學給我介紹了一個女朋友。不，我的意思是"女的朋友，"還不是女朋友呢。她姓<u>馬</u>，叫<u>紅</u>。她很好看，也很和氣，學識也很好。我們認識以後，星期六和星期天不是去看電影，就是去飯館吃飯。有時候她請我，有時候我請她。我們很談得來。

　　我們下了課也寫電子信。談學校的功課，談我們喜歡的作家跟電影。她的數學很好，要是我有不會的她就告訴我。她寫報告的時候，也問我的意見。有一個可以談得來的好朋友真好。她會是我的女朋友嗎？

　我想告訴海英也給她們兩個人介紹介紹。我想晚上給海英打一個電話，看她這個星期六晚上可以不可以跟我和馬紅去飯館吃飯。

問 題

1. 金建怎麼認識馬紅的？
2. 你想金建喜歡馬紅嗎？你怎麼知道？
3. 金建跟馬紅下課以後作甚麼？
4. 金建甚麼功課好，馬紅呢？
5. 金建為甚麼要給海英打電話？
6. 你想海英會跟金建、馬紅去吃飯嗎？為甚麼？
7. 你想馬紅會是金建的女朋友嗎？為甚麼？
8. 為甚麼我們得有好朋友？
9. 你跟朋友去飯館吃飯的時候，誰請誰？
10. 你星期六、星期天做甚麼？

Appendixes
附錄

VOCABULARY INDEX

Pinyin	Character	Meaning in English	Lesson	Page	
				(P)	**(C)**
dào	道	road, way, path; channel(N)	5	127	143
dào	到	arrive, reach (V); up until (CV)	9	264	279
de	的	(subordinating particle)	2	36	50
dédào	得到	get, obtain, gain, receive (V)	9	264	280
děngdào	等到	by the time, wait until (V)	9	264	280
dì	弟	younger brother (N)	3	64	80
diàn	電	electricity (N)	10	293	311
diànbào	電報	wire (N)	10	293	311
diànhuà	電話	telephone; phone call (N)	10	293	311
diànyǐng	電影	movie, film (N)	10	299	315
dìdi	弟弟	younger brother (N)	3	64	80
dìng	定	set, decide; certainly, definitely (V)	9	267	282
duō	多	many, much, excessive; odd (SV)	6	162	179
duōshù	多數	majority, most (Adj)	6	163	180

F

fàn	飯	cooked rice or other cereals; meal (N)	10	297	314
fàncài	飯菜	meal, cuisine (N)	10	298	314
fànguǎn	飯館	restaurant (PW)	10	298	315

G

gào	告	tell, inform, notify (V)	6	164	181
gāo	高	tall, high (SV); a surname (N)	9	263	279
gāodà	高大	tall and big, tall (SV)	9	263	279
gāomíng	高明	brilliant, wise (SV)	9	263	279
gàosu	告訴	tell, let know (V)	8	234	250
gāoxìng	高興	glad, happy, cheerful; be willing to (SV)	9	263	279
gāozhōng	高中	high school (N)	9	263	279
gè	個	individual (N); (MW for person or thing)	3	64	80
gèrén	個人	individual (person) (N)	3	64	80
gōng	功	work, achievement (N)	6	163	180
gōngkè	功課	schoolwork, homework (N)	6	163	180
gòu	夠	enough, sufficient, adequate (SV)	9	267	282
gòuyìsi	夠意思	really something; generous, really kind (IE)	9	267	282

Pinyin	Character	Meaning in English	Lesson	Page (P)	(C)
guǎn	館	accommodations for guests; a shop; a place for cultural activities (N)	10	298	315
guó	國	country, state, nation (N)	2	36	50
guójiā	國家	country, state, nation (N)	3	63	79
guówáng	國王	king (N)	2	36	50
H					
hái	還	still, yet; even more, also, too, in addition (Adv)	5	129	144
háihǎo	還好	not bad, fortunately (IE)	5	129	144
háishì	還是	still, nevertheless, had better (Adv); or (Conj)	5	129	144
hǎokàn	好看	good-looking; interesting (SV)	8	235	252
hòu	候	time (N); wait (V)	7	197	214
hòunián	後年	the year after the next (TW)	4	98	114
huān	歡	joyous, merry, jubilant (V)	5	130	145
huānsòng	歡送	see off, send off (V)	5	130	145
huì	會	will; know how to, be able to (AV); meeting(s), get-together, assembly, conference; association (N)	7	195	213
huí	回	return, go back, turn around (V)	8	234	251
huí guó	回國	go back to one's country (VO)	8	235	251
huìhuà	會話	conversation (N)	7	196	213
huílai	回來	come back (V)	8	234	251
huíqu	回去	go back (V)	8	234	251
huí xìn	回信	write in reply, write back (VO)	8	234	251
huìtán	會談	formal talks (N/V)	7	198	215
J					
jǐ	幾	how many (QW); a few; several; some (Nu)	4	96	111
jiā	家	family, household, home; a specialist in a certain field; a school of thought (N)	3	63	79
jiàn	見	see, catch sight of (V)	9	265	281
jiànshi	見識	knowledge; experience (N)	10	296	313
jiào	叫	call (V/EV)	2	35	49
jiē	接	receive; come in contact with; catch; meet; pick up (V)	9	263	279

Pinyin	Character	Meaning in English	Lesson	Page	
				(P)	(C)
jiè	介	be situated between (V)	3	63	79
jiēdào	接到	receive (V)	9	264	280
jièshào	介紹	introduce, present; recommend (V)	3	63	79
jièshàoxìn	介紹信	recommendation letter, reference (N)	8	229	247
jìnbù	進步	advance, progress, improve; (politically) progressive (V/N)	9	268	282
jīnnián	今年	this year (TW)	4	98	114
jīng	經	through (V)	8	231	248
jīngguò	經過	pass, go through, undergo; happening (V/N)	8	231	248
jīngyàn	經驗	experience (N)	8	231	248
jiù	就	already, as early as; just, only (AV)	7	201	217
jiǔhuì	酒會	cocktail party (N)	7	195	213
jiùshì	就是	exactly, precisely; even if (EV/Adv)	7	202	218
jiùyào	就要	be about to, be going to, be on the point of (AV)	7	202	217
K					
kāi	開	open, make an opening; start; operate (V)	8	232	249
kāihuì	開會	hold or attend a meeting (VO)	8	233	249
kāikǒu	開口	open one's mouth; start to talk (VO)	8	232	249
kāimén	開門	open the door (VO)	8	232	249
kāimíng	開明	enlightened, open-minded (SV)	8	233	250
kāishuǐ	開水	boiled water (N)	8	232	249
kāixīn	開心	feel happy, rejoice (SV)	8	232	249
kāixué	開學	school opens, term begins (V)	8	232	249
kàn	看	see, look at; read; think, consider (V)	8	235	251
kàn bào	看報	read a newspaper (VO)	8	235	251
kànjian	看見	caught sight of; saw (V)	9	266	281
kǎo	考	give or take an examination, test or quiz (V)	6	164	181
kǎoshì	考試	examination (V/N)	6	165	181
kè	課	subject, course, class (N); (MW for lessons)	4	96	112
kě	可	can, may (Adv); but, yet (Conj)	7	200	216
kě'ài	可愛	lovable, likable, lovely, adorable (SV)	7	200	217
kèběn	課本	textbook (N)	4	96	112

Pinyin	Character	Meaning in English	Lesson	Page (P)	(C)
shíqī	時期	period (N)	7	197	214
shì zì	識字	learn to read, become literate (VO)	10	295	312
shù	數	number (N)	4	98	113
shū	書	book (N)	8	236	252
shūbào	書報	books and newspapers (N)	8	236	252
shūmíng	書名	title of a book (N)	8	236	252
shùxué	數學	mathematics (N)	4	98	113
sī	思	think, consider; think of; long for (V)	2	37	51
sì	四	four (Nu)	4	97	112
Sìshū	四書	The Four Books, namely, *Daxue* (The Great Learning), *Zhongyong* (The Doctrine of the Mean), *Lunyu* (The Analects of Confucius), and *Mengzi* (The Mencius) (N)	8	236	252
sìyuè	四月	April (N)	4	97	112
sù	訴	tell, inform (V)	8	234	250

T

tán	談	talk, chat, discuss (V)	7	198	215
tánhuà	談話	conversation, talk, chat; statement (N/VO)	7	198	215
tántiānr	談天兒	chat, make conversation (N/V)	7	198	215
tánxīn	談心	heart-to-heart talk (N/V)	7	198	215
tiānqì	天氣	weather (N)	8	233	250
tiānzhēn	天真	innocent; simple and unaffected; naive (SV)	9	265	281
tiàowǔ	跳舞	to dance (V / VO)	7	199	216
tóng	同	same, similar, be the same (SV)	1	5	19
tóngxué	同學	be in the same school, fellow student, schoolmate; a form of address used in speaking to a student (N)	1	5	19
tóngyì	同意	agree, consent, approve (V)	2	37	50

W

wǎnfàn	晚飯	supper, dinner (N)	10	298	314
wǎnhuì	晚會	evening party, an evening of entertainment (N)	7	195	213
wǎnshang	晚上	(in the) evening, (at) night (TW)	6	162	179

Pinyin	Character	Meaning in English	Lesson	Page	
				(P)	**(C)**
xìnxīn	信心	confidence (N)	8	230	247
xìnzhǐ	信紙	letter sheets (N)	8	230	247
xīng	星	star (N)	7	196	213
xīngqī	星期	week (TW)	7	196	213
xīngxing	星星	star (N)	7	196	213
xìng	興	interest, excitement (SV)	9	263	279
xuǎn	選	select, choose, pick, elect (V)	4	95	111
xuǎn kè	選課	select courses (VO)	4	95	111
xué	學	study, learn; imitate, mimic, knowledge, subject of study (V)	1	5	19
xuénián	學年	school (or academic) year (N)	4	99	114
xuéqī	學期	school term, semester (N)	4	95	111
xuésheng	學生	student, pupil, disciple, follower (N)	1	5	19
xuéshi	學識	learning, knowledge, scholarly attainments (N)	10	296	313
xuéwèn	學問	learning, knowledge, scholarship (N)	1	5	19
xuéxiào	學校	school, educational institution (N)	5	128	144
xǔkě	許可	permit, permission, allow (V/N)	7	200	216
Y					
yàn	驗	examine, check, test (V)	8	231	248
yàng	樣	appearance, shape, sample, type (N)	6	159	177
yàngzi	樣子	appearance, shape, manner, sample, model (N)	6	159	177
yàofànde	要飯的	beggar (N)	10	298	314
yì	意	meaning, idea, intention (N)	2	36	50
yǐ	已	already (Adv)	8	230	248
yǐ	以	use, according to, because of (CV)	7	201	217
yídìng	一定	definitely, certainly, surely (Adv)	9	267	282
yǐhòu	以後	after, afterwards, later, hereafter, in the future (Conj/Adv)	7	201	217
yǐjīng	已經	already (Adv)	8	231	248
yìjiàn	意見	idea, view, opinion, suggestion; objection (N)	9	266	281
yìsi	意思	meaning, idea, opinion (N)	2	37	51
yìtiāndàowǎn	一天到晚	from morning till night, from dawn to dusk, all day long (IE)	9	265	280

SENTENCE PATTERN INDEX

Flash Cards

1.1 tóng	1.2 xué	1.3 shēng	1.4 shì	1.5 lǎo
口 同	子 學	丿 生	日 是	老 老
1.6 shī	**1.7** shén	**1.8** me	**1.9** bù / bú	**1.10** mǎ
巾 師	甘 甚	广 麼	一 不	馬 馬
2.1 jiào	**2.2** míng	**2.3** zì	**2.4** měi	**2.5** de
口 叫	口 名	宀 字	羊 美	白 的
2.6 guó	**2.7** yì	**2.8** sī	**2.9** yīng	**2.10** wén
口 國	心 意	心 思	艹 英	文 文
3.1 jiā	**3.2** jiè	**3.3** shào	**3.4** gè	**3.5** dì
宀 家	人 介	糸 紹	人 個	弓 弟

3.6 liǎng	3.7 bà	3.8 wǔ	3.9 qī	3.10 méi
兩	爸	五	七	没

4.1 qī	4.2 xuǎn	4.3 jǐ	4.4 mén	4.5 kè
期	選	幾	門	課

4.6 sì	4.7 zhōng	4.8 shù	4.9 nián	4.10 nǎ / něi
四	中	數	年	哪

5.1 le	5.2 zhī	5.3 dào	5.4 nán	5.5 xiào
了	知	道	難	校

5.6 hái	5.7 yīn	5.8 wèi	5.9 xǐ	5.10 huān
還	因	為	喜	歡

6.1 zěn	6.2 yàng	6.3 xiàn	6.4 shàng	6.5 duō
心 怎	木 樣	王 現	一 上	夕 多
6.6 gōng	**6.7 xiě**	**6.8 gào**	**6.9 kǎo**	**6.10 shì**
工 功	宀 寫	口 告	老 考	言 試
7.1 huì	**7.2 xīng**	**7.3 shí**	**7.4 hòu**	**7.5 tán**
日 會	日 星	日 時	亻 候	言 談
7.6 zuò	**7.7 wǔ**	**7.8 kě**	**7.9 yǐ**	**7.10 jiù**
亻 作	舛 舞	口 可	人 以	尢 就
8.1 xìn	**8.2 yǐ**	**8.3 jīng**	**8.4 yàn**	**8.5 kāi**
亻 信	己 已	糸 經	馬 驗	門 開

8.6 qì	8.7 sù	8.8 huí	8.9 kàn	8.10 shū
气 氣	言 訴	口 回	目 看	日 書
9.1 gāo	**9.2 xìng**	**9.3 jiē**	**9.4 dào**	**9.5 zhēn**
高 高	白 興	手 接	刀 到	目 真
9.6 jiàn	**9.7 gòu**	**9.8 dìng**	**9.9 bù**	**9.10 zhù**
見 見	夕 夠	宀 定	止 步	示 祝
10.1 diàn	**10.2 zuì**	**10.3 rèn**	**10.4 shí**	**10.5 péng**
雨 電	日 最	言 認	言 識	月 朋
10.6 yǒu	**10.7 fàn**	**10.8 guǎn**	**10.9 yǐng**	**10.10 ba**
又 友	食 飯	食 館	彡 影	口 吧

k   like k in kid.

            kàn   see, read.

x   like sh in shock

            xǎo small

h   like ch in Bach (German)

            hǎo good

r   like r in radio

            ràng let

ai   like 'y' in flys

            kāi open

ao   like 'ow' in now

            hǎo good

ei   like ay in day

            hēi black

ou   like ow in low

            zǒu walk

b	like p in 'spool' (oy) bào newspaper
p	like p in 'pool' pǎo run
d	like t in stool dào way
t	like t in tool tào set
z	like ds in fads zǎo early
c	like ts in cats cǎo grass
zh	like 'j' in Jane. zhǎo search
ch	like ch in cheese chǎo fry
j	like j in Jeans jiào call
q	like ts in mats qiǎo bridge.
g	like k in skate gāo tall

th $\rightarrow$ j / ch $\rightarrow$ ch / sh $\rightarrow$ sh /